I0165406

Praise for *Our Best Work*

"Nilofer Merchant draws on her wealth of experience and rare common sense to uncover 24 perversive and soul-crushing norms that damage innovation, well-being, and profits. *Our Best Work* provides powerful and proven antidotes for leaders who are bent on banishing these bad old ways of doing business. I am smitten with her solutions, including 'a hero harms us,' 'forge A-teams by not fixating on A-players,' and that 'strategy and execution are one and the same.'"

—Robert I. Sutton, professor emeritus at Stanford University and *New York Times* bestselling author of *The No Asshole Rule* and (with Huggy Rao) *The Friction Project*

"In her latest book, Nilofer Merchant challenges the limiting assumptions in our existing playbook and forges a new path to innovation. Creative, story-filled, and practical, *Our Best Work* is a must-read for creating teams ready for the future."

—Sanyin Siang, founding executive director of Duke University's Center on Leadership and Ethics and author of *The Launch Book*

"This book may blow the lid off everything people think they know about how to lead and manage organizations. Nilofer Merchant takes on virtually every slogan in the manager's informal handbook and shows them to be either fatuous or false, and destructive (not merely useless) to the organizations that live by them and the people who work in them. Much of what Merchant has to say will surely be controversial, but if people take her arguments seriously, when the dust clears, life in these organizations will be much improved, as will the goods and services they offer. Merchant is especially well positioned to write such a book, with a long history of leadership positions in some legendary companies."

—Barry Schwartz, visiting professor at Haas School of Business, UC Berkeley, and author of *The Paradox of Choice* and *Why We Work*

"With her engaging, powerful voice, Nilofer Merchant invites readers to move beyond outdated and individualistic management paradigms toward more collaborative—and more human—approaches to value creation. Refreshing and rigorous, this book takes on entrenched norms that stifle innovation and joy. Prepare to be challenged and inspired!"

—Amy C. Edmondson, Novartis Professor of Leadership at Harvard Business School and bestselling author of *Right Kind of Wrong*

"Finally, a business book that dares to expose the invisible forces holding back innovation—and that offers a viable path forward. Nilofer Merchant has delivered a bracing blueprint for any leader who wants to combine purpose and profit."

—Daniel H. Pink, #1 *New York Times* bestselling author of *The Power of Regret* and *Drive*

"*Our Best Work* expertly exposes the invisible norms that limit innovation and value creation in today's organizations. Drawing on decades of Silicon Valley experience and extensive research, Nilofer Merchant reveals how inherited workplace practices systematically overlook the talents and contributions of the majority of our workforce. But Merchant doesn't just call out the problem—she is redefining what effective management means for our time, offering a powerful new vision for leadership based on enabling rather than controlling. By identifying hidden barriers and providing practical solutions, she delivers an essential playbook for building truly collaborative, high-performing organizations where everyone can contribute their full talents. At a time when companies struggle to innovate and adapt to changing cultural norms, *Our Best Work* provides a blueprint for human-centered leadership that will define successful organizations in the future. *Our Best Work* offers transformative ideas that bridge the gap between management theory and lived experience, demonstrating how including all voices is essential for creating sustainable business value."

—Kristy Tillman, former head of workplace experience design at Slack

"Brilliantly reframing what it means to create value, *Our Best Work* pushes us to question the systems that limit our best work and our truest selves."

—Chip Conley, *New York Times* bestselling author of
Emotional Equations and *Learning to Love Midlife*

"As the head of the Athena Center for Leadership at the feminist powerhouse Barnard College, I have the mission of cultivating the next generation of leaders—those ready to challenge the status quo and drive transformative change, like alumnae Grace Lee Boggs, Chai Feldblum, and Greta Gerwig. So when I say this, I mean it: *Our Best Work* is the book I—and the college students and early-career innovators I work with—have been waiting for!"

—Umbreen Bhatti, Constance Hess Williams '66 Director of the
Athena Center for Leadership, Barnard College, Columbia University

"A delicious book, *Our Best Work* reminds us of what happens when we choose trust over fear and design a future we can be proud of together."

—John Maeda, vice president of design and AI at
Microsoft and author of *The Laws of Simplicity*

"Merchant understands the importance of tackling structural change to ensure that the voices often unheard are the ones driving the future."

—Reshma Saujani, founder of Girls Who Code and *New York Times* bestselling author of *Brave, Not Perfect*

OUR BEST WORK

ALSO BY NILOFER MERCHANT

The New How: Creating Business Solutions Through Collaborative Strategy

11 Rules for Creating Value in the #SocialEra

*The Power of Onlyness: Make Your Wild Ideas
Mighty Enough to Dent the World*

OUR BEST WORK

Break Free from the 24
Invisible Norms That Limit Us

Nilofer Merchant

HARPER
BUSINESS

An Imprint of HarperCollinsPublishers

Without limiting the exclusive rights of any author, contributor or the publisher of this publication, any unauthorized use of this publication to train generative artificial intelligence (AI) technologies is expressly prohibited. HarperCollins also exercise their rights under Article 4(3) of the Digital Single Market Directive 2019/790 and expressly reserve this publication from the text and data mining exception.

OUR BEST WORK. Copyright © 2026 by Nilofer Merchant. All rights reserved. Printed in the United States of America. No part of this book may be used or reproduced in any manner whatsoever without written permission except in the case of brief quotations embodied in critical articles and reviews. For information, address HarperCollins Publishers, 195 Broadway, New York, NY 10007. In Europe, HarperCollins Publishers, Macken House, 39/40 Mayor Street Upper, Dublin 1, D01 C9W8, Ireland.

HarperCollins books may be purchased for educational, business, or sales promotional use. For information, please email the Special Markets Department at SPsales@harpercollins.com.

hc.com

FIRST EDITION

Designed by Kyle O'Brien

Emoji art © Cali6ro/Shutterstock, Inc.

Library of Congress Cataloging-in-Publication Data has been applied for.

ISBN 978-0-06-346573-2

25 26 27 28 29 LBC 5 4 3 2 1

To Kiddo,

Some of these stories involve you. Thank you for letting me tell them.

For years, I thought my truth was the problem. Now I see it's the path to freedom.

And because I trust that there's no such thing as one-way liberation, I write this for us.

—Mom

The truly new looks truly wrong at first.

—Alice Fulton

Contents

Caged

Our best work.

The phrase sounds simple—aspirational, even. Like a promise of all that is good. But what it delivers changes based on how we scope each word.

Our: depending on who is included in the collective pronoun, it could benefit a few or many. *Best*: it could be about maximizing profits or solving meaningful problems. And *work*? It's not clear if that's about the contract or the calling.

These aren't just linguistic choices. They are at the heart of the question: What is the point of work?

On one level, the point of work for all of us is simply that it's a necessary means to an end. We all have bills to pay, that's true, but the bigger truth is that the majority of our adult life is spent at work. And at one time or another, we have all thought the same thing: *Is this it?*

That's the question so many of us are asking. Sometimes bitterly. Often exhaustedly. Always in the quiet of our hearts.

We were told that work would mean something. That if we gave it our best—our time, our passion, our ideas—we'd get somewhere that felt worth it.

But most days, our hope for doing our *best* work seems like a mirage.

I've been brought in to help teams—small and large—around the world innovate, grow, and reinvent. And no matter the company, title, or mission, what I hear is the same: Work isn't working.

The problem with work isn't you. It's that you're set up to fail.

It's not about your workplace—it's about a system designed to prize profits over people.

And it's not just about capitalism—it's about an entire culture that values obedience over originality.

There is an intangible power—felt but not seen—that limits us all.

Making it so that no matter how hard we try, something's always out of reach. That we're being measured against the wrong things. That the rules are written in invisible ink.

We show up wanting to do work that matters. But we're handed tasks, checklists, busywork. Lather, rinse, repeat. When we try to add our distinct bit to the world, we learn that they don't want that from us. We're always asked to do *more* but never encouraged to do *better*. Let alone our *best*. In truth, most jobs—like 70% of them[1]—weren't designed for our true Self to shine; they were built to keep us in line.

We worry: *Is it me?*

Many of us have watched our parents pour their lives into their jobs—early mornings, late nights, weekends—only to be rewarded with burnout, layoffs, and a hollow "Thanks for your service." We see through the façade now. Work isn't about growth, loyalty, or merit. It's about extraction. Profits for a few. Disposability for the rest. And that corporate ladder our parents climbed? It doesn't even exist anymore. The game is rigged, and we're way too sharp to fall for the trap.

We wonder: *Is it possible to opt out?*

Some of us became team leaders, hoping to build something better through collaboration, creativity, and meaning. But all work seems to deliver is frustration. We are asked to motivate others when we're barely inspired ourselves. Our days are clogged with bureaucracy, meetings that solve nothing, and decisions that are half a loaf. Becoming a leader was supposed to be empowering; instead, it's a big disappointment.

We hope: *It's better elsewhere.*

Some of us started our own thing. A consultancy. A startup. A side hustle that became a life. We set out to do meaningful work on our own terms. To make something real, solve a problem, bring an idea to life.

We worked relentlessly—mornings, nights, weekends—believing effort would lead to progress. But somewhere along the way, we noticed success became about followers and personal brand and how well we could pitch our story to others. We hustle harder and do everything "right," and yet the breakthrough is elusive.

We keep asking, *Why isn't this working?*

And if you're the one in charge, the weight of all this is incredibly heavy. You're expected to have all the answers—as if that were even possible. The board wants you to be in control as they push for endless growth and profits, while your team demands clarity and meaning. Even on vacation, you're working, because what choice do you have? *This is success,* you think, *even if it doesn't feel that way. It's just what capitalism demands.*

You don't even ask, *What alternative is there?*

We're told to pull ourselves up by our bootstraps. But the boots don't fit. And the straps? They were outsourced long ago.

We live in a world run by algorithms, global trade deals, and decisions made in rooms we'll never enter. All we hear is that success is about increasing efficiency and making progress, but no one seems to ask, *progress for whom?* Those with money influence the system, and to such a degree that it no longer feels like any of us can effect change. Every day, more tasks get automated, and it's not just factory workers or cashiers whose jobs are at risk anymore. White-collar professionals, coders, designers, even creatives—no one is safe. What took years to master can now be done in minutes by an algorithm that doesn't need sleep, healthcare, or a work-life balance. We're told to be brave, show grit, and do our 10,000 hours, but for *what?* To outcompete machines? AI doesn't just threaten our livelihoods—it undermines our purpose, leaving us pondering . . .

What else is there?

These questions are the quiet chorus of our modern workplace. They hold the pain, frustration, and despair of modern-day work. They name the limits we feel.

It is *good* to admit just how bad it is, to *let* it break our hearts.

But let's also let it fix our sight.

Because each question assumes we must twist ourselves to fit.

- Answer the question *Is it possible to opt out?* and you're trapped in a false choice: Either play by the rules or refuse to play, but the game itself remains unchanged.
- Answer *Is it better elsewhere?* and you'll get a new boss who is the same as the old boss.
- Answer *Is it me?* and you will constantly be trying to fix yourself—attending seminars, reading self-help books, taking personality tests, practicing communication skills—trying to fix what was never broken.
- Answer *Why isn't it working?* and you seek answers with even more effort.
- Answer *What alternative is there?* and you concede that capitalism's worst excesses can't be tamed.
- Answer *What else is there?* and you settle for crumbs, accepting the table as it stands, never imagining how to flip it.

These questions limit rather than liberate us.

Each blames or shames.

What we really need are better questions.

I know better than anyone what happens when we ask better questions. I helped launch the first web server in the tech industry at Apple Computer, heralding the internet we all depend on. I helped reform the California Community Colleges system from a trade school model to a low-cost entrance point for higher education, creating the kind of access we all need.

I've personally helped launch more than 100 products, netting a whopping $18 billion in sales. Iconic companies like HP, Nokia, L'Oréal, Yahoo, Walmart, IBM, Google, Symantec, Adobe, and GE have all asked me to help them grow—but even more often, I'm brought in when they need to rethink everything.

I've even helped people get off their tushes by giving a talk in which I said that sitting is the new smoking,[2] which is why 195 million Apple Watches alert you to stand up every hour. The question I asked for that talk: *Do you know that what you're doing, right now, at this very moment, is killing you?*

That's why I believe in the power of generative questions.

They don't just help us name what's broken. They help us build what's possible.

So let's start here: *What is it that limits our best work?*

The Network of Barriers

All our workplaces rely on inherited norms—those informal, mostly unwritten, always invisible rules that define what is "normal."

These norms dictate and set the tone for acceptable actions and behaviors, whether in business or nonprofits, government, or education. Norms make our lives easier. They spare us from having to make constant decisions about how things should work.

But that equally means we're not making intentional decisions about how things *should* work.

Norms invisibly direct our every action from the shadows of the past. They just hang in the air like ghosts, whispering in our ears: *This is just how it is. This is how we do things around here.* They shape who gets heard *or not*, who always wins the political fight *or not*, and who always gets to lead while the rest of us have to do their work.

A limit isn't just a perimeter, a barrier we cannot cross. A limit is a firm hand holding us in place, shaping our choices and our aspirations.

Left hidden, the norms can't be investigated or interrogated, let alone redesigned.

And until they are, work will not change. Leaders will not change. Power will not change. Capitalism will not change.

Here's the problem: Today's economy runs on value we don't know how to name, let alone measure.

Only about 16% of what drives a company's market value shows up in our financial accounting systems: buildings, inventory, salaries, patents—tangible things.[3] Today, those capital-based things represent a shrinking share of what drives breakthrough performance. But the rest, the far more important part, falls into a vague and mysterious category: *intangibles.*

That's not just a measurement gap. It's a strategic blind spot.

Without metrics for the intangibles, work optimizes for what it *can* track. But that hyperfocuses work on rate-of-return measures like profits, efficiency, and productivity or fragmented metrics like brand value, NPS, and engagement scores. Which inversely means that they—which is to say we—cannot manage the real drivers of today's value creation engine.

What does that elusive 84% represent?

- Whether people are enabled to *add* their distinct value.
- Whether ideas are being *joined* together to create real and robust solutions.
- Whether we're *building* the solutions of tomorrow.

The cost of this is cumulative and compounding: missed innovations, inequitable workplaces, and a future built on yesterday's limits.

The urgency of this gap spikes exponentially with AI technology. If we can't value the intangibles, we risk designing systems that won't utilize humans effectively, or at all. AI is incredibly good at replicating the routine. But it can't invent. It can't care. It can't dissent. It can't hold tension or sense when a decision lacks integrity. If we don't sharpen our visibility into how value is created, we won't just lose sight of it, we'll design it out entirely.

Modern economic drivers come from access to novel ideas, and purposeful networks to scale those ideas.[4] We need to update our practices to reflect this: Value is no longer just capitalized—it's co-created. And co-creation depends on something that economists and business leaders don't yet know how to measure but that everyone in the workplace feels: the invisible norms that shape who is heard, who creates, and who benefits.

I've identified 24 specific and concrete norms that, in both subtle and significant ways, stop us from doing our best work.

Why 24? I'd like to say it's one for every hour of the global workday—because that sounds pithy and powerful—but really, it was the result of a foundational question.

Given everything we already know about what allows us to do good, meaningful work—collaborative leadership, psychological safety, the power of novel approaches—why aren't we doing those things?

Studying that, I've isolated each element that keeps us stuck. Similar to what we learned in high school chemistry class, that all of life is made up of just 92 invisible elements, I found that work, too, is made up of invisible elements. Instead of oxygen or carbon, these are work norms.

When I share this, people almost *always* ask me to simplify it—to reduce the list to something smaller.

I get it. Ten would be much more manageable.

But we miss a lot when we oversimplify things.

It's like looking at just part of a cage and wondering why the animal inside doesn't escape. If you studied any *one* wire, up and down its length, you might believe that the animal could simply push past. If you see just *some* of the wires, you'd wonder if the beast actually wants to stay where it is. But until you see the *whole*, you miss the point. And that's when it hits you—how the wild thing is fully ensnared, caged, trapped.[5]

Not because it chooses to be.

Not because it lacks power.

And certainly not because it doesn't try hard enough to escape.

The genius of norms isn't how *persuasive* they are—it's how *persistent* they are.

It's not just *one* or five or ten things that trap it in place, but the way those things intertwine and twist together, a tangled network of systematically related barriers that hinders flight, hinders escape, hinders freedom. It is their relationships to each other that make the seemingly lightweight barriers as confining as the solid walls of a dungeon.

Just as the cage is not built of one wire, what limits our best work isn't built of just one thing. It is embodied in beloved concepts like servant leadership, performance reviews, and high-impact players—norms held up as the gold standards of good management.

These norms keep us trapped.

Caged.

No one intends this. The people who champion these norms mean well. They're following what they were taught, just like the rest of us. To understand how these norms harm, we have to see where they came from—not to cast blame, but to trace inheritance. Because these aren't new ideas. They weren't invented in corporate boardrooms or MBA programs. They've been with us for centuries. They come from the hierarchies of ancient empires, from the logic of kings and conquerors, from the systems that upheld slavery, colonialism, and apartheid. They've survived through patriarchy and supremacy, and are passed down to us through expectations, language, roles, and rewards. Old ideas shape our modern reality. This is our inheritance, but it doesn't have to be our legacy.

Which is why we must name the 24 norms that limit our best work. So we can see our collective cage. If we don't see it, we unknowingly maintain it. We participate in it. Perpetuate it. And become complicit in our own oppression—limiting our own freedom without realizing it.

Don't Go It Alone

The next generation will *surely* fix work, people say.

That's how things will change.

That's the hope.

I doubt it.

Not because I don't believe in young people or a fresh perspective. But because of data. Researchers at Oxford University did a longitudinal study around power.[6] They studied the same 30 or so university students over four years, doing a total of 98 interviews. These students—bright, capable, and studying with some of the best-ranked professors—were learning that systemic barriers exist and how those barriers were marginalizing them, invalidating them, and erasing their voices.

They learned how they were trapped.

At the beginning of the research, it made complete sense that the students believed either that things weren't solvable at all—systemic change, after all, is hard to achieve—or that the solutions could be simple (just be more assertive, work harder, do better, speak up, and so on). Yet even years into the study, even after those students knew more of what was really keeping them stuck, these same students said things like "It's not *so* bad" and "It only affects me *some* of the time" or "I'll be the exception to the rule, strong *enough* to power through it."

They *knew* what was harming them—theoretically, at least—but they downplayed or denied the very forces that held them back.

The researchers called this the agency myth: the idea that individual effort alone can overcome structural constraint.

But let's be clear: This problem is not a myth.

What's mythical is the belief that knowledge can free us. It's not enough to name the problems—we must know how to enact our own liberation.

Not in the singular. But together.

When we change how we participate, the system has to change with us. For example, if I stop dancing the tango with you, the dance stops. And if we start a line dance, the tango may still exist on the dance floor, but it no longer holds our attention. If the line dance exists, others can join us. The system shifts.

That's why we're not just naming what limits us; we're also naming the practice that we want to do, toward leading indicators. In economics, leading indicators are those things that change before the overall economy does, thus providing an early sign about the future direction. I use leading indicators—instead of laws or rules—because the ever-changing world we live in needs less rigidity and more signposts to help us know if we're on the right track for where we want to go.

The only thing we need to change is everything, and this is not work we do alone.

Many want to name the barriers to what limits our best work as one big thing: power dynamics. But this simply isn't useful; it's not precise enough. Power dynamics are everywhere and therefore nowhere. Calling the issues out at the systems level is like naming Earth but not a city. We cannot navigate to Earth; it is everywhere and nowhere. Having a precise name isn't just a descriptor; it's a definer. It's both a map and a path. And the more precise a name is, the more we can navigate the situation. Rather than Earth, it's the City of Light. And not just Paris, but the 7th arrondissement. Even more precisely, we'd name the metro stop, which tells us the specifics to navigate—the markets, the schools, the streets. Precise naming says this is *where we are*, which gives us the navigation tools to get to where we want to go *next*.

Precision gives us language, clarity, and the power to act.

And this all matters for us as individuals, as teams, and as leaders because the future requires iteration and innovation. So let's be real—there are 80,000 books on innovation (I've counted), and there are more innovation consultants and advisers than are countable. We know about the need for collaborative leadership. We have tools and systems, best practices, and models. We have Harvard Business Review and Fortune conferences. And there are talented people (like you) who are doing their very best to drive growth. And yet innovation is ever elusive. Knowing is not enough to escape what chains us to the past.

Naming the 24 norms is a crucial *first* step. But it's not the full step. People often have big conversations about change with me from the perspective of not knowing. They answer the question of what to do next with *I don't know.* And I respond: *Assume you do know. Now what?* Almost every time, they do. Which is to say, we do.

The only way change happens is when we put what we know into practice. That is why at the end of each of the 24 chapters in this book, I share an Innovation Practice, a way of navigating out of the limiting norms of the past and into the leading indicators of the future.

This allows us to practice the future, so we create a new reality.

Work Is Where the Self Meets the World

There's a transformative power in naming things.

Colonization—the act of appropriating a place for one's own use—often began by renaming the places. Names change how we refer to something, how we identify it, and how the world is made. The new name alters identity, possession, and reality itself.

Once, renaming was a tool of conquest—claiming something as *theirs*. Today, the power of naming can make it *ours*.

To name something is to pull it from the shadows and give it form, weight, breath. Unnamed, it hovers like a ghost—felt but not seen, known but not understood. The moment you find its name, though? It solidifies, becomes real, claimable. Think of a child's first word—how they say *ball* or *mama*, and in that utterance, they don't just name the thing; they make it their own. Naming gives them the power to pull the object into their world. Naming has a magic like no other; it doesn't merely *describe* reality but *directs*, maybe even *determines* it.

Once something has a name, we know what it is we need to talk about.

This is the alchemy of naming: It turns the invisible into the possible.

When we name the 24 limiting norms that surround us, they can never hide again. If we can name what is happening, we know what to address. If we can introduce ourselves to the leading indicators, we will become the warriors of freedom.

And this matters.

Not just because work is where we spend most of our time but because work is where the Self meets the world, as a famous poet once wrote.[7] Work is how we add our bit to the whole. Work is how and where our essence shapes the world around us, where our being gives rise to doing. In work, we bridge the gap between our personal interests and the external world to see how we matter—to make an impact. The definition of the verb *impact* is "to have a strong effect or influence on a situation or person." It is not about being more forcible, as we've been told we need to be, but about creating a dynamic space where the deepest, truest parts of ourselves emerge, not just to fulfill tasks but to create, connect, and transform both ourselves and the world we touch.

We won't fix everything, everywhere, all at once. But we can join together to do something, somewhere, soon. We can't create the future using the language of the past. We must let go of what limits us and practice what liberates us.

I wish I could say we have forever to discuss this.

But we don't.

The world is burning.

So take it in, and then let's go.

Toward freedom.

Toward the future.

1

Trade Comfort for Change

Limiting Norm: Planning Change
Leading Indicator: Practice Changing

No one likes to think they are averse to change. Yet they are. Which is to say, we all are.

Change means moving into unfamiliar territory—a vast, unknowable, uncertain, and therefore risky place.

This book is not just asking you to move into unfamiliar territory; it's demanding it.

Loudly.

Emphatically.

Unapologetically.

Unequivocally.

This is not a negotiation where the past and the future meet halfway and work it out. No. This is where we admit that change is required of all of us, for us all. For every industry, company, leader, team, and person. We must be prepared to face it. Head-on.

It's going to get uncomfortable, but that's how progress and innovation happen.

Change can elicit two distinct reactions: excitement or anxiety. (Sometimes both at once!) When change happens from excitement, we tap into possibility, creativity, and the desire to invent the next thing. But if we're anxious, we'll self-protect, disconnect, and resist anything and everything. A positive approach enables us to create what is needed; a negative one nips change in the bud.

No real surprise there.

The eye-opener comes in realizing that very few of us can tell when we're in that second bucket, the resistant state. At least not at the moment. And certainly not by ourselves.

And this is a big deal. It's why this change topic is the first one I address in this book on how we spot the norms that limit our best work. Without the ability to face change? Nothing changes, ever.

Yet most change at work is really control in disguise.

When Power Speaks

Clicker in hand, power pose in place, I stood at the front of the conference room.

A lot was at stake. I was presenting the "State of the State" to the incoming CEO, who was deciding which products would be killed, and which of us would be canned. Despite the lack of sleep from making last-minute changes to the presentation based on team feedback, my naturally wild hair was professionally blown out, to go along with my straitlaced navy blue Ann Taylor skirt suit and pearl earrings. *Professional.* Even as I stood there, I told myself that I could sleep when I was dead (or fired). *Committed.* With the jargon, buzzwords, and lingo of our industry in mind, I had memorized, practiced, and trained myself to speak in the declarative. *Prepared.*

It was do-or-die time. And I was ready.

The slide behind me? It featured the Apple logo. Because the incoming CEO was Steve Jobs. Returning from his exodus to save the company.

Before I said even one word, Jobs—who had walked in wearing a T-shirt, ratty jeans, and gross flip-flops that desperately needed to be replaced—spoke.

"Fuck the Channel. We don't need the fucking Channel!"

This was, I suppose, in response to the 20-foot title slide being projected behind me, which had the word *Channel* on it, for the specific part of the business division that I led.

I looked over at my boss, John, for guidance. I got a shrug. All the other team managers lined up against the wall shuffled their feet, looked down, looked away.

I was on my own.

And despite being thrown by Steve Jobs cursing at my PowerPoint, I delivered my prepared remarks. I shared what our team had done to grow the Server product line from $2 million to $180 million in a short 18 months. How we were on track to make our first billion dollars. That we had won an industry award for our innovations—the only award given to Apple in years. And how we were doing what no one else in the company was able to do: growing both margin and revenues when Apple was struggling financially and losing market share.

As I talked, I noticed that Jobs didn't ask any questions. I grew more panicked by his lack of interest than by his earlier aggression.

What the fuck is happening? I screamed in my mind, over and over again (hey, if he got to curse, so did I).

Most change at work is really control in disguise.

No one told me the answer to that question. I had to work that out for myself. It took decades for me to understand that what happened in that room had nothing to do with me, the team, our results, or my presentation deck. It had to do with Steve being in control. Showing how he held all the power, no matter our team's success. Signaling that there was only one voice that mattered: his. Nobody said this aloud. The powerful don't need to assert their power. That's how power works.

It's invisible. Felt but never questioned.

The Only Truth Is Change[1]

In the field known as change management, the process is described like this: You—as the catalyst or leader—are open and ready for change; you just need to convince, direct, guide, enroll, and motivate other people. The good part about this process is that it acknowledges that change is necessary. Across the many frameworks, change is characterized as what happens when teams have three things: (1) the *will* to change, (2) a *plan* for change, and (3) *others executing* that plan.

This method is often shortened to the phrase "Plan the work and work the plan."

This was Jobs at the meeting: showing his will, his plan, and directing others to that plan. First by what he said, second by what he didn't say.

In this view, change is what you *direct* and *make* happen—that's the norm. But let's slow down for a moment. Do you notice that the norm assumes that someone *needs* to motivate, to enroll, to direct; how change is something one *makes* happen by getting others on board?

As if change isn't the most *ordinary* and *everyday* thing.

Because isn't everything changing all the time? You, me, our environment, the rules, even evolution. Even change changes. The capacity to change—which I define as *the way we find out what works best now*—is what keeps any organism alive. Our cells are constantly changing and re-creating us. Human minds, too. We are constantly changing, adapting, and developing from the day we're born.

We change when we want to.

Because change is who we are.

It is a constant.

And something we're already, naturally, quite good at.

If we are allowed to do it.

Chase It Down

Before I was presenting my division's case to Jobs, we had to create one.

It all started in a hallway. I was on my way to lunch when the president of Apple USA stopped me, showing me a spreadsheet. "Do you know why this product is so profitable?" he asked. I didn't, and I told him so.

"Can you find out?" he asked.

This was an opportunity, I thought. Lunch could wait.

I rushed back to my boss, Michelle, expecting excitement. But instead of giving me a high five, she shook her head. "You've been handed a dog project," she said. "Everyone else has passed on it."

Great. I felt like a sucker, an idiot for not having known to avoid it.

But I had already said yes, so there was no turning back.

I didn't know much, if anything, about the product or the market. The spreadsheet had data about where the product was selling. Top of the list was Chicago, Illinois. I called the regional office, found out the name of the right salesperson to speak with and learn what he knew. After talking to him, I asked who else was involved and reached out to them. One conversation at a time, I uncovered what was working. Apple's partners and sales reps weren't just pushing a standard product; they were trusted by Apple's best customers in ways corporate didn't understand. And together, they were building full-on solutions to our customer's problems, jury-rigging things out in the field to do so. This was the early, early days of the internet, and Apple's field team was figuring out how to help traditional designers expand their businesses by creating websites using a mix of software and hardware.

After 50 or so conversations, I had a perspective: If we joined with these channel partners, gave them the support they needed, we could scale this.

When I shared my findings with Jim, the president of Apple USA, he asked me to present it to his whole leadership team.

Not one person in the room agreed with me. It wasn't even subtle— there was disdain for the very idea of working with one-off solutions. And why trust outsiders? Why give power to people not in the room? I seemed to be the only one at corporate seeing the potential in a collaboration.

And then Jim turned to me and said, "Why don't you lead this project?"

I blinked. "What?" I wasn't even sure I'd heard him right. "You know I have zero sales experience, right?"

But he handed me the project. Michelle shook her head when she heard. "It's a setup," she said. "This can't work." And one part of me *fully* agreed. And yet because I'd had these conversations with people doing the work, I knew there was *something* there, something good, something worth pursuing. Not because of what I would do but because of what we could do.

That's how—18 months later—I found myself standing in front of Steve Jobs, representing our entire division. Sharing our results. Those first calls I made to the regional field office asking the super simple questions "What's working?" and "Why?" and "What else do you need to grow?" led to programs that led to new ideas for the product, and so on and so on.

Revenues? Boom.

Growth? Boom.

But the real transformation wasn't in the numbers. It was in how we got there. A bunch of people, from different corners of the company and beyond the walls of the company, came together to create something valuable for all of us. We asked and answered, *What is possible?* And supported what emerged.

Change doesn't happen because one person has all the answers. That's not change. That's control. And while Jobs's bravado was compelling in some way, it's still a king telling his people what to do. Having one party tell everyone else what to do limits our imagination, our ingenuity, our collective and best work.

Following the top-down model of change management causes value to be lost. Read that again.

The data shows that nearly 70% of fresh, new, value-creating ideas are lost because they are silenced or ignored.[2]

During a fellowship at the University of Toronto's Rotman School of Management, I worked with economics and policy researchers for nearly two years, and together we calculated that number.

70%. Seven. Zero.

The number is stunning. It means the *vast* majority of ideas are right in front of us but unseen. Intangible. Invisible. Missed.

It plays out like this: Some people—those with positional power or social status—receive higher initial receptivity for their ideas. Their work gets early support, a "Hey, I can see how that half-baked idea could be made to work," and then receives what is needed to make it a better idea. This early support means their ideas get encouraged. Equally, those without status or power are ignored or denied that important early energy so that their ideas die off before they even get a shot.[3]

Most of us want to believe that all ideas are equally evaluated and the good ones rise to the top while the bad ones fall. The research shows the opposite: Some ideas are set up to be considered, and the rest are treated as if they are invisible.

And, of course, we can self-silence. We can see that others are not listening to us, so we think our ideas must not matter. We can feel the lack of support in how people don't meet with us, and so we believe we're stuck without their buy-in. This self-silencing is not anyone being stupid or not being brave or being uncommitted to their work. No, this is just how the 70% respond to the social cues they are given. Humans, after all, are social animals. Our ability to sense those social cues is a survival skill and necessary given our need to belong to one another.

But it comes at a huge cost.

That same research at Rotman sized up the economic cost: It represents at least $1 trillion of untapped value. A number so large, most of us can't even figure out what it means. And this is far more than economic value. It's the loss of rich human capacity, of the value each of us has to offer. And this distinctive, if invisible, value affects the widest set of stakeholders—beyond the firm, its employees, or its owners. It's a gap for our various communities. These dynamics easily explain why we're not seeing cures for cancer or solutions to address climate change or whatever else could be solved with new and novel ideas, or fresh approaches.

And that's why each of us has to chase our ideas down.

Chase it down. It's a phrase I use often that was inspired by the story of a poet who could feel a poem approaching her from across the landscape when she was out working in the fields. This sensation was like a thunderous train of air barreling toward her. Upon sensing its arrival, the poet would run like hell to her house, aiming to capture the poem on paper before it passed by. If she was too slow, the poem would continue across the landscape, looking for another poet. At times, she would almost miss it, but by reaching out with her other hand, she could catch the poem by its tail and pull it backward into her body as she transcribed it, resulting in the poem's appearing on the page perfect and intact but backward, from the last word to the first.[4]

New ideas occur to us all the time, but we need to chase them down, pull them through us and into the world. We all need to be our own kind of poets.

Change isn't so much about seeing what no one else has *seen* or thinking what no one else has *thought* but about *acting* in a way that creates—or rather, co-creates—the future.

Years after I left Apple, I ran into Jim at some industry event. By then, he was working for Spencer Stuart, a big leadership and talent search firm. After catching up for a bit, I couldn't help but ask him, "What in the world made you give me that role back then, when no one believed it would work?"

He paused for a moment, then smiled. "You believed," he said simply. "And that was enough. I had to trust that if your curiosity had taken you that far in just a week, it would take you wherever we needed to go. Everyone else doubted anything was possible, but you didn't. You were willing to explore, to do the next right thing. And that's how change really happens."

I stood there, taking it in.

And now I can see that this is how change works, every time. Organically. Iteratively. Change is ever-present, and emergent. Despite what we've been taught, change is not about an edict or an event, and someone "making" it happen to others. That's domination and control being packaged up and sold to us as change.

Anytime we participate in controlling relationships, whether professionally or personally, we are saying that it's okay to be controlled. And it's never okay.

Fear of Uncertainty

When change seems impossible, we are told what to do: *Persist. Stop asking for permission. Pick yourself first. Be brave. Never give up.* But these edicts suggest that the limiting factor is ego or willpower. It's not.

Humans block change for a very specific reason: We fear the unknown. We fear it because it affects several foundational things:

- Our sense of purpose. Even if we don't like or know our current purpose, it grounds us. The unknowing—that feeling that we don't know what matters next—unmoors us.

- Our identity. If we can't imagine who we will be and become in the future, we resist change; we never want to annihilate ourselves.
- Our dignity. What if we can't handle the new and uncertain thing? Then we lose face and thus our social standing—which is a very big threat to Self.

Jonathan Fields, a friend of mine and the author of a thoughtful book on the workings of change, once shared with me one reason that a particular book of his didn't sell in high volume. The title: *Uncertainty.*[5] "No one chooses uncertainty," he said with a laugh. "At least not willingly."

Yet we all live with uncertainty; to deny that is to deny reality.

The limiting norm of change management as something you make happen through schedules and plans and directives is just an effort to control uncertainty.

And we only ever try to control that which we don't trust.

If we don't trust ourselves—that we can handle the unknown—we impose rules for how change should happen. If we don't trust others—to care, to participate, to allow themselves to be changed—we say that we can't move forward until they buy in. Controlling behavior is just a sign that we don't trust that it'll be okay. That we'll be okay.

So when change isn't happening, three reasons are given:

1. So-and-so doesn't want it enough (as if the issue is willpower).
2. The plan for change was wrong (as if people are stupid).
3. Someone didn't execute the plan (as if people are lazy).

These are all ways to "blame and shame" rather than acknowledge the fundamental human condition—our fear of uncertainty.

And, interestingly, the research says that when people are blaming and shaming, it causes responses that physiologically limit our best work; specifically, our levels of feel-good hormones—dopamine, oxytocin, serotonin, and endorphins—all drop, affecting our reward systems, bonding, and mood. This biochemical response leads to an increase in the stress hormone cortisol, which literally puts our brain in survival mode and thus takes up the resources for higher brain functions, like generating creative solutions.[6] Our increased anxiety also narrows our perspective, so we literally cannot see the world around us and can't tap into the resources at our disposal.[7] Not to mention that anxiety often leads to avoidance, which keeps us stuck.[8]

We literally stop *being able* to change when we are blamed for having a natural, human, and right reaction to uncertainty.

This is a bind most of us find ourselves in.

Again, not *those* people.

Us.

And when in a bind, humans will default to what humans naturally do to survive: *seek out comfort.* Comfort is freedom from distress, an easing of constraint. Optimizing for comfort is good, even savvy, if things are fine as is. It allows for stability, continuity, and consistency.

But what if things aren't fine as they are? What if the status quo isn't working? What if, for example, we are collectively facing a global climate crisis, rising inequality, or deteriorating health conditions? What if your team isn't delivering what you know they're capable of, or the situation requires something new of you all? What then?

If we're comfortable, we're repeating what's already worked in the past. Or even repeating what hasn't worked because it is still the thing that's known, and therefore comfortable.

To be clear, chasing comfort is not good or bad. It's just a thing. (We won't end this dilemma by judging the dilemma.) No one chooses comfort to harm anyone. We choose comfort to *protect* ourselves. To keep *safe.* To *survive.*

It's primal. Kind of a big deal.

So the right to comfort is not to be judged as *incorrect* but needs to be addressed because it leaves us *incomplete.*

Seeking comfort rather than change is what limits our best work. Because it limits progress. Change is an important attribute for all things. New information, experiences, and demands that broaden our minds are meant to challenge our earlier beliefs. They open the door to new ideas and allow for multiple points of view to be valued and integrated.

Change is necessary so we keep advancing and growing and creating. To not change is to be stagnant. To change is to be expansive. These patterns show up in our personal lives, our professional teams, and the marketplace.

And now one tough piece of news.

If we have the *privilege* to choose comfort—our own, that of our bosses, that of those who would like the continuity of the old guard—we need to see that it's coming at someone else's expense. When we default to comfort, we're inadvertently voting to perpetuate what *has been*, which means we're protecting the past and stifling progress. To protect the past is to protect all the ways that white supremacy, patriarchy, classism, colorism, or any other system of privilege is encoded in the organizations we operate in. To choose comfort in that light is to stand in the way of growth and change, and to lose that 70% of ideas we so desperately need.

And that's why I am loudly, emphatically, unapologetically, and unequivocally asking you to step up. To step in. To chase what matters to you.

As you change, all the bullshit that limits us changes also.

Get Uncomfortable

Given that our brain is wired to seek comfort, can we shift and make room for change?

Yes, we can.

We do it by creating a new neural pathway. And we start that process by creating a mental pause—putting a smidge of space between the default response and the conscious choice.

How do we do this exactly? By *practicing* it.

A gym I belong to is part of a chain called Orangetheory Fitness (OTF). They're known for high-intensity workouts, especially this thing they call "All Outs." The idea is that the body needs to have a wide range of activity levels to get fit. We can't just do the same old thing and expect anything to improve. As the name suggests, All Outs are when you go as hard as possible. For example, I run about a 10-minute mile in the neighborhood, but All Outs have me running the equivalent of 7:30-minute miles, or, on good days, 6:40-minute miles.

During All Outs, I nearly always feel like I'm going to die, that this *all out* is also the *end of me.* And in this way, the all-out experience mirrors what change is at work. At our core, "change" always seems dangerous.

As my heart rate rises—to 91 or 95% of its maximum, which feels life-threatening—I often question if it makes sense to go so hard. I start to think of good reasons to stop or at least slow down. I remember not sleeping well the night before, eating lunch late, or being dehydrated. I imagine a twinge somewhere. I start telling myself a story about why I should take it easy and not overdo it. In other words, I start rationalizing how to stop or stall change and accept the status quo. We protect ourselves because we instinctively know how to survive—stay comfortable.

But all that changes depending on how the All Out is teed up.

Before an All Out is called, some trainers will say, "You're going to go all out for one minute." And then they'll add, "It's supposed to be uncomfortable." And often, they'll explain that it won't last forever by saying there will be recovery afterward, say walking for 30 or 90 seconds.

The tee-up allows someone that mental pause to shift from unconscious resistance to conscious choice. Without it, any of us (picture me raising my hand high) can easily default to comfortable choices and find plenty of good reasons to do so. Knowing that it's expected to get uncomfortable and that it won't last forever lets us interrupt that self-protective, comfort-seeking part of ourselves and choose to stay all in.

As we practice dealing with discomfort, consciously, we create the space for change.

The same theory applies to our approach to change at work. Instead of saying, "Oh, we're all good with change," why not admit that any—and every—particular change brings up some specific scaries? Denying the scaries doesn't make them any less real. Even if you're unaware of your own fears and anxieties—or someone else's—they still exist.

We can do for each other what the OTF trainer is doing for the class.

Instead of leaving people to their own devices, we can help one another be open to change by asking some version of the question *Are we willing to be uncomfortable?* And reminding one another that the discomfort won't last forever.

We can ask our colleagues, "What about not knowing is uncomfortable for you?" Our ability to have these uncomfortable conversations shifts every-thing. By asking and observing, we're not solving things for each other. We're simply making room to see the situation we need to address clearly. As my friend and professor of innovation Tim Kastelle says, a conversation is the smallest unit of change.[9]

Because you can't solve a problem you aren't willing to have.

Trying to discuss change without acknowledging how much we are already protecting against change isn't going to work; that's why it hasn't yet. This is the kindest way I have of explaining why we collectively mostly keep doing what we were doing a long time ago.

Where true change exists, so too does choice.

Until we can name our contradictions—the stories, feelings, and tensions—we'll inadvertently protect ourselves and stall progress.[10] If we want to stop perpetuating the status quo, we must try new approaches. We can choose to get uncomfortable. This especially applies to leaders who can ask others to "change" but not expect the same of themselves. And the thing is, just like at OTF, the discomfort won't last forever.

Once we face the uncomfortable part of change, we can grow new muscles. And in doing that, grow new capabilities.

Crawl Toward the Future

I should share—in all transparency—that I complain nearly every inch of the way at OTF. It's deeply uncomfortable to be growing, changing. This complaining is similar to what a baby does when learning to crawl. Babies cry not because something's wrong but because they're expressing what it feels like to expand their own comfort level. They are learning that first a hand has to move, and then the opposing knee—or else a face-plant happens. This process, known as *motor frustration*, is not only normal but crucial. It's signaling how we're actively living through discomfort to develop skills and reach a desired goal. The gap between a baby's *desire* to crawl and their lived *capacity* can be frustrating. Maybe it even *should* be frustrating. But that frustration, those tears, is part of the process of growth—just like ours, when we struggle through something new.

Complaining isn't, by itself, a sign of failure. It might very well be an expression of progress, as we'll discuss in chapter 2.

But you know what is a sign of failure? When we live within the comfort of what we know now. When we settle for easy certitude and common fears instead of choosing freedom. When we want something to be perfect from the outset, we stall its existence; the first task is to make it exist, then you can make it good. All of these are the equivalent of the baby sitting on their butt and not making the developmental motions that lead to crawling and later walking and running.

Oh, and one last thing. Babies don't crawl for the sake of crawling. They crawl because they want *something*. And they are tired of trying to get someone else to get it for them. They want autonomy. They crawl for a purpose.

So many teams try to generate change through prescriptive design: someone telling everyone else what's going to happen. Or bosses who determine the levels of contribution by defining specific roles and responsibilities. Or HR setting clear expectations for performance and then asking people to conform to their predictions about what one can contribute. Or team leaders carving up big meaningful work into bits and pieces. Or a founder who creates a three-part schedule for insights and measurements and operationalizing change, as if we can plan when the insight comes.

Let me ask you this: Why would we ever cage people and limit the ever-expanding capabilities they have? Why would we try to deterministically know ahead of time what contributions are needed? Why wouldn't we instead just enable the unexpected levels of contribution once we engage together?

To change.

This insistence on knowing in advance what is possible is a contemptible way to live in the world because we limit what is possible. "Change management" is just masked control, and a limit of our imagination.

No one starts organizations wanting them to suck. They are created so that we can do bigger, better things—together. We all want to accomplish something we cannot do alone. Yet that passion gets mutated through change management into procedures, rules, and roles. Instead of a bold mission, we get policies. Instead of generating aliveness, we get squeezed, flattened, emptied. Trapped.

Instead of wanting to *engineer* change, how about we simply *embrace* change? Instead of *planning* change, we *practice* change.

This is the path to our liberation.

To our future.

INNOVATION PRACTICE
Date Fear

Goal: Practice being uncomfortable, so we learn it won't kill us.

Fear—and its cousins shame, guilt, and anxiety—often drive our actions invisibly. A date with fear is a chance to sit with discomfort, listen to what's useful, and still choose a path consciously. It's a rhythm, a practice of being.

The practice? Being in uncomfortable conversations. Because conversations are the smallest unit of change.

This isn't a solo or purely intellectual exercise. We can't think our way into transformation. We need each other. When we turn toward discomfort together, we create a social container that makes change possible.

Practice Prompt

One person asks. One reflects.

- What's scary about this specific change?
- What part of us is scared? (Name the parts—each has a reason.)
- How does this fear serve us?
- What story could we let go of to be present in the now?
- What new story might let us face what is?

By naming what's present, we loosen its grip. We're not trying to silence fear—we're choosing not to act from it. When we date fear, we don't become it. We act from freedom.

2

The One with the Pain Is(n't) the One with the Problem

Limiting Norm: Demonize the Person
Leading Indicator: Deal with the Problem

My boss just told me I'm being too demanding, Shauna texted. You'll never believe what's happening as I try to do what I was hired for. Oh, wait, maybe you will.

I did. And so would *any* change agent—those of us who love to make things better.

Those of us who raise issues often get blamed in a tone that says, "How dare you be upset with us" and "Don't call us out on our stuff." We're called "overly critical" and made out to be the *source* of the pain rather than the one *revealing* the pain in order to heal it.

You might even be thinking that about me as I bring up these norms that limit our best work. When someone is bringing up something uncomfortable—which is at the heart of all progress—it's natural to deal with that discomfort by *demonizing* the person rather than *dealing* with the issue. Casting someone as the culprit serves as a shield to progress, similar to choosing comfort over change. It's the flip side of the same coin.

To be sure, being "too demanding" is negative. It's the boss who insists on a weekend meeting without specifying a time, leaving you unable to make plans. It's the *Devil Wears Prada* fly-me-outta-here-in-the-middle-of-a-hurricane boss who is impossible to please. It's the Steve

Jobs persona who dominates the conversation, draining the room of all the oxygen, leaving everyone gasping for air. And that person who just gripes endlessly without a solution in sight? They're not only exhausting but also a soul-sucking force of nature who drags everyone down.

But Shauna was doing none of that. She was just being labeled that way. Why?

Labeling people as the problem is how defensive people go on the offense. To get someone to back *up*, back *down*, or simply *get out*.

Yet what does the "critical" person want for us?

It's what we want for ourselves: to grow.

Demonized and Divisive

For nearly a decade, Google had tasked Ross LaJeunesse with protecting human rights in China. In this role, he developed the company's plan to stop censoring search results. Google was celebrated for this support of free expression and data privacy.[1] LaJeunesse, who held various executive roles at Google, was trusted throughout the company and received rave performance reviews. That changed in 2019 when LaJeunesse felt the company moving away from the values he—and they—had championed.

So he tried to sway minds.

At one point, he joined 1,400 employees in signing an internal letter criticizing Google's failure to be transparent about its plans in China.

Visibly at odds with the company's leaders, he was told he was being problematic. One day, he was accidentally copied on an email.[2] An HR director said LaJeunesse seemed to "raise concerns a lot" and instructed staff to "do some digging" on LaJeunesse himself instead of the privacy issues.

Google was *demonizing the person* bringing the problem to their attention instead of *dealing with the problem*.

This happens despite the evidence that denying dissent just leads to conformity, not creativity.[3] It happens in every size of company, and across industries, throughout marketing to sales to product teams, and at every level. And perhaps most surprisingly, it doesn't matter how powerful or popular the person was before they started agitating for change.

First, they are told they shouldn't *raise* so many problems. *Check.*
Then, if they continue, they're told *they* are the problem. *Mate.*
Checkmate!

The person is now in an inescapable position. So is everyone else. Stuck.

Labeling people as the problem is how defensive people go on the offense.

Having been checkmated far too many times in the past, Shauna had anticipated issues.

During her interviews to join this big bank, she had been told that "everyone knew" there were obstacles to growth. Still, no one had been able to put together strategies to address the necessary changes. The organization was creating a role for someone to champion change. As an incoming senior director, Shauna would report to the VPs of both marketing and product development as her job scope spanned those areas. So she had insisted on having the two leaders interview her together. She wanted to look them in the eye and have them tell her together how they would back her when the time came.

"I was so proud of myself for setting the stage for success by having this conversation; I thought it meant the path was paved to address the actual problems, you know?" Shauna told me.

Then she dug in, spending her first 60 days on the job studying the situation.

She attended meetings, asked questions, and researched the marketplace responses to different campaigns. Then, using all this data, she did a classic "gap analysis" between what the firm said they wanted when they hired her (a customer set that reflected the broader demographics) and how well they reached that goal (not so well). She previewed her analysis with colleagues who had more history with the issues, and those people confirmed that her insights were on point. Then, as her bosses had requested, she put together a three-part strategic plan to bridge the gap.

"I did everything carefully, and with the best intentions," she told me.

And this is an important thing she's saying.

Change agents do the change-work never to *cause* pain but to *relieve* pain. Yes, of course they know it's going to hurt a little, to make everyone a little uncomfortable. But they are keeping their eye on the prize: growth for us, benefit for all.

Despite all her prep work, Shauna got pushback when she shared her take—lots of it.

"Whhhhat is happening?!" she vented to me a day after our texting. "They hired me to improve this stuff, but now it's like all they want to hear is that they are already great."

In another meeting just a month later, she tried to provide even more context: To ease into the topic, she reminded people why she was hired. Then she described the process they used (which everyone had already bought into), to tee up the insight.

But, again, when she named the problem, she sensed something off in the room.

"As I was talking about the challenge, I could swear that one of my bosses was translating what I was saying into something I wasn't. I was saying, 'It sucks,' and he heard it as 'You suck.' I started to question if I was being too harsh or maybe saying something that could be easily interpreted as 'You all sucked before I got here.'"

Rather than the truth being recognized as a vehicle for freedom, it became something to fear.

Every change agent can wonder if the pushback they get is deserved. Did they state things too strongly? Were they personalizing the issue? Was it not clear why they were pointing out the gaps? Each of us owes it to one another to name issues effectively, so they can be heard.

Given the response she was getting, Shauna started to couch her words, saying things more "kindly" and using more euphemisms. Instead of saying, "This isn't going to get better until we fix it," she said, "Some things we might want to consider are . . ."

She was backing up.

After a while, she couldn't even tell what she was advocating for. She had stopped doing what was right for the business in an effort to avoid being seen as a shit-starter, rabble-rouser, or pot-stirrer. For as much as we collectively value *disruption*, none of us like being labeled this type of *disruptor*. It's scary to be on the outside.

But Shauna noticed that softening didn't make a difference. If anything, backing up and toning down her words muddied the waters, making the subject less clear. Kindness is often described as that *soft* place to land when what we need is a *solid* way to work. This is how defensiveness emotionally manipulates the change agent to fail. To be defensive is to act like the victim of the situation, falsely making the change-agent the villain.

So the champion for progress starts to back *up*, back *down*, or *leave*.

And all of us suffer.

After all, we can't solve things if the truth of them is denied.

Shauna's bosses had a meeting—without her this time—and said to one another, "The one with the pain is the one with the problem." How did she know this? It was documented in her performance review, where she was also labeled "divisive to the team."

Le sigh.

Divergent, dissident voices are the key to growth and innovation.[4] All the research backs that up. Even if you're "incorrect" in what you propose, just asking a question and voicing an opinion can enhance your team's performance by 30%.[5] Dissident voices add something to a group that, on balance, makes them generate more creative ideas and make far better decisions.

Yet blaming the person rather than dealing with the issue is a management norm.

It's a redirection like when a magician draws your eyes away from the deck of cards to perform a sleight of hand. *And for this next trick, I'll make our problems disappear* . . . Redirection limits our best work because it means we're not facing the challenge at hand.

This has a long history that precedes the business moment.

In America, refusing to acknowledge the widespread genocide of Native Americans leaves the country unable to address those traumas. In fact, the word *genocide* is almost never used in standard K–12 curricula, even though scholars' and the UN's definition of genocide clearly applies to Native peoples. That's *denial*. In 2021, researchers at UCLA published a study to quantify the theft of land, and one estimate was that $1.5 trillion in land wealth was extracted from Native Americans to give to white settlers under programs like the Homestead Act. America didn't just erase lives; it stole and redistributed that wealth. Descendants of those homesteaders still disproportionately benefit from that wealth transfer. Today, many Native communities are depicted as drains on our economy, with stereotypes like that of the drunken Indian. As if the problem is some individuals and not the large-scale policy that led to destitution. And teaching a concept of "manifest destiny" justifies the theft, a *redirection*. When scholars try to document the full history, their books are banned. Banning books that don't sugarcoat the history of America is another redirection. So groups then discuss the book ban, not the original topic.

That's what's happening at work, too: denial and redirection. It's far too easy. After all, the person voicing the problem begins to sound like the problem, especially for those who don't know what the problem is. The tension then becomes Shauna vs. boss and LaJeunesse vs. Google. In those power dynamics, boss and Google will nearly always win, and individuals are silenced. The topics of broadening the customer base or addressing human rights in China get lost in the fray.

The more challenging the situation, the more likely a person will be penalized for bringing the issue forward. That's why in equity-related topics like sexual harassment or equal pay, it's common to demonize the players involved and, in some cases, fire the leaders agitating for change rather than take on the issues themselves.[6]

The solution lies in the simplest, most often overlooked step: Be open to a critique.

The Gift of Complaint

Claire didn't just move to Arizona for a change of scenery—she went for a shot at something bigger. After sitting in her salon chair for eight years, I saw how good she was at thinking of ways to grow. Herself and the business.

Being a hairstylist wasn't the endgame for her. She loved working with her hands, but she knew the limits on how far she could go financially. And that she'd eventually age out of the work because it involves spending long hours standing on one's feet. Thinking ahead, she wanted to learn the business side.

So when she got the chance to help manage a salon, she took it without hesitation.

Even though this meant moving out of state and away from friends and family, Claire found a way to make it work. (She spent one week a month in California to take care of her loyal clients, easing both the financial and emotional impact of her transition.)

At first, Claire was patient at the new salon. She watched, listened, and waited for her moment. She'd been hired as an "assistant to the CEO," and she was supposed to have an opportunity to grow the salon. "I was looking to see where I could help most," she said.

As she asked questions like "Why are we doing this instead of that?," she found herself getting pushback. Over time, her questions sharpened. "Why aren't we using social media to push our higher-margin services?" But she still didn't get a response. The more she learned, the clearer it became—things weren't changing, and no one (other than her) seemed all that interested in growth.

The salon then did to Claire what Google did to Ross LaJeunesse and the bank did to Shauna. Claire got labeled as divisive for wanting what was best for the firm. She was told that she was "complaining" too much. "Don't complain, because it brings everyone around you down," the salon owner said. "That's not how we grow."

This is the kind of comment that makes me seriously frustrated. On behalf of Claire, and on behalf of all of us who get shut down.

Because complaining is a *necessary—critical*, even—part of how we grow.

We complain as we identify the gap between where we are and where we need to be. It's the baby crawling and experiencing motor frustration we talked about in chapter 1. Complaints in adult life are us highlighting the underlying issues that might otherwise be overlooked, thus facilitating opportunities for discovery, discussion, and improvement. Sharing complaints with others is how we express our own desire for something else. And when it's heard, it fosters a kind of solidarity, essentially leading to the question *Don't we deserve better?*

I listened to Claire as she shared her struggles. I listened to her question herself, wondering if she was overreacting or even overreaching.

And I told her then the same thing I'm telling you now. The same thing I've had to tell myself a million times over.

Being labeled as critical or divisive for wanting what is good for everyone is a form of manipulation.

To be fair, by the time any of us ask for a problem to be solved, we've probably gone past the patient stage, the curious phase, and maybe even the calm phase. We've likely become a little strident, anxious, and bothered. We can get frustrated and show frustration with those who are not as interested.

But those who would rather keep things the same use this against us. They say our style is the problem, redirecting attention away from the fact that progress is stalled. They say our tone is unhelpful. And because we know we've crossed a line from initial curiosity to bold naming, because we know we're making people uncomfortable with what we see and name and raise, we can question if we're handling things as well as is needed. This introspection process is healthy, just as our questions driving growth are healthy. But this is also how someone uses our capacity to pause, reflect, and grow against us. When someone tells you that your tone is wrong—*tone-policing* is the name for this—they are doing it to dismiss or derail the message by criticizing the delivery. That part is not healthy. Not for any of the people involved, nor for our collective growth.

Unwinding Checkmates

If we're being honest (which is kind of the point here), we've all been guilty of what Google, Shauna's boss, and Claire's boss did. It's sneaky little habits that show up whenever we're faced with feedback, criticism, or any moment of discomfort that might call for our own growth. And if you're thinking, *Nope, not me, I don't do that,* congratulations, lovebug—you've just deployed the first of the 3 D's that create organizational checkmates: *defensiveness.*

Imagine someone is trying to talk to you about how you could improve in a specific area, and instead of engaging with how to do so, you find yourself bringing up new and different topics. "Yeah, well, you know, you have problems, too. I hate it when you do A, B, and C." Welcome to the next D, *deflection*, where you try to dodge your own accountability by changing the subject. Bonus points for changing the subject to include the person raising the issue.

And then there's the third D: *deference*. This one can be a bit sneakier. It shows up when we feel somehow powerless or when we're trying to avoid conflict. Someone calls you out on a mistake and you respond, "You're right, I guess I just don't know what I'm doing, maybe you should just take over," effectively handing the reins back to them, absolving yourself of responsibility while looking like the humble victim. You roll over, give up.

Sound at all familiar? Maybe a little too familiar? Feeling called out?

Don't worry—you're not alone.

And also, this is a call-in. We've all been there (whether we want to acknowledge it or not). These 3 D's are part of the human condition. They're what we do when we're feeling threatened, overwhelmed, or unsure of ourselves. We protect ourselves.

But here's the kicker: Every time we let defensiveness, deflection, or deference take the wheel, we're robbing ourselves of the opportunity to consider if and how the critique makes sense, and therefore grow.

We *know* this, but we rarely *know what to do* about it.

Not when we're doing it, and not when others are doing it to us.

So let's just process each D and see if we can recognize what's happening in real time to then redirect the conversation back to something of use, which is growth-oriented, and hopefully even enlivening.

Let's start with defensiveness. It's a reflex, a knee-jerk response that is someone acting as if they're under attack. People get defensive when they equate feedback with judgment, and nobody likes feeling like they're being judged—especially when the thing they're being judged on is something they care about (or, worse, insecure about).

Defensiveness in action was "Ross is making problems for us by raising issues about China at the same time the US government is saying we're not managing privacy issues well. Why is he bringing this up now? We are just trying to do good things!" Google's leadership and HR teams might not even have realized that they were doing it, but by being defensive, they blocked their own growth.

To address defensiveness, one can say: "I hear that you're feeling attacked, but this is not about assigning blame."

In other words, *name* the defensiveness and ask the person to *recenter* on the real issue at hand. This may require you to return to the topic later.

Next is deflection. Ever bring up an important topic, only to end up in a 20-minute conversation about an upcoming budget meeting, or your colleague's recently diagnosed gluten intolerance? Deflection is avoiding responsibility by changing the subject.

Deflection protects people from facing their own uncomfortable truths, so they divert attention from their own actions and point the spotlight elsewhere—*anywhere* else. If they attack the other person involved? Well, *that* is the gold medal of deflection skills. "Even though I *never* brought up whatever other topic before, I am bringing it up now, so let's discuss that first."

Pain Olympics, I call this.

Don't fall for the deflection game. Gently but firmly *redirect* back to the issue. "Let's talk about one thing at a time; we can talk about that *after* we've effectively dealt with this."

And finally, there's deference. Deference in action is when someone bows out of a situation by handing all the power over to you. It's them going limp, knowing you can't possibly drag their body over the finish line. They'll say, "You're right," not because they agree but because they're saying whatever they need to in order to escape the conversation. It feels like you've won, but no surprise here: You haven't. Deference is sneaky because it can look like agreement or acceptance, but in reality, the person is just sidestepping their responsibility to engage. Telling you they'll leave everything to you is not agreement; it's saying whatever they need to in order for them to not have to deal with things. Deference sounds good, but think about what someone is doing. Deferring. Putting off. Putting aside.

You want to handle it by encouraging *involvement* instead of surrender.

You might say: "I appreciate your trust in me, but for this to work, it has to be a team effort. What part of this project do you feel comfortable leading?"

When you encounter one of the 3 D's—defensiveness, deflection, or deference—the key is to recognize that these responses are all about self-preservation.

We want to guide the person away from feeling *cornered* and toward feeling *capable* of handling the situation. And if you're the person employing one of the 3 D's—which, again, is natural—teach yourself that your job is to be comfortable being uncomfortable. When you slip up, just notice that you did, pause, and return to the conversation like the grown-ass adult that you are, or at least want to be.

By naming the 3 D's, we face the issues. We *deal.* After all, the danger isn't the critique. No, the real danger is when we resist change and stop growing. It's when people stop raising issues that depletion, stagnation, and economic flatlining set in.

Revealing the Pain Reveals the Possibilities

When we name the gap between where we are and where we want to be, it is not done to harm.

No, we are reaching for better. For a better future. Even our best future.

Yet revealing the painful parts evokes an emotional reaction in people.

I can guarantee that some will say that by raising the issues I raise in this book, I am being a downer. They will say that I am not helping by showing the gaps, ask why I don't focus on the benefits of collaborative leadership. They will suggest that I be more positive, as if my tone in writing about what holds us back is the issue. They will perhaps criticize the use of personal stories because that changes the topic to the vulnerability and the underbelly I am showing.

They will call me divisive. They will pull out every single one of the 3 D's.

And in anticipation of their reaction, I might *back up* or *back down* or *quit* altogether. But here's the thing: If I backed up and backed off because of those concerns, we'd all lose.

The person willing to be critical is deconstructing what we love so it can be reconstructed into something better. The person creating the conversation for change is fighting for the things we love. For we only ever invest our energy in something we love. So that person who knows the issues well enough to say, with real intimacy, that better is possible? They are fighting for you. And you need to stop fighting them.

What no one says is how a "divisive" voice is someone who can do three things at the same time. They not only can *imagine* that better is possible, but they've also got the *operational chops* to figure out where the gap is, and they are *willing* to handle any necessary conflict; that combination is both rare and needed. They can be of help to those who are more conflict-avoidant, the don't-rock-the-boat types. They serve the whole.

Why? They are willing to name the hard thing to help us do the hard thing. Having people raise issues is a leading indicator that they care and are willing to fight for improvement and growth, which should be celebrated. Our pain isn't the problem; the problem is the problem.

And here's the final truth: If you deny people a chance to help you, they'll go somewhere else and help another company defeat you.

INNOVATION PRACTICE
Dodge the 3 D Ball

*Goal: Practice the art of steering the
conversation to get back on track.*

Get Ready:

- Grab a peer and a soft ball (a tennis ball works great).
- Write the 3 D's—defend, deflect, defer—on different parts of the ball.

How It Works:

- One person tosses the ball. The catcher glances at the word facing up and acts it out—gets defensive, deflects the issue, or defers responsibility. Don't overthink it; just stay in the moment and channel someone who does this in real life.
- The partner's job? Bringing the conversation back on track. Practice redirecting with clarity and calm.
- Then switch: The responder becomes the actor and tosses the ball again.
- Keep the pace brisk. Do 10 rounds each (20 total). In groups, take turns or rotate pairs—aim to finish in 10 minutes.
- Repeat. Do the exercise a few times over a few weeks.

Example:

- Catcher sees "Deflect" and says, "Yeah, I didn't double-check the numbers, but don't you think we need a bigger budget anyway?"
- Responder redirects: "Let's talk budget later—right now, how do you want to double-check those numbers?"

3

Disrupting Value

Limiting Norm: Just Do It
Leading Indicator: Do the Right Thing

For years, I, like many, believed that work was largely about one thing: making money. It's why I got so darn good at making money for the boss and the company. Business's job is to make the money, and after you've made enough, you give some away so charity can do good. Everything else was a veneer, a façade, a distraction.

But then something changed for me. I took an elective course in my MBA program called Spirituality in Business.

Now, as a student of applied economics *and* spirituality in business, I've learned that the word *value* has deep roots in both fields. Yet the implications are vastly different. In economics, we measure value by doing what leads to either more or less. More is always good, and less is always, well, less-than-good.

You see this applied at work when people say:

"Just do it."
"Move fast and break things."
"Profit now, perfect later."

These business idioms celebrate action over aspiration. They trumpet outcomes and profits as an organizing principle because without profits, you can't go on to do good. This take on value—*monetary value*—leads teams to prioritize whichever direction leads to *more* money, size, profit, revenue, or stock valuation. It's all about being bigger, the bottom line, and the bank account.

Then there are these ideas at work:

Do what matters.
Create value, not just products.
Make a dent in the universe.

These sayings represent a different take, one that celebrates *humanistic values*. Viewed through this lens, value is not about measuring things but about making a judgment call. Value here is about the *best* way to act or live. It's principles and purpose, what's good and not-so-good. This perspective directs you to what has the most meaning. In business, this means being ethical and responsible, caring about more than the immediate gain, considering the environment and sustainability, and providing social value through your work. This focus on humanistic values gives purpose to the endeavor.

It's the difference between "Just do it" and "Do the right thing."

This difference? It's significant.

At the heart of the question *What is our best work?* is the distinction between these two completely contrasting measures of value.

Now we must decide what we, well, *value*—in the third sense of the word—what something is worth to us. As we do, we're deciding who and what matters *to us* in answering the following questions:

• What should we create?
• Who benefits from that work?

This isn't just an intellectual exercise. These questions and the choices we make shape every single decision. They shape the way we act. And define the economic future we're creating.

In chapter 1, we talked about why we need to address our own discomfort to break free from the norms that limit us. In chapter 2, we explored how to deal with others' discomfort—and the 3 D's—when challenging the status quo.

Now we need to clarify what we truly value—so we know what we're aiming *for*.

What Do We Stand For?

When Paul Polman took the helm of Unilever, he didn't just inherit a mess—he inherited a reckoning.[1]

Unilever was already one of the largest consumer goods companies in the world, ranked among the top 5, but it was underperforming compared with its main competitors, Procter & Gamble and Nestlé. While it had a diverse portfolio of over 400 brands reaching more than 190 countries, the company was focused more on cost-cutting than on innovation. And while there were pockets within this huge firm doing purposeful work, the widespread concern[2] was that Unilever was yet another soulless corporate machine that extracted more value than it generated.

People like Polman aren't brought in to fix the small stuff. He was already known for his strong belief in sustainability and long-term value creation. And now he could put his values into practice. He was there to ask the big questions and find the big solutions: not just how to keep Unilever afloat but how to redefine its very purpose.

Polman's aim at Unilever? To integrate the two distinct disciplines of value.

Enter Dr. Myriam Sidibe, a public health expert and Unilever employee who had created a business model to do just that.

At first glance, all Sidibe was doing was selling a simple bar of soap—just an ordinary product that's been around for thousands of years. But by making it small enough, she made it affordable enough for those who budget day by day, or week by week. Then she made sure that the local kiosks that serve these communities could participate in the profits so that they wanted to stock these little bars of soap. And it wasn't enough to have the right product at the right price in the right places. Soap solves so many preventable deadly diseases like dysentery. But to get people to use soap, she needed a campaign to reach the community and change their social norms. And that was not work that a company can do alone. So she got together with other soap brands, as well as social good organizations (the

UN, nonprofits) and government officials who cared about health in these developing countries and started a campaign that had the reach and impact needed.[3]

This was well on its way before Polman arrived.

But it proved what he believed was possible, what he desired—a purpose-profit model that worked. Not only did sales of the soap brand Lifebuoy grow, so did Unilever's reputation as a company that cared.

When he learned about Sidibe's initiative, he asked her, "How did you manage this?"

"It wasn't just about selling soap. It was about building a coalition," she told him. In these communities, Unilever's role wasn't to sell yet another product, she explained, but to solve a real-life problem. It had to transcend the brand's goals; it had to be a brand on a mission. And, of course, she shared how the business model shifted. Success wasn't just about how Unilever got what they wanted (a purposeful company + profits), but how those kiosks and world health organizations also got what they wanted (solutions that mattered + a portion of the value capture).

- Value was not just *monetary* but also *humanistic*.
- And the value created wasn't just distributed to *one* party but *many*.

Polman was inspired by what he learned. "I came to Unilever because I believe this company can lead in a new way of doing business—where purpose drives profits, not the other way around."

And with Lifebuoy, he had a business model template he *could* and *did* use across the company. Polman leveraged Sidibe's model for the one product for many of the 400 Unilever brands.

Which is its own book,[4] but a few snapshots: Under Polman's leadership—between 2009 and 2021—Unilever's shareholder returns skyrocketed by 300%.[5] And the company changed humanistic social norms for the benefit of many. You might even remember how Dove— another Unilever brand—launched a Real Beauty campaign that showed how women see themselves as compared with how others see them. That coalition, which included the media, struck a powerful chord, sparking a broad conversation about the messages that girls and women receive and accept about their self-worth. Participants in the Dove Self-Esteem Project included parents, schoolteachers, youth leaders, mentors, employees, and organizations such as the World Association of Girl Guides and Girl Scouts. Since its inception, the project has reached over 60 million youths across 150 countries. Independent studies have reported both short-term and long-term boosts in body image and mood among participants after they engaged with the project's workshops and online tools.[6]

Two Steps Forward, One Step Back

After leaving Unilever, Polman continued to believe in the purpose-plus-profits model, and made the rounds at conferences like the World Economic Forum and the Conscious Capitalism CEO Summit. He talked to his contemporaries about what was possible when the two forms of value became integrated.

It was inspiring. And engaging. Even encouraging.

And I wish the story could end there. The feel-good factor paired with the facts: that humanistic values are deeply interconnected with monetary value-creation. But unfortunately, the story took a turn.[7]

After Polman left in 2021, the constant economic challenges post-COVID pushed Unilever to the wall again. The new leadership team was working to find more profits—and fast.

In the fall of 2023, I had a conversation with a Unilever executive at a conference in Cannes, France. He shared the latest thinking of the C-suite: "We can talk about *values* once we've created enough *value*."

I knew what this one sentence meant.

We all know.

It meant that as soon as the profits came under pressure (and once the leader prioritizing purpose was long gone), the integration of the two forms of value just . . . fell apart.

This happens a lot.

As soon as an organization stops "winning" in the profit domain, the purpose-plus-profits strategy is nearly always jettisoned, abandoned, ditched.

This is why many say the purpose-profit marriage is just an illusion.

The economist Mariana Mazzucato calls the purpose conversation that companies play nothing more than a "shell game,"[8] and *New York Times* opinion columnist Anand Giridharadas calls it "an elite charade."[9]

Maybe they are right.

Despite the many bold pronouncements by companies about pursuing purpose and not just profits, evidence shows no real action. In fact, many companies that use these words have aggressively sold addictive drugs such as opioids, instituted mandatory arbitration for sexual harassment, offshored profits to avoid paying their fair share of taxes, and funded politicians to undermine their customers' human rights (women's, transgender, civil). They're even more likely to have higher regulatory compliance violations and emit more carbon.[10]

But it feels like more than just a big con.

And I don't think it's about bad actors.

It seems more persistent than that.

The very norms that form the foundation of our modern economy are driving this. But they are intangible—invisible, even. Unseen, they remain unchallenged, quietly controlling everything.

Lies We've Been Told

Many, if not most, corporate leaders say that *humanistic values* must come after *monetary value*. This is not by accident. We've been taught this norm.

Economist Milton Friedman argued in his 1970 article "The Social Responsibility of Business Is to Increase Its Profits" that a corporation's primary responsibility is to its shareholders and that any focus on social or ethical values should *always* be secondary to maximizing profits.[11]

Economist Adam Smith launched this ideology far earlier, in *The Wealth of Nations* (published in 1776), by saying that if business owners (the butcher, the carpenter, and so on) simply pursued their self-interest, it would *naturally* lead to overall prosperity.[12]

Michael Porter, a famous Harvard management professor whose ideas are taught in virtually every business school in the world, stated that the "essential test of whether a firm should pursue a social objective is not whether a cause is worthy but instead, *only if* there is a chance to create profits while also benefitting society" (italics mine).[13]

Always. Naturally. Only if. Collectively, they are saying that monetary value is *always* more important than humanistic values. And they are saying that it's *always* the firm that should primarily benefit from value-creation.

And this reasoning is why after Polman left Unilever, the newly appointed leadership slowly but surely reverted to the Friedman-Smith-Porter norm. While Polman integrated purpose and profits, once he wasn't there to advocate for both, the default norm slipped back into place, like a needle settling into a well-worn groove on a record.

And some of you will be thinking, *Duh, girlfriend; this is how it is. Capitalism 101.*

My point is that it is how it is, but not what it could be. It remains stuck, limited, only if we accept their value systems as our own.

After all, this tussle over profits vs. purpose is a red herring, in that it distracts. Asking the question of whether the focus should be on purpose *or* profits is creating a tension that leads us to collectively believe there is a trade-off.

It's a way of thinking, a framework, that purposefully misleads us.

Mind you, we've all used this framing to great effect in one way or another.

It's when you ask a colleague whether they want to meet at 4 or 5, not if they want to meet at all. Or when you ask your child if they want peas or carrots. The question isn't *if* they want vegetables, because you've already decided that Kiddo has to have their veggies. And so the kid has *some* choice, *some* self-determination, but in a way that is very limited, an illusion of choice. Now, it's one thing when we presuppose that our colleagues want to meet with us, or when parents do stuff to (hopefully) serve their kid's best interests, but another thing altogether when a pre-set framework is used to tell us the point of work.

The data is consistent: Values do not negatively affect *value*. Not by any stretch of the imagination. Companies that prioritize ethical values, corporate social responsibility, and long-term sustainability perform better over time.[14] A study by *Harvard Business Review* found that companies with strong environmental, social, and governance (ESG) practices nearly always have lower costs of capital, better operational performance, and stronger stock market returns.[15] Similarly, research from Deloitte suggests that businesses with a strong sense of purpose aligned with values experience greater employee engagement, customer loyalty, and long-term success.[16] And then there's the NYU Stern Center for Sustainable Business meta-study of more than a thousand research papers that concluded that companies with strong ESG propositions have lower cost of capital, better operational performance, and higher stock price performance over the long term.[17]

There is *no* question.

And you know this. We all do, actually.

- When people feel encouraged, their performance rises.
- When we take time to listen to new ideas, innovation happens.
- When we have empathy, we build for equity, accessibility, and sustainability.
- When we focus on enhancing the quality of life for all stakeholders, we design for a larger audience.
- When we care about the intrinsic well-being of others, we foster the kind of psychological safety that leads to creativity.

At the practical level, those of us doing the work of work—whether it's called innovation, entrepreneurship, problem-solving, collaboration, design thinking, digital transformation, user experience (UX), growth strategies, business model generation, or psychological safety—*already* apply humanistic values if we're any good at our value-creating work.

Yet most of us accept a framework that firms and shareholders deserve most or even 100% of the benefit of the value created because they're the ones who capitalized it. Well, that's *one* way of thinking. But it's not the *only one*. Ecological, feminist, and Indigenous ways of working—long neglected in mainstream management—show us another. They offer us ways to conceptualize the way we create and distribute value as a web of relations, where the firm is not at the center nor even the first among equals but simply one collaborator among many.[18]

So why do we buy into the status quo? Why do we not challenge those who sell us the prioritization of monetary value above all else? After all, the people who invented the ideas of how self-interested people work in markets that operate efficiently and that a manager's job is to profit-optimize do not seem that connected to reality. Adam Smith, who championed the self-interest idea in economics, did so while his mother quietly managed the household, feeding and caring for him.[19] Yet Smith's entire economic model ignored the very thing that sustained him: love. Found in the form of unpaid emotional and household labor. But he wrote as if she didn't exist, severing his economic thesis from what made his work, his life, possible. There's a beautiful book on the topic, *Who Cooked Adam Smith's Dinner?* by Swedish author Katrine Marçal.

Friedman's philosophy laid the groundwork for deregulation, privatization, and the reduction of government spending. Many governments today spend their energy to enrich the wealthy instead of helping everyone keep our promises to each other, as fellow citizens, neighbors, friends. The promises of education and libraries, of health and care, of being supported as we get old because we paid into the system. And Porter's argument that subordinates societal good to profit reinforces the very system that causes the harm.

Phew.

That's a lot to digest about what is flawed in these economic theories, even for me.

And so let me just say this.

Powerful people tell us that caring for each other doesn't matter.

They tell us that doing things for the common good is stupid.

And that money and the things that lead to more power is the goal.

The *primary* goal.

And if we believe those things, accept their values as our own, that's a choice.

But if you don't believe these things but believe you don't have a choice, that's the trap. If you tell yourself that this is the way it has to be—that money is the ultimate goal, that efficiency is the highest virtue, that the market will always correct itself—you have sacrificed your own humanity, your community's well-being, and the planet's future. And so the trap is self-imposed. The way out requires something harder than most of us feel we're up for. Yet if we're going to move toward freedom, this is the way. We need to open ourselves to the uncomfortable possibility that we can believe something different than the existing norm.

Which will make us feel like we're on the outside, and that's scary— that is, until we realize that we don't want to live in that cage.

It's a chance to reclaim or claim a vision of economics that includes each of us.

The word *economics* traces back to *oikos*, the Greek word for "home" or "household." It was once a measure of *our* community's health, the activity that kept *us* alive. Economics was therefore human *and* monetary, *and* tied to the well-being of most of us, not just a few. Now, it was never perfect—inequality has always existed, and some have always been left out. But the original economic definition answered the deeper question: What is the point of all this? An economy was more than profits; it was about sustaining life, about keeping our shared lives flourishing. That's something powerful, something we can reclaim.

Many argue that profits have to come first, because that's what lets us drive growth. But that denies that there are many ways to make money. Structure follows strategy. Take Southwest Airlines, an oldie-but-goodie example of how a company came in and completely changed the airline industry with their values of humanity, humor, and accessibility. Those values shaped their entire operating model, from boarding procedures to fleet design. They made money even though "everyone" thought that what they did was "impossible." Money follows meaning.

Profit is simply an outcome of what you choose to design for.

Take Uber. It didn't invent ride-sharing; it built a business model around convenience and scale. But if the founding value had been transportation access, it could've looked entirely different—worker-owned networks, transparent pricing, advocacy for public transportation, localized algorithms. Would it be a different business? Absolutely. Less viable? Not at all. I say this as someone who builds business models for a living: There are many, many ways to make a load of money. So, the question is never *if* you can make money by centering values. It's *what becomes possible* when you do.

Now I want to address why so many don't believe this shift is possible. Those who say you *have* to prioritize chasing the mighty dollar over serving a larger mission. Those who say you *have* to serve their shareholders above all else. And why they can only *make* purpose work if it's a win-win.

I hear you that you believe that, but I want you to see something.

It's that you don't know what else is possible. It's almost as if you don't understand that you deserve better.

I've been exactly where you are. Not just in business, but in the deepest, most personal way.

Most business books, if they include the personal at all, do it in a sanitized, instrumental way: "Empathy improves innovation." "Resilience helps retention." "Trust drives performance." But what do empathy, resilience, and trust feel like? They're not clean or convenient. They're messy—made of confusion, joy, grief, curiosity, or betrayal. In other words: lived experience. And that's what this book includes. I use personal stories not to make this work about me but to make visible what usually stays hidden. Work is personal. It has to be. Because it involves us humans. By bringing lived experience into the insight of what's limiting our best work, I'm not departing from my field of strategy—I'm grounding it.

Strategic insight doesn't float above lived reality. It rises through it.

Proving One's Worth

I'm embarrassed.

That's how I feel as I share this story. A story I once told with joy.

I was at a lecture-hall desk at Santa Clara University. MBA class. Eighty students. I had slouched down in my chair so far that my eyes were nearly at desk level. To others, it might have even looked like my chair was empty. The professor, David Caldwell, was a white-haired, lean, wiry figure—Santa-esque if Santa went on a keto diet. If he saw me hiding, he didn't comment.

Sitting next to me was the man I would later marry.

We didn't really know each other then. We had shared another class, so we knew each other by sight but barely by name. Still, he noticed my slouching.

"Do you want my sweatshirt?" he asked warmly.

"No, thanks," I said, being polite.

"Are you cold?" he asked a few minutes later, starting to take it off.

I sighed, or maybe I huffed because I wasn't being listened to. "No. Why do you ask?"

"Your arms are crossed," he whispered.

Then, for the next 10 or so minutes, while the class struggled to answer the prof's question, he kept pressing. *What's wrong?*

There was nothing wrong per se. The class was just obstinately stuck on some organizational development (OD) question, which was the course topic.

Eventually, I gave in to his persistent demands. "I'm bored."

He didn't ask why. Instead, he immediately dismissed the possibility. "You can't possibly know the answer." Flat. Confident. He was so sure of his rightness. If he—and the rest of the class—didn't know the answer, how could I?

He wasn't curious. If he had been, he might have learned that I was leading a $200 million division of a major corporation, responsible for growing it to $300 million within a year. That I'd been doing some kind of OD work for over a decade.

That was my context, why I was so bored in the mandatory MBA class I wasn't allowed to test out of.

But I didn't say any of that. I did what I was trained to do. What so many of us are trained to do: I proved myself. I scooched myself up in the wooden chair, raised my hand high, got called on by the professor, provided the correct answer, and watched the class discussion move—ever so slowly—forward.

I looked over and gave my challenger a little smirk as if to say, *See?*

And he *did* see. He approved. I'd passed his test.

And here's why I share this story. Not to cast anyone as villain or victim. For we are all—each of us—fallible. And equally redeemable. We're all stumbling our way through the mess of being and becoming. And the norms that limit us in that effort. What I seek is not blame or fault, but the truthiest truth—because only when it's spoken plain can we loosen the grip of the old, and break free.

My instinct to prove myself, to perform worthiness, wasn't just personal. It was the norm. And in cooperating, I was participating in my own oppression. That same impulse—to do what is expected of us—is what I see in so many leaders today. They think the point of work lies in maximizing profit, earning investor approval, hitting the quarterly mark.

Not because they *want* to, but because that's the norm.

That's not leadership.

Or someone living their values.

That's performing what others expect.

It's obedience in a suit.

And I know how hard it is to see.

For years, I told this story of meeting Hubster with warmth, thinking it was sweet. As if he fell in love when I blew his mind.

But I couldn't hear what I was saying:

- That he got to decide if I was "right."
- That rightness even mattered.
- That a third party was the arbiter of my goodness, the authority who mattered.
- That I wasn't listened to, believed in, even though I spoke my truth.
- That I wasn't operating by my own values but by his.

I wish someone had named this for me back then. Maybe these words name it for you: Until you know what it is you value, you'll default to what others value.

The Treadmill with No Stop Button

During that long-ago first interaction with my future husband, I couldn't see what values were driving us; the rules were opaque. But they shaped our entire relationship: He demanded that I prove my worth to him, and I tried to do so.

Unsuccessfully.

Because it is an impossible task.

No one can prove their worth to another. That's because each of us is already worthy. The person who demands that you prove it has made themself the judge of you and put you on a treadmill that has no stop button. A love that has to be earned isn't love at all. When someone requires you to prove your worth, that's not intimacy—it's captivity. It may look like a joining, but it's one person holding the key, while the other learns to live inside the cage.

For the longest time, I believed this is just how the world works. Of course, I have to give attention to the guy demanding it. Of course, I have to prove my worth to whoever questions it. Of course, I must play by the rules as they exist.

That same logic is what's driving us at work today. Of course, leaders have to prioritize chasing the mighty dollar over serving a larger mission. Of course, they have to serve their shareholders above all else. Of course, purpose is permitted only if it passes the profitability test. Just as in love, the rules of worth distort what connection could be—and we are held captive.

Until you know what it is you value, you'll default to what others value.

Our future requires something different from us.

We have to define what we value. To know what matters to us. To shape our decisions.

So we don't keep speaking to someone who isn't listening.

So we don't do what they want us to do just because they insist on it.

So we don't keep choosing monetary value over humanistic values.

So that—at a minimum—we know what we are working toward.

This is our best work, we can say. And believe it, too.

INNOVATION PRACTICE
Even/Over Statements

Goal: Know how to name what matters most to you.

Values aren't just what you say you care about—they're what guide your choices, often invisibly. To see them more clearly, ask yourself three questions:

1. What upsets me? Notice moments that frustrate, hurt, or piss you off. These often reveal a value—like respect, autonomy, or kindness—being stepped on.

2. What do I do with my day? Look at where your time and energy naturally go. These actions reveal what truly matters to you.

3. What do I do all the time, regardless of context? Notice if you're always the hospitality person, or the person who calls it like it is, no matter whom you're with.

Now name three values you see behind those patterns. Write them down.

Next, ask yourself: When my values compete, what do I choose—even/over another good thing?

"Even/over" means naming what you choose even when it costs you something else you also care about; it's not picking a good thing over a bad thing but choosing between two good things. For example, honesty even/over harmony. Rest even/over achievement. Connection even/over self-respect. Clarify not just what you value but what you prioritize when it counts.

Finally, share your "even/over" choice with someone you trust. Say it out loud. Notice how it feels. That conversation can surface new insights—or affirm the ones that are already true for you. And know that values are not static; they are shifting, and we can always be tuning in to them.

Having clarity about your values creates the ability to navigate to your future. This is central to what we mean by our best work.

4

If You Don't Ask, You Don't Get

Limiting Norm: Vilifying Politics
Leading Indicator: Visible Politics

Why does one team always get preferential treatment and resources?

Politics.

Why do the people who talk the loudest and sound the smartest in meetings always get ahead, while those who do the actual work go unnoticed?

Politics.

Why can the boss prioritize their own self-interest without any consequences?

Politics.

We hate office politics because it's the root of everything wrong with our team dynamics. Politics isn't just a nuisance. It's the invisible hand that shapes our work, often for the worse.

If there is a clear villain at work, it's politics.

Or is it?

Don't Put Yourself in Harm's Way

When Talia started her new job, she stumbled across a report outlining five critical areas the company had to address—or risk its future. Curious, she took it to her boss and asked, "Are we doing something about this?"

The response was blunt: "No. There's no money."

No money? For something crucial to the company's future?

Talia was tempted to tackle one of those five areas herself, which made me want to tackle her.

"When a boss says there's no money," I told her, "it's not about money. It's about priorities." We all find money for the things we care about. And so if you push for something management is not yet ready to solve, you're out of sync with everyone. There's honor in chasing good ideas into reality, but if you're doing it *after* the company has said they won't support it, you're just throwing yourself into the gears, risking everything for nothing.

A year later, a new VP arrived and asked Talia to lead in the area where all those problems, unsurprisingly, persisted. The VP hinted it could lead to a new role, maybe even a promotion.

Of course Talia wanted to solve the problems. She'd been eager to do so long before her new boss dangled the management carrot. She knew how much the problems were costing the company, and it meant managing a larger team, which she excelled at. Most importantly, it would mean progress.

But I wondered if she was set up to succeed. I asked her if the assignment came with the staff and budget to fix those five critical issues so that she wasn't being handed the problem without the backing to solve it.

This is a common problem.

What if you sign up to do something but are deeply under-resourced? You could work hard, and your team might even solve some issues, but if the issue is not fully addressed and the company tanks, you'll be blamed. If no one's decided the solution is worth resourcing, they're just putting your name next to the problem.

"Worse yet," I told Talia, "you'll feel like you failed."

Failure at work often feels *personal* when it's *political*.

How We Decide What Matters

What exactly do we mean by *political?*

When someone is described as being *too political*, it's that they are focused on navigating the social dynamics, with its power structures and relationships, rather than focused on the work. We often label political people as *self-interested*, but that's not the real issue. After all, we each need to advocate for ourselves. The problem with political people is that they are self-advocating but aren't *also* invested in the common good. They prioritize their own needs *always*; they will toss the shared goals under the bus or climb over our bodies to get what they want. But what most pisses off those of us who are trying to meet both personal *and* shared goals is that the person who is political often succeeds at our expense.

It's why so many of us say, *I don't do politics.*

And I get that.

Seeing the *icky* aspect of political behavior makes us want to be *non-icky.*

But politics? It's not something that *can* be avoided. Because it touches *every* aspect of work. And authority. It affects our team goals and resourcing. It affects whom we report to and our span of control. If we unpack "politics," we see how it shows up in the minutia of work, like:

- Time allocation
- Prioritization
- Authority
- Assignments
- Budgets
- Rules and policies
- Schedules

Politics is the tension and tussle that decide priorities, budgets, and timelines. But it's always bigger than budgets or timelines. When we're being political, we're arguing over *whose needs get to count.* And so these tussles are essential—to be valued, not vilified. But just as we had to know we deserved better before we could demand better when it came to values, the same is true for politics. First we have to know what values we're fighting *for*, then we need to engage in the necessary tussle—to give our values their due shot.

And so let's be far more precise about what politics is.

Politics is simply a process: *how we decide what we decide.* It isn't inherently good or bad; it's just a process that can be executed well or poorly.

It's about making decisions and navigating power dynamics involving resources and status. Essentially, politics is the art of negotiating our needs.

Yet somehow, we don't.

Not all of us, anyway. Many of us have been conditioned to think that politics is the stuff other people do, or that it is icky and shouldn't be engaged in at all.

The powerful have taught us this. Think of politicians who blame politics for what is wrong with the government, even while asking to do the job of politics. They have taught us to vilify politics so they can have the domain all to themselves. That's why they do this: to take away the agency of the many and create a dependency on the few.

But if politics is how we get our needs met, then everyone *needs to* play, not just those in charge.

Those who abuse power reinforce and exploit the aversion we all feel for the topic. At work, it means the boss can blame politics for why core issues are not being addressed and thus avoid being called to task for under-resourcing different projects. And if politics is the problem, no one needs to discuss and address why one team gets preferential treatment, information, and access. And firms can claim they're apolitical to shut down tough but uncomfortable conversations—like about inequity, social injustice, and human rights—conversations that decide who gets to count. It's better to have the players resign or redirect themselves to accepted norms than to have them question why shit is working the way it is.

All this steering—the 3 D's in action—pushes us to overlook the obvious.

There's a well-known experiment about this: If you're asked to count how many times the white-shirted players pass the ball during a basketball game, you focus on that task. Meanwhile, a gorilla walks right through the scene. A huge, hairy gorilla. Yet with our attention directed elsewhere, half of us miss it entirely.[1] This is selective attention at work—we filter things out based on what we're guided to see, even things that are right in front of us.

There's something similar going on in our places of work. We're looking right at the crappy allocation of resources but not seeing how our attention is being redirected to make us think politics is the problem. And so we're missing something big. The gorilla in the room.

Obscuring the process denies power to many.

The Villain of the Story

"We already tried that."

It was one of the first things I heard when I was hired to help REI grow their customer base. At first, I believed them. After all, it would seem illogical that anyone would steer the group away from exploring a needed solution. But however counterintuitive it is, it happens all the time.

Even at companies that excel in tackling complex problems.

REI—Recreational Equipment Inc., the American retailer renowned for outdoor recreation services—is known for large-scale projects to preserve the outdoors as a transformative space for current and future generations. They understand that sustainability isn't about simple, absolute solutions. It's not just about choosing a specific material if it means that material must be shipped from halfway around the world. It's not about eliminating packaging if that leads to unusable, returned products. As a result, they have a comprehensive approach to product lifecycle management, which includes using sustainable materials, improving the durability of their products, and creating programs for product repair and reuse. This not only reduces waste but also supports a circular economy.[2] One of their main suppliers, Patagonia, even endorses buying nothing as a part of their strategy. I share all this not to love on REI but to show that their teams recognize that every decision to do "good" involves trade-offs, costs, and implications. To them, there are no easy answers, only the careful negotiation of competing interests.

In other words, they do politics really well.

Which is why I was surprised to see this attitude of "Been there, done that" at REI.

When I asked what exactly they had tried, I found out they'd abandoned one growth strategy because someone had claimed the boss wouldn't like it. I also heard that a Tennessee team likely would have overruled it, as they "always" got their way. Additionally, there was no budget for the plan, as this part of the business rarely got the resources needed.

Politics was always to blame. It was the villain of the story, intractable and unmovable.

But it's not that politics is unmovable. It's that it's often invisible.

Okay, I'd say. You say the boss wouldn't have liked it; is that your assumption, or did you discuss it with him? What exactly didn't he like?

Someone had failed to ask for what they really needed. They had abandoned options due to the assumed preferences of the boss or other teams. Instead of relying on empirical evidence and strategic insight, they let their decisions be swayed by perception.

This is how politics' invisibility limits our ability to do our best work.

How is it that these team members—the ones who knew how to negotiate the impact on the planet, from suppliers to materials to user behavior—went limp when it came to negotiating the internal dynamics of bosses and preferences?

And here's the tough news that I had to deliver: We don't win if we don't try. That's giving up before we even show up. And not only have you not moved forward but you're also going to hate yourself just a little bit for not asking for what you need. It's one thing for someone else to deny your needs; it's another thing to abandon your own interests.

We can often negotiate for other people's needs to be met, but asking for what we need is harder.

That's what was going on at REI.

Each team member I worked with always seemed hurt that I didn't want to accept their understanding of how things functioned. It always felt like they were trying to protect me or us. From what? From wasting our time. From the pain of rejection. From the shame of failure. They were also worried about being perceived as power-hungry, demanding, or pushy. And maybe even losing whatever authority, autonomy, and agency they had. After all, logging a loss on the board shouldn't be punished, but it nearly always is.

So they decided—albeit unconsciously—not to negotiate for their needs.

As an outsider to the organization, someone who hadn't bought into the existing norms, I knew that what they were saying was true for them, yet equally untrue. What I could see was that they weren't being dumb, or avoiding the situation, or not trying to solve the problem. They were just trying to avoid politics because it might result in political fallout.

I get it, I'd say, but this matters to you, right?

We need to manage how we decide what we decide.

Avoiding issues due to politics means we miss out on potential solutions and the chance for the best outcome. It's okay, I always tell teams, if leadership rejects our proposals; our responsibility is to present specific ideas that align with our objectives and advocate for them. If our ideas are shot down, that's not on us. To get shot down highlights the gaps between our different ideas, which tells us something. We get information. We might learn something. But if we never even make the case, we can't illuminate any gaps between us.

Only by engaging in the game do we move the ball forward.

I told Talia and the REI team the same thing: Ask for what you need.

Discuss what the business needs for the work to get done right. Make the debate about the business and the goals of the work, because that's the issue at hand—not just for Talia and her company or REI and that organization. But for all of us.

Making politics visible is another way we free ourselves.

When we voice our needs at work, there's always the risk of disappointment if others dismiss or deprioritize them. This fear of rejection can lead us to withhold our needs altogether, avoiding the potential sting of being told they don't matter, which is to say we don't matter, or that those needs will be put on the back burner.

Yet by not negotiating our needs at work, we have abandoned the one and only person whose needs we're responsible for. We often surrender our needs before we've had the opportunity to see whether others are willing to fulfill them, limiting what is possible.

Even if our voices tremble, our needs must be heard.

Getting What You Want

We've all got interests, and those interests are not always aligned. It's easy to think of this as a negative, to get caught up in the stress of not already being on the same page and lose sight that this is okay. But can I remind you of the obvious? We're not all supposed to be the same. Our variation of what matters is both natural and valuable.

The key, then, isn't to get someone to give in or give up.

It's about finding the solutions that serve our shared goal.

Back when I was attending community college, when I was all of 19 years old, I was asked to sit on a statewide board of governors as the student voice to advocate for community colleges to become what they are today, an accessible step toward higher education. I represented the 1.6 million students, others represented the faculty, and others represented the fiduciary concerns and so on. Lots and lots of interests were represented. Someone, somewhere hired William Ury to teach us how to do this work well. Ury has a famous "Getting to Yes" framework,[3] a powerful method for negotiation politics that became foundational to my thinking.

Separate the People from the Problem

The first principle of Ury's framework is deceptively simple: Separate the people from the problem. When politics are at play in the workplace, it's easy to confuse someone's position with their identity. We often see people as obstacles if they disagree with us. But this way of thinking leads to conflict, not solutions.

Instead, recognize that each person, however frustrating you may find them, is just that—a person.

Each of us has our own concerns, fears, and pressures. Each of us brings our own history and experiences, visions and hopes. None of us are the problem. The problem is the issue at hand, whether that's how to allocate resources, meet deadlines, or structure a project.

Even if our voices tremble, our needs must be heard.

Your goal is to work *with* others to solve the problem, not to "win" against them. This is why you don't want anyone to feel bad about the fact that you disagree; you don't want to shame them by saying, *Hey, the last time you did this kind of thing you f'd it up, so you'd better listen to me this time.* You want to focus on facing this challenge together.

Now, before I go on, I have to address the people who believe other people *are* the problem. The ones who think the reason they didn't get into a certain school is because someone "less qualified" took "their" seat. Or the person who believes that immigrants are the reason good jobs don't exist for them. I get why someone might think that, but that thinking is not their own. This idea that you're losing out because of someone else's opportunity is rooted in a scarcity framework designed to pit people against each other. It's an idea that those in power spread around to divide and conquer—keep us fighting for scraps while the real wealth and opportunities stay concentrated at the top. Instead of blaming some people, let's talk about why there isn't enough educational access or why jobs aren't available to all of us and who benefits from keeping it that way.

Repeat after me: People are not the problem; the problem is the problem.

For example, say a coworker consistently shoots down your ideas in meetings. Instead of seeing that person as antagonistic, ask yourself *what's going on there*. Maybe their boss has given them a competing goal to the one your boss has given you. Maybe they don't sleep well, so they are being short in their comments. By exploring the question of what's really at work, you create space to name the real issue, which is often hidden to all.

Focus on Needs

In office politics, people often dig into positions: "I need this budget"; "I am in charge." These positions can feel immovable, where if you want something different, you are in a tug-of-war. William Ury suggests focusing on what he calls "interests" instead of "positions."

I recommend we go even deeper, to ask what someone *needs* that is fueling their approach.

For example, a colleague might insist they have more control over a project. Their language might even be "I need to lead," but that seems to me more a position. Their need is more primal, perhaps a desire to feel seen or recognized or to prove their competence. Or maybe they are struggling to support you given other competing interests, so they are telling you to do things a certain way because that's the only way they can fit you in. If you address the core need—offering opportunities for recognition or responsibility, or even just naming the issue as "no one here needs to prove their worth"—there's room to move from positioning and posturing toward solutions.

The key is to ask questions. Don't just accept what people say at face value. Dig deeper: *Why do they want that? What do they really need?*

And to do that well, assume for a second that it simply doesn't matter what the outcome is, that the only thing that matters is the connection between you and your colleague. Then, and only then, ask: *What's going on?* This shift is how you actually pay attention to the other person's needs and not just listen so you can jockey for what you want.

And all of this means that we need to discern what we ourselves want and need. Because politics isn't only about getting clear about other people's needs; it's about getting clear about our own.

Invent Options for Mutual Gain

Once you've separated the people from the problem and uncovered needs, the next step is generating options for mutual gain. In workplace politics, there's often an assumption that there are only two options—yours and theirs—and only one of them can win. Instead of win-lose, Ury wants us to think win-win.

But I think that's still too limiting a frame. I want to expand on it.

Before meeting with anyone else, I want you to do a practice of generating 25 ideas for what *could* work. Try as much as possible to not ground these in "reality" but to imagine you are in a science-fiction film; lots of things that we can't yet do in modern life might be possible in the future because of technological advancements.

Be expansive. Be creative. Be otherworldly.

For example, say you and a colleague are vying for the same limited resources to support your respective projects. Rather than fight over the pie, think about how you could expand it. Could you collaborate on a shared initiative? Could you seek additional resources together? By expanding your time horizon or whom you could include, you'll find levers of change. A wild approach expands the boundary of what is possible. Because, in truth, all things are possible.

These three steps make politics *visible* instead of the *villain*.

Politics isn't about winning and losing but about how we participate in creating what comes next.

And who doesn't want that?

To be sure, some don't. I'm not naïve.

Some want you to try to negotiate needs and spend your energy while they do whatever they want. I am not trying to deny how the powerful can say whatever and then simply block change. It's what we learned in chapter 1; leaders can choose comfort and deny everyone else progress. But we do not change that dynamic by accepting that change is impossible. We change the interaction by making the political framework transparent, apparent. By showing what is happening rather than letting political stuff stay hidden behind the curtain.

Making it visible changes things.

Out in the Open

Back at Apple, a few of us noticed something strange in our management meetings. No matter what topic was under discussion, it felt as if the decisions had already been made. We'd go in thinking we'd tussle over something, only to leave wondering if we'd just been going through the motions.

It was like some invisible hand was steering everything.

The more we thought about it, the clearer it became to us. Decisions weren't really happening in those meetings—they were happening somewhere else. Then we connected the dots. We noticed that certain members of the leadership team had an off-site meeting the day before our key meetings. By asking the admins, we learned that this "meeting" was actually a game of golf. Just the guys on the leadership team, no one else.

We started to question what might be going on. Were they talking things through while playing? Pre-deciding everything out on the course, where none of us had access?

One of us decided to test this out. Marie Schmidt—who was 6 feet tall and incredibly athletic, having played nearly every competitive sport while in college—started taking golf lessons on the weekends. She bought the right clubs, put in the hours, and got good. Once she was confident that she could hold her own, she sent an email to the leadership team, laying out her golf stats and asking to join them for their next round.

A simple, polite request to participate where the decisions were being made.

We realized that their power required our participation. If we opted out or acquiesced to their golf games, we were giving them our proxy. But when you believe you have a role to play, you can signal that you don't consent. Even if the result doesn't change in the moment, at least now you've shown that you're not fine with what is happening.

In our case, the off-site meetings quietly disappeared. There were no more golf games, no more pre-decisions happening outside the office. And for the first time, meetings became places where the real discussions happened. Decisions were debated, ideas were tussled over, and the invisible barriers fell. It's not that the people once excluded won every battle. But that politics, once invisible, became visible in the room—where it belonged.

INNOVATION PRACTICE
Political Mapping

Goal: Make the power dynamics in your organization visible.

When something feels stuck at work, don't just ask what needs to change—ask who is keeping it in place, and why. Power is not an immutable, indelible structure set in stone but an intangible entity resting on sand that we can shape into many things. But first we have to make it visible.

Practice Prompt

Step 1: Ask Three Simple Questions

Next time you're frustrated, grab a notebook or chat with a friend and explore:

1. Who benefits if nothing changes? (Ask not from a place of blame—just observation. Who's doing okay as-is?)

2. Who wants this new thing most—and why? (Hint: That might be you. But is there anyone else who'd back it?)

3. Who has the power to shift things—even a little? (Don't default to "the boss." Power is often informal—who influences whom?)

These questions help you see the landscape instead of assuming that you have to push harder. Power isn't a wall—it's a web.

Step 2: Talk It Out

Share what you noticed with a colleague, friend, or mentor. Ask:
"Does this map ring true to you?"
"What else might I be missing?"
Politics is not just about the subject matter; it's about the who and the why. Once you know that, you have more fidelity.

5

You Can't Sleep When You're Dead

Limiting Norm: Give It Your All
Leading Indicator: Give and Get

We're supposed to give work our all. This ethos is woven into the very fabric of business: the journey from the mailroom to the C-suite requires it. It's how you go from a humble garage to an IPO, from rags to riches, from obscurity to influence.

And it isn't just about doing what's necessary—it's a testament to our dedication and commitment to our jobs, teams, careers, and dreams. We are told to bring *everything* we have to the game and leave *nothing* behind on the field. Work can be the path to earning more than money; it's also how we gain dignity, respect, and skills. It's why so many of us juggle, get help, and color-code our calendars. To make it all work.

And yet here I was, feeling as if nothing worked.

Feeling like a failure.

At home.

At work.

At life.

I was giving my all, and it wasn't enough.

Question the Premise

"What happens when you're alone with your mother?" the psychologist asked.

I watched from behind the glass at Stanford's children's hospital, breath tight in my chest. My 6-year-old son—Kiddo, as I call him—sat with chunky Lego blocks, explaining that he was never really alone with me.

"*NEV. ER*," he said, breaking the word into two, emphatic when she questioned it.

She asked why.

He told her how we'd play together, curl up under his favorite blanket, wander the aquarium in awe of jellyfish and otters—until my phone rang, and I'd rush out for a work call.

"We aren't alone. She has her phone."

I moved my hand to my heart as if I could hold the pain in.

For a working mom—is there any other kind?—this is the ultimate gut punch.

This meeting was our Hail Mary. His teachers, guidance counselor, and principal had all told us that Kiddo was "acting up" at school; they pointed to his bringing matches to school, assuming he was going to set the place on fire. His towheaded friend Alison, who had asked my son to bring the matches, got "talked to," while Kiddo got suspended. (It was years later that I learned they just wanted to have a fun campfire.)

This wasn't an isolated incident. Kiddo was the one sent to sit outside the classroom for being "too active." Evaluated and re-evaluated. Diagnosed with ADHD. Autism. Oppositional defiant disorder.

Given every label but one: boy.

A brown boy in a predominantly white school.[1]

I loved my job at the strategy firm I'd founded—solving complex problems and helping leaders and companies flourish—but hearing Kiddo's words made me question if that love was misplaced.

The psychologist then asked Kiddo about time with his father. He shared how Dad worked on the computer while he played nearby. His father's distance didn't bother him; it was a constant. And, somehow, fine.

The double standard landed hard. Society had already taught him that a father's work is normal; a mother's is neglect.

The psychologist shared her summary. "The problem," she said, "is that he wants attention."

She said it as if it were a flaw. As if wanting to be seen—fully, wildly, and with all his fire—was a diagnosis.

My husband nodded, relieved to have an answer from an authority. Together, all the people in power agreed: Kiddo was "broken."

And I was "the fix."

Neither was true. But this "solution" meant no one at the school nor his father had to change.

I quit my job to focus on being a parent.

I had been the primary wage earner. By a lot. My husband took jobs that weren't fulfilling. We both sacrificed, giving everything we had for our family. To be clear, I don't regret it—every life has a sister ship,[2] the one you don't sail.

But in our devotion, we didn't stop to ask why self-sacrifice by some in the room was the default answer for fixing systemic problems.

Never Enough

It's 5:45 a.m. in small-town Ohio. Judy slips out of bed quietly, careful not to wake her husband, dons her blue vest, and heads to Walmart. Across town, Judy's best friend, Sarah, does the same. They're in their late 40s, early 50s, with husbands who once earned enough to support the family. But those jobs are long gone, and now it's the women's turn to provide. It wasn't supposed to be like this. Judy's husband, Mark, was a machinist; Sarah's husband, Joe, worked in a factory; and both men had served in the military. Paid $14 an hour, Judy and Sarah make just enough to cover the mortgage, groceries, and electric bill. But there's no health insurance, no paid time off, no margin for error. Get sick? You don't get paid. Miss a shift? You lose hours that you can't afford to lose. They regularly work double shifts, grateful for the opportunity to pull overtime whenever they can, so they don't feel like they are on the brink.

Judy tries not to think about how this is all they have now. Sarah doesn't dwell on what will happen if her husband's unemployment runs out.

They just keep showing up, giving it their all.

For Mark and Joe, it's a different story. They're angry. At the economy, their politicians, and, of course, themselves. But mostly? They direct their anger toward their wives, the women who once made their lives a joy, because their wives now spend more time at Walmart than at the kitchen table. Their simmering frustrations grow as they feel their status eroding.

While the men wouldn't say it this way, their job was always about more than a paycheck. It was their way of adding their bit to the world. It was the connection between what they could offer and how they could create value. While it's poetic to talk creativity in the form of writers and poets and artists, what Mark and Joe did was creative in its own distinct way. To understand them, and each of us, we can see work as the way we create. Regardless of role. Writers write. Teachers teach. Managers manage. Leaders lead. Founders found. Welders weld. And servicepeople serve. It's our way of sharing who we are.

Judy, Sarah, Mark, and Joe gave what they had, but it was never enough.

Making It All Work

Here's the irony, if that's the right word for this: None of them—Judy, Sarah, Mark, or Joe—blame Walmart.[3]

Not hardly.

They see the largest retailer in America as a lifeline, a safety net that keeps them from total free fall. They don't talk about Walmart's labor practices or the fact that, by design, the women's jobs keep them stuck in this precarious balance of gratitude and exhaustion.

Instead, they blame themselves.

They internalize the belief that they just need to work harder, push further, "give it their all." It's the American creed—hard work equals success. This creed is exported more than anything else America creates. So if someone isn't succeeding, the fault must lie with them, not with a system that allows billion-dollar corporations to pay so little that workers depend on government aid to survive.

Let's put some numbers on that.

In 2024, Walmart's CEO, Doug McMillon, earned approximately $26.97 million in total compensation, which included base salary, stock awards, and bonuses.[4] This compensation was 976 times greater than the median compensation for Walmart employees, which was $27,642 during the same period.[5] Meanwhile, the Walton family—heirs to the Walmart fortune—had a combined net worth of over $432.4 billion in 2024, making them one of the wealthiest families in the world.[6] Despite this immense wealth, many of Walmart's hourly workers rely on federal assistance programs like Medicaid and SNAP (food stamps) to make ends meet.[7]

If Walmart raised its average worker's annual salary from $27,642 to $50,000—a jump that would allow employees to actually live their lives without depending on the government, second jobs, or constant overtime—the cost would be staggering by most measures: an additional $46.95 billion per year. But for the Walton family, the hit would hardly be catastrophic. Given that they own roughly 46% of Walmart, their share of the cost would amount to around $21.6 billion—a mere 4.9% of their fortune. And that's assuming they covered the increase entirely out of their own pockets, without adjusting Walmart's logistics, operations, pricing, or financial strategy in any way that could fund a Good Jobs strategy.[8]

In other words, the family that built its wealth on low wages and cost-cutting could single-handedly transform the lives of 2.1 million workers and still walk away with over $400 billion. They could jump-start the change, funding it while the operational issues were worked through. The real question isn't whether they can afford it. It's why they won't.

Oddly, these arguments never seem to reach the people living through it. Judy and Sarah don't see themselves as victims of corporate policy; they see themselves as lucky to have jobs at all. Walmart equals opportunity—that's what Walmart tells them is true.

The world tells us to be grateful we have jobs at all. And no one wants to be the victim in a story. But we shouldn't be exploited.

And yet it feels like giving until you hurt is the only option, because it's the norm. When we accept self-sacrifice as the answer, we only blame ourselves instead of looking for the solutions that would address the situation. It's not just workers at big companies who do this but also entrepreneurs who blame themselves for not having figured out how to scale growth but don't see the situation fully. This is meritocracy at work, one of America's most cherished myths: the belief that success is earned through talent and hard work alone, that the best rise because they deserve to. But this belief breeds both hubris and humiliation—it flatters the winners into thinking they are solely responsible for their success, and it blames the rest for falling short.

If you talk with the top executives at Walmart—and I have talked with them—they will tell you that there is a good reason to do things this way. It keeps the cost of goods down. So the end-user consumers can benefit and buy a 60-inch television for just $200. The executives also argue that it's not their job to institute the standard for wages; it's the government's job. And they deflect when challenged on why they spend a ton lobbying the government to avoid paying people a living wage. In these conversations, the executives take the position that their primary charter is to make money for their shareholders, as we discussed in chapter 3.

Given that employee salaries are tangible and the effect of paying a substandard wage is intangible, they manage for what they can measure.

For them, this just makes sense.

But for Judy and Sarah, it irrationally *also* makes sense. They deny the invisible pressure of always needing to work, despite bad backs or suffering from the flu. They make allowances for the fact that they need to work double shifts just to meet their most basic needs, that the jobs at Walmart pay *just* enough to keep them afloat. And while they know deep down that it's not a great solution, they aren't sure what else to ask for, or even if they're allowed to ask for more. Which makes sense, because how can anyone be expected to come up with solutions or solidarity when they're so darn exhausted?

That's the trap: working hard to make it work, being the kind of employee worth hiring and rehiring, yet never questioning why it's always about how much they have to give and not about how much they get in return.

This is nothing new.

A Long History

Giving work your all feels virtuous and right—heroic, even—because we have been indoctrinated with the idea that on the other side of giving it your all, you live in the land where all your dreams come true.

But the hard truth is that many are giving it their all, and it's not working for them—somewhere around 57% of the global workforce struggle to make ends meet.[9] In the US, this equates to 160 million people barely scraping by.[10] Many pick up extra hours or second jobs, giving it their all just to get by. Jobs are set up from 9 to 5 while schools aren't, so the lack of childcare—available in nearly every other developed nation—adds another source of financial stress. Some people will also be on a government support system for healthcare because it's not a social guarantee in America; America spends more on healthcare than any other country—almost twice as much per patient as its peer nations. But the outcomes don't match the cost. Americans die younger, face more preventable illnesses, and are more likely to skip care because they can't afford it. Prices are higher across the board—for hospital visits, for prescriptions, for administrative overhead. Despite spending nearly twice as much per person, the US ranks last among wealthy nations in life expectancy, avoidable mortality, and maternal and infant health— core measures of whether a health system is working. And yet what's most distinctive about the American system isn't just its cost, or even its inefficiency. It's that health insurance is tethered to employment. We've made access to care a function of having a job, and often, of keeping one. That choice—unusual among wealthy nations—limits individual freedom, locks people into roles they might otherwise leave, and concentrates power in the hands of employers. In much of the world, health is treated as a social guarantee. Here, it's a bargaining chip.[11, 12, 13]

And then there are entire generations of kids—Generations X, Y, and Z—who have grown up witnessing their parents give work their all, only to watch their families not get enough in return. For example . . .

- The 24-hour nature of an always-on work culture means there's a teammate who always needs input, so you feel like a bad colleague if you don't help them. One part of us is always at work and, therefore, never 100% present in our lives.
- Instead of accrued vacation, workplaces instituted an "unlimited PTO" model, characterized as "treating employees

like adults." But when the norm is to "give work your all," many workers don't take any time off. And when job changes inevitably happen, people leave as empty husks of humans without the cushion of accrued dollars to let them rest between gigs.
- People naturally want to put their gifts to use, to be recognized and valued. So when we're told that the strategic plan needs our "particular input," we want to help even when we're still expected to do our regular work. We say yes to helping out even when it means giving up sleep and our nights and weekends.

We joke, *I'll sleep when I'm dead.* But the problem with that is, well, we're dead.

Work turns the loving, generous, and creative spirit of us wanting to care and "give it our all" into a one-sided economic benefit for the firm.

Until this is rebalanced, we limit the potential of each and every one of us. Let's be clear: Effort matters. No one's saying hard work is irrelevant. Most people who succeed do work hard. But so do millions who never get a shot. What makes meritocracy a myth isn't that merit is fake—it's that merit alone never determines the outcome. Structural advantage shapes who gets seen, who gets mentored, who gets forgiven, who gets funded. And those advantages often feel like nothing at all—just a good school, a second chance, a door left open. That's the trap. As Tressie McMillan Cottom writes, privilege hides in plain sight, cloaked in the language of personal excellence, of effort, of sacrifice. If you've worked hard, it doesn't mean you didn't earn your success. It means you didn't do it alone.

"Self-sacrifice" solves things through individual actions rather than by the design of a better model.

When top leaders complain that their staff is not giving their all, their comments are centered solely on the firm's interests. And we participate in perpetuating this idea. So many of us, frustrated by our own overwhelm, think our colleagues should "step up more." As if the answer is to ask for more and more, when it's just as likely that the issue is chronic under-resourcing. The higher-ups will get bonuses based on increased productivity, the owners will get stock growth, while the rest of us end up with nothing left to give.

That's a power imbalance of pretty epic proportions.

Work is like the casino, where the "house" always wins.

And this power disparity has deep roots.

When the system of slavery was legally abolished in America, nearly 4 million formerly enslaved people were set "free" but had no land, jobs, money, or ability to sustain themselves.[14] At the same time, the former slave owners still needed labor to cultivate their land. So a new system emerged: sharecropping. With a sharecropping contract, those struggling for physical and economic survival were granted small plots of land to farm. Instead of paying rent, since they had no money of their own, they were required to give a portion of the crop yield, called shares, to the landowner. Laws were put in place that entitled the owners to set the value of any crop. Not only that, sharecroppers were also forced to buy the necessary fertilizer, tools, animals, and machinery from the landowner or local merchant on credit, often at exorbitant interest rates. The farmer set the price of what they used and of what was sold (often invisible to the sharecropper). The result of this power imbalance was that sharecroppers were barely able to make ends meet and were always indebted.

The formerly enslaved people were technically "free" but now trapped in a different way. And they were told that if they weren't "succeeding," it was on them.

An entire economy built up around this power dynamic.

And while some may argue that this was their choice—to sharecrop, that is—when all the choices in the model are tilted toward those in power, choice is just an illusion, a mirage, or an outright lie.

And what's worse is that sharecroppers were expected to feel *grateful* for the opportunity to work a farm and *expected* to give their work their all.

The road from there to here, from then to now, is a direct one.

You are lucky to have a job.

You should be grateful to work here.

You owe it to us to give your best.

We've either heard it or said it, and nearly every one of us has bought into a system that has programmed us to believe it.

A Hierarchy of Human Value

Self-sacrifice is often celebrated.

Like the fact that our children should come first—above everything else, especially for women. At work, it's why we need to take on that extra project. Why we need to show up no matter what and fight to get ahead, even if we're exhausted, even if our lives are falling apart.

Sacrificing everything for work has become the measure of success, but what good is giving your all if you lose yourself in the process? What if giving your all means having nothing left? Giving our all accepts the premise that there *is* a hierarchy of human economic value. It implies that certain people matter more, and their needs must get centered over those of others.

Just like the idea that a child's care is fundamentally more important than a mother's fulfillment at work, or that a man's ongoing emotional neglect of his child is acceptable, the hierarchy of human value surrounds us.

At work, this hierarchy looks like this:

- A company should do what serves its own self-interest, not society's.
- An employee's worth is tied to their immediate output or contribution to the company, and they deserve no long-term commitment from the company.
- Higher-ups lead strategy and make decisions; subordinates execute.
- Subordinates receive feedback from their superiors, not the other way around.
- Directives are communicated from higher-ups to subordinates, ensuring order.

Even the language we use at work (superiors and subordinates) is hierarchical. Which is why so many teams now use different terms (associates, for example), as if that name change obscures the underlying expectation of who gets to give it their all without getting what they need.

We're using the word *hierarchy* a lot here. Yet it's worth stepping back to clarify that this is not the same as the hierarchy of the organization. We tend to conflate these two very different things: the *structure* that helps groups organize, and the *evaluation* that ranks some people as inherently more valuable than others. A friend of mine, Bob Sutton, the Stanford organizational theorist, has made an argument that hierarchy is essential—not because some people matter more but because complex work requires coordination, clarity, and decision-making. That's a functional need. The danger comes when we mistake structure for status—when a role designed to manage complexity becomes a reason to confer more dignity, more voice, or more humanity. Which happens far more often than we acknowledge. Sutton quotes a CEO who puts it plainly: Never confuse the hierarchy you need with the respect everyone deserves.[15]

When all the choices in the model are tilted toward those in power, choice is just an illusion, a mirage, or an outright lie.

Whether at work or in life, when we accept a hierarchy of value in the structures we live in, we are saying we can solve problems for one side of the equation—those who "matter" most—and not for everyone involved. Some are expected to be "unconditional" about their commitment to others, while others benefit from being conditional and holding back. And so some of us end up hating ourselves and each other instead of fixing the models in which we function.

Self-sacrifice is not just an imbalance; it's depleting and extracting. To move to a regenerative model where work is a place to feel joyous and juicy, not sucked dry as husks, we need to find a different way. We must design for mutually beneficial work and solve for and learn to serve multiple interests at the same time.

Companies can no longer build a better balance sheet through unbalanced people.

This is not the future, but the vestige of a shameful past.

Game-Changer Moves

Now, interestingly, surprisingly, astonishingly, Walmart does something dramatically different from their corporate MO in their sustainability work.

There, they are a leader. Setting the standard for what is possible.

It started decades ago. Around the mid-2000s, Walmart brought in some of the top people in the sustainability space to discuss the role of the environment in business and how business needed to step up. In those conversations, private from public scrutiny, Walmart recognized the environmental impact of its global reach.[16] In 2005, the company made its first major environmental commitment by hiring a Chief Sustainability Officer and pledging to cut greenhouse gas emissions. Walmart's early efforts focused on reducing its operational energy use and waste, like installing solar panels on store rooftops and introducing energy-efficient store designs.[17] It seemed like a drop in the ocean compared with the company's vast supply chain, but it helped them see how to move forward.

We all crawl before we walk and walk before we run.

By 2017, Walmart had taken a bold leap with the launch of Project Gigaton, aiming to eliminate 1 billion metric tons of greenhouse gas emissions from its supply chain by 2030.[18]

This was a game-changer move.

Walmart recognized that most of its carbon footprint came from suppliers, not its own operations. By enlisting suppliers to reduce emissions across transportation, energy, and manufacturing, Walmart sought to turn its vast network of partners into a force for environmental change. Alongside this program, Walmart began to focus on sustainable sourcing, with major commitments to responsible products like sustainable seafood and cotton. In 2020, it expanded its scope to regenerative agriculture, aiming to improve soil health and reduce environmental damage from farming practices.[19]

As of 2025, Walmart's sustainability strategy is deeply woven into the company's business model. Its renewable energy initiatives now power 50% of its operations, with a goal of 100% by 2035. The company also continues to innovate in circular economy practices, focusing on reducing packaging waste and encouraging suppliers to follow suit. Walmart's work to integrate sustainability into its core operations has led to measurable progress, with millions of metric tons of emissions already reduced.

I don't mean to say that Walmart is perfect in this area, because God knows we all could do more for the environment. But I share all this to ask one question: Why is it that in one part of their business, they push to make advancements but in the domain of labor practices, they remain hell-bent on maintaining the old ways?

In one case, they fully accept a hierarchy of economic value—their people must earn as little as possible to ensure "everyday low prices." Conversely, they recognize that depleting Earth's resources to run their business will not work out over time.

It depends on what you question and what you don't.

It depends on what you give and what you get.

The Give/Get Ratio

We often talk about fairness at work in vague terms—feeling "valued," "recognized," "seen." But underneath those sentiments is something more measurable, if still hard to name: a give/get ratio. It's the relationship between what you put into a situation—your time, energy, ideas, emotional labor—and what you receive in return. That return might be money, yes, but also opportunity, respect, autonomy, or simply the chance to rest.

When that ratio is right, work feels enlivening. Business models are generative, not extractive. And people flourish. Contributing their best because they're not being drained—their needs are being met. But when the ratio tilts too far in one direction, when the giving outweighs the getting by too much for too long, something shifts. Exploitative business models leave people unable to make rent or feed their children. It doesn't always look like cruelty or coercion; sometimes it looks like praise without promotion, loyalty without stability, impact without credit. And we rationalize it—telling ourselves the payoff is coming later, or that this is just how it is for people like us.

At its core, the *give/get ratio* is two things:

1. The relationship between what you *put* into a situation (your efforts, contributions, etc.) and what you *receive* in return.
2. A representation of the exchange; the *balance* of value.

And getting the ratio right is the difference between work that is generative and work that is exploitative. The give/get ratio matters because it names what's often left unspoken: the exchange happening beneath every job title, every team dynamic, every mission-driven promise. It gives us language for asking a better question—not just "Am I doing meaningful work?" but "Is this meaning built on mutual value, or am I the one holding the weight while someone else cashes in?"

The answer to the question costs us more than hurt feelings.

When we show each other that we will take care of each other, everyone can go all in. If each side knows the system is set up to fail them, everyone is being drained.

This is a microcosm of what happens in larger teams, organizations, and even industries when we fail to consider the collective give/get ratio. Yes, in the near term, it is "economical" to do it a certain way. But that's not the whole picture, is it? When the focus is on the transactional level, the related innovation, morale, and potential for growth are missed. The give/get ratio can't just be about one person or one team; it needs to be a shared understanding, a framework that acknowledges the importance of reciprocal exchange across the board. How do we give/get to grow the pie? How do we give/get so we have the quality of life we all deserve? Instead of one person shouldering the burden of progress, everyone is engaged in the act of giving and receiving, and the value created is amplified by the efforts of all involved. It's like building a team where every member contributes not just their skills but also their needs and expectations— leading to more aligned, transparent, and fair collaboration.

In a workplace that brings out the best in us, the give/get ratio isn't a personal calculation—it's the foundation of the economic model.

Which brings us to a key distinction: Work is different from a job. A job is a specific role, shaped by an organization's needs. But work is bigger than that. The word *vocation* comes from the Latin *vocare*—to call. The root is voice. Work is how we express who we are and how we contribute to something larger. It's not just effort. It's expression. When we treat work as if it's limited to a job, we miss what makes it meaningful. Work—the way the Self meets the world—is how we do our best work. It's a way we can be fully alive. Work is an expression of us, and we are an expression of work.

When leaders and teams are aware, they make sure that the work is distributed equitably and that everyone's contributions are recognized and rewarded. It's not only about salary, though that matters, but about whose ideas are heard, whose effort is visible, and who gets investment to grow. And it doesn't stop there. The shift to a collective understanding of the give/get ratio requires us to challenge the systems that normalized uneven or one-sided contributions. It means telling those around us what we need—not only to survive but to thrive, and not just for our own flourishing but for a flourishing of the whole.

It's when what works for the business also and equally works for the person. So we can each say out loud, *If it doesn't work for me, it simply doesn't work.* This is the future, the baseline, and how we unlock new possibilities that drives us all forward.

A New Strategy

In 2021 and 2022, many industries, especially retail, were facing a severe labor shortage. Globally, we had just suffered from COVID drama, and companies were struggling to attract and retain workers, which led to high turnover and rising costs to replace employees. For IKEA, a Swedish-based but global retailer with thousands of workers, the cost of recruitment and training new staff became increasingly unsustainable. With an annual attrition rate of 62,000 workers, IKEA was facing high costs in lost productivity and hiring. This prompted the company to reassess its compensation strategy to keep workers longer and reduce turnover, which could save money in the long run. As *Bloomberg* reported, raising wages and improving benefits became a financial necessity rather than just a goodwill gesture.[20]

But what drove them to change their give/get ratio wasn't competitive pressures, it was public pressure—aka political participation as we explored in chapter 4—from consumers and activists who demanded living wages, especially in the wake of the pandemic.

IKEA recognized that failing to address their employees' grievances could tarnish its brand reputation, especially with the very Gen Z consumers they most need to buy their products.

People believed they deserved a better ratio, and they got it.

So while the company may have framed these decisions as part of their ethical commitments, they were certainly driven by a need to remain competitive in a tight labor market and preserve their workforce stability. It's all about economics.

We get what we need when we address it together, not individually.

A New Structure

Change happens at many levels—individual, relational, systemic. Yet too often, we misplace our attention. We tell individual people to work harder, to communicate better, to lean in or speak up. Asking those who are being harmed to do something about it makes some sense; after all, they are the ones most affected. Helping them stand up for themselves seems to be the most direct intervention. It is a call to action with those who have the most skin in the game. This, however, suggests that the problem exists and can be solved solely at this micro level. Or, we do the opposite: We lay the blame for the macro-outcomes of cutthroat capitalism on "the system." And while there's merit in that argument, given the complex and layered interactions that formulate any system, it's not a lever most of us can influence.

What we neglect to notice is that between the micro and macro lies the messy middle, the relational layer.[21] How the "system" is fed by our interactions, our collective behaviors. This is where collective change is not just possible but a pivotal approach. The key to change isn't just effort; it's knowing where to push:

- **Individual** (or micro)—personal beliefs, behaviors. Change happens through self-awareness and related action.
- **Relational** (or meso)—the social expectations, scaffolding, and structures that shape our workplace norms. Change happens in how we interact. Resistance being one interaction, new patterns another.
  » Social expectations set *standards*, such as that children go to school vs. work in a factory.
  » Scaffolding includes *programs*, like the 20% rule at Google that allowed them to recruit well by "giving" people space to work on their personal passions (obviously, Google benefitted from this, Gmail being an example of something that came from a personal project).
  » Structural *policies* include equal pay, living wages, healthcare, and childcare.
- **Organizational** (or macro)—institutional outcomes like profit, revenues, or GDP growth. *Change happens by defining an alternative metric.* No metric is neutral; someone is deciding what profit is, and who benefits.[22]

It's hard to see the levers of change. When we need to feed our family, and therefore need to keep our job, choosing to seek a better give/get ratio feels personal. Individual. That's why so many of us think the problem is ours alone. But framing the situation as a personal problem is a sleight of hand. It turns an economic conversation into an interpersonal one. As if the issue is that some people disagree. Or that some people are just not trying hard enough. When the issue is actually a policy question: How do we design a model that enables our best work?

And so that's where we start. The Walmart women thought they had to work harder to help their families. I thought quitting my job to stay home for my son was the right sacrifice. But each of us was limited in our view. Because the problems weren't individual failures or private negotiations—they were relational issues camouflaged as personal ones.

And I get why the Walmart women and I did what we did. We think we're being *responsible*, but what we're really doing is *sacrificing ourselves*, which stops us from building a solution that actually works. As in. Works. For. Us.

When we sacrifice ourselves to solve the structural—that is to say, business model—issue, we're giving up our own vitality. When we pour everything into a system that doesn't change, so will the next person who follows in our footsteps. Nothing will shift. There will just be more people being made to feel that they are the ones who need to fix things. Making choices that ignore their own well-being. It strips us of our freedom, and, if I can be blunt, it's the very opposite of our intention. It is irresponsible to sacrifice ourselves at the altar of whatever. The one person we're responsible for? Ourselves.

To create real change, we have to tell a different story—one that names the structure, not just the struggle.

INNOVATION PRACTICE
The Give/Get Ratio

Goal: Practice making the give/get ratio clear.

When teams feel stretched or stuck, the issue isn't just workload—it's often imbalance.

Try this together.

Step 1: Discuss (as a Team)

In pairs or as a full group, notice patterns:

- Where are we asking too much of some people?

- Who's overutilized, underutilized, or under-recognized?

Step 2: Adjust (Together). Ask:

- What shifts could restore balance? (Think structures, not individual actions.)

- Are there unspoken norms—like always relying on the same people for emotional labor or last-minute fixes?

- Can we redistribute giving or increase what people get?

Balance doesn't mean that everyone gives (or gets) the same amount. It means that the mix is generative, sustainable, and openly acknowledged. Make this a regular rhythm—especially before big pushes. When people feel seen and valued, teams flourish.

6

Serve Progress, Not Power

Limiting Norm: Speak Up
Leading Indicator: Share of Voice

Have you ever noticed that Power doesn't need to introduce itself? We've known it since forever. We recognize it instantly, no matter its disguise. Whatever Power demands, we know exactly how to respond.

Luke certainly did.

He glanced around at the 10 people in the conference room before rising from his seat. The group chatter paused as someone called out, "Luke, why are you moving?"

"Oh, I just need the outlet over here," he replied smoothly, though his knowing glance at me suggested an ulterior motive as he walked over. He settled into the chair beside me, his presence warm and comforting.

Leaning in, he smiled as he advised me, "Help Colin out with his idea. It's in your sweet spot; it'll show everyone in the room just how sharp you really are."

At first, it sounded like encouragement. A gentle push. The kind of advice women or young people often get: Speak up! But I've come to see that advice for what it is: not a hand up but a nudge that serves only the powerful.

Luke and I had been invited to the room as fellows with an economic institute. A handful of us had been selected to research and discuss how to create economic prosperity. Brainy stuff. Some were experts in policy—for example, why it helps the economy when the government funds childcare. Others studied what enabled cities to be vibrant economic hubs. Others figured out how to have companies that typically paid low wages operationally shift so they could fund good-paying jobs.

We had each been invited because we had something to add and something to learn by working together.

Let me repeat that.

We had *each* been invited because we had value to offer.

That was the backdrop of Luke's encouraging advice to "help Colin."

What Advice Serves You?

It's hard to spot when advice serves you.

It's when you're between gigs, and all the guidance you get follows this pattern: A startup person says you should join startup land, a tech person says you should join tech, and so on. In broader life, it's why people are told to go to college, join a big company, and save for retirement. Nearly every conversation with an older generation (and boomers in particular) assumes that what worked for them will also work for you and doesn't consider how the paradigms of college tuition, corporate life, and retirement have shifted. This advice is about them feeling good about their choices and telling you to follow in their footsteps, regardless of whether those are right for you. This is imitation advice: "Do what I did."

Other advice is tailored to you. It pays close attention to your specific circumstances and what you need to know to progress. It's advice that allows you to tune in to your own self-wisdom to let it guide you. Advice that isn't asking you to make the "right" choice but to trust that any choice you make is inherently the right one for you. It acknowledges that every life ship has a "sister ship," one that follows quite another route, reminding us that there are many equally valid paths toward becoming who we are becoming.

Then there's power-preserving advice, guidance that seems helpful but reinforces the status quo. Like when some—regardless of their talent and capability—are nearly always expected to prove themselves. How some folks are consistently asked to "speak up," as if the problem of their being ignored in so many rooms will be fixed if they do even more. Or how younger men are conditioned to reinforce the men-in-power's ideas rather than the best ideas. Or how despite being invited into the room, one can still be excluded while in the room. It's the most dangerous advice because it turns systemic exclusion into a personal failing.

None of this is easy to spot. To sort. *Especially* if it's delivered with warmth and a smile. It's hard to know whether we're getting advice that will let us serve something greater than ourselves or that will serve someone who thinks they're greater than we are.

Serving Power

The "Colin" that Luke was talking about was the head guy, the one who had spent months recruiting all of us to join the institute. Getting this group in one room took a lot, and we had a big agenda. People had traveled not only from different states but from different countries. However, nearly the first thing Colin did was go off-topic, sharing a business model he was "especially excited about," even though it seemed unrelated to why we were all gathered together.

Something about Luke's singling me out made me want to take his advice.

And yet something else told me I'd seen this movie before.

I've seen how people get accustomed to their every word being absorbed—how they take the floor and slip into a monologue. A story, or a stray shower thought, and just like that, the shared agenda vanishes. We often let it slide, thinking, *Whatever, he's just doing his thing,* as if it's harmless disorganization we're witnessing. But monologues aren't harmless; they hijack the room. They're a quiet power play, taking all the oxygen as if no one else needs any. Every time it happens, we trade what we could have made together for one person's need to feel important.

I also wondered if what I was witnessing was *himpathy,* a term coined by Kate Manne in her book *Down Girl.*[1] Empathy when directed at women is seen as coddling, but empathy directed at men is seen as reasoned and admirable. In this way, himpathy doesn't just *support* the most powerful men—it *perpetuates* patriarchy itself.

To process what was going on around me, I opened my Moleskin to a pristine page and wrote out questions:

Would Colin want any advice that I have to offer?

Whom in the room do I need to convince of my value?

Can I convince anyone of my expertise if they don't already see it?

Why am I being singled out by Luke?

Is my advising Colin to make his idea better the best use of our collective time?

Writing while listening, it took a few minutes, but I organized my thoughts. As discreetly as possible, I passed Luke a note: "Not even Colin seems to care about what he's talking about. Give him 20 more minutes to hear himself talk, and we'll likely all move on."

Luke read my scribbles, raised an eyebrow, then returned his full attention to Colin.

At the 23-minute mark, the subject changed.

Luke and I have yet to discuss his advice to me or my response. I wasn't avoiding the exchange, but a conversation about this kind of advice just felt so . . . *unnecessary.*

Why?

Well, let's unpack Luke's specific suggestion that I help Colin with his idea to demonstrate my expertise to the others.

- He assumed that I *needed* to prove my value to the room.
- He advocated that I spend my political capital, energy, and time on *someone else's* agenda.
- He didn't seem to notice (or care?) that the topic had little relation to why we had gathered.

This isn't great advice. It prioritized the powerful. It tokenized me. And distracted from our common cause.

What did Luke advocate? To serve Power rather than Progress.

Who Is Nearly Always Heard

Work—those norms and standards of modern work—has a default preference for who is heard.

It listens to loud, full-throated people over quiet[2] folks because it believes that's what passion and dedication look like. Work listens to confidence rather than competence because persuasion is overvalued. Work listens to experienced people over fresh perspectives because it thinks that knowing all the right lingo is a measure of value.

So distinct points of view—the source of value creation in our modern ideas economy—are left unheard.

And yet plenty of media, books, and experts ask the ignored people to speak up more. Facebook executive Sheryl Sandberg got published and gave a related TED Talk asking women to "lean in" to seek equal pay.[3] Another iteration of "Speak up." At the time, she was a C-suite executive at her company and a Corporate Board Member of Facebook; she could have advocated for an equal pay policy there, but she didn't.

Sandberg's advice was similar to Luke's: it served Power, not Progress.

I didn't know back at the Prosperity Institute what to do with Luke's advice. I was caught in a bind. Research shows that when women do "speak up," they are penalized for taking up anywhere close to their fair share of time.[4] Which is how Sandberg's advice resoundingly set women up. Told to be more assertive by Sandberg, women (especially women of color) who are will be called aggressive and, therefore, not team players. And punished. This is what's known as the double bind:[5] The very behaviors that might earn you respect if you were someone with power get you penalized if you're seeking power.[6] Mentored to build their presence to get ahead, many quickly learn that this is seen as "self-promoting" behavior, making them "unlikable." The data on the backlash is as consistent and clear as the data on bias. I knew from all the research that what Luke had asked of me was a sacrificial mission: Any attempt to act in one's own interest is futile, leaving the individual more trapped and powerless, as every choice leads to a negative outcome.

Luke, interestingly, knew this body of research as well as I did.

This norm has deep roots. The smile. The singling out. The supportive tones. These are what *benevolence* looks like: the appearance of being nice while extracting exactly what one wants. Originally, a "benevolence"—a voluntary contribution, or gift—was a tax imposed by kings in the 15th century. The tax *had* to appear to be a choice so the king could raise more money outside the existing parliamentary systems and keep it all for himself.[7] So the king would send commissioners into the local community to convince people that giving to the king was a sign of altruism and that serving the powerful was a privilege.

Serving the powerful is a privilege, says the norm.

It's what many of us accept as true and needed. Even necessary.

But let's call it what it is: Modern-day benevolence is how the elite "help" the non-elite—but always in such a way that it enhances their reputation, and they remain on top. The unheard get exploited while those dispensing advice are given more opportunities and more power.

To ask people to solve a problem that is not their own is exhausting, not encouraging; tearing down, not building up; and harmful, not helpful. Despite the tone or appearance of niceness. Despite anyone's *benevolence*.

The opposite of asking the unheard to speak up more is not for some to STFU and listen. No, that is just a polarity. The opposite of telling people to *speak up* is to change the room so all voices are heard well.

So what does it look like when someone uses their power to change the room itself?

Make the Room Change

In the mid-1950s, when Black people had a hard enough time getting work, and Black women even more so, Marilyn Monroe saw an opportunity.

Monroe lobbied the owner of the famed Mocambo club to book Ella Fitzgerald. If he did as she asked, she promised to take a front table every night and bring friends. Monroe knew what this would do. It would fill the club and create sold-out events. So the club owner would not only benefit economically but also be associated with the in-crowd.

With that tempting offer that no one could have turned down, the owner said yes.

And Monroe delivered. She booked a front table and brought friends to fill that table night after night. She also asked her team at her studio to help, to let the press know where she would be. The press went overboard to cover these events, photographing Monroe's outfits and the people she brought. Beautiful people in beautiful fashion is always a media draw.

The press coverage raised Fitzgerald's profile and people's interest in her music and style. This led to more gigs being booked, both domestically and abroad. And more opportunities being presented to her. By 1955, Fitzgerald had transitioned from bebop to recording broader genres. In 1956, she released the first of her eight songbook albums, *Ella Fitzgerald Sings the Cole Porter Song Book*, which she credited for helping her to break through with non-jazz audiences. An international career followed, and during her life, she recorded nearly 2,000 songs, earning 14 Grammy Awards and the Presidential Medal of Freedom in 1992.[8]

Instead of asking Fitzgerald to "speak up" or "lean in," Monroe did the work to fix the room and make the room receptive to newness.[9]

Of course, this wasn't self-sacrificing. When those in power change the room, they don't necessarily lose anything. In Monroe's case, it broadened *her* audience, too. It made her more than a bombshell; she became more interesting.

By her stepping up instead of asking someone else to speak up, more value was created—not for one but for all.

Modern-day benevolence is how the elite "help" the non-elite—but always in such a way that it enhances their reputation, and they remain on top.

And that is the irony in what happened at the economic institute.

Colin could have benefitted from having the institute deliver big ideas. He could be shaping policy globally. He personally would have become more relevant, but he couldn't allow that as long as Power needed to be serviced first.

Yet it's what he's been taught. And no one has yet to help him see that there's another way.

To be clear, I'm not saying, "Share the microphone," as if only one person can have their voice heard. What I'm advocating is making the room more interesting by giving *all* the voices their fair shot to be heard. In practice, sharing the mic is not about relinquishing power but about expanding who holds it. Binary thinking distorts the concept, framing it as an all-or-nothing proposition: either one person speaks or another does, leaving no room for the idea that many voices can be included. Complex conversations require all of our additive contributions, and power can be more equitably distributed without anyone's losing their voice.

When you amplify others' voices, your own grows. It's counterintuitive.

Truly powerful people don't limit what voices they listen to.

Just the opposite.

Because when we listen to all voices, we grow the power of our ideas. And our economy. And the community that economy serves.

Change the Here

Instead of asking individual leaders to say something like "We're open to ideas," the best gathering protocol is to have a round-robin process with an option to pass, so that each person has a chance to weigh in. This is how we ensure that those who may otherwise be silent or ignored—new people, young people, introverts, women, people of color—are socially and structurally included by design.

This would be an example of one strategy I regularly use.

In the marketing world, there's a concept called *Share of Voice*.[10] It measures the market share that a brand owns compared with its competitors. It gauges brand visibility and how much the brand dominates the conversation in that industry. The more marketing Share of Voice one has, the greater the popularity and authority among users and prospective customers. Share of Voice then is a battleground between players to occupy the buyer's mind.

It pisses me off that a concept of *sharing* is twisted like that.

Let's take back the term and reclaim it from the competitive marketing concept to what the words mean. Share. Of. Voice. Share of Voice could be about setting up the arena so all voices are heard in the arena, which is a different goal altogether. In the end, we all want to be part of something greater than ourselves. We are ready to tussle together and build ideas that matter. This is what we're striving for, and it is the reason our individual voices matter in the first place. To work toward our shared goals.

We have tons of solid data that shows how biases limit us from doing our best work, whether it's about loud/quiet, young/old, white/non-white, or male/female. Using that data, it's possible to intentionally design/redesign how we run gatherings to address biases we know exist.

In chapter 3, on value disruption, we talked about how you deserve better than the model that says money is everything and caring for each other is stupid. In chapter 4, we addressed how to demand better by getting involved in the political process. In chapter 5, we talked about how your job is to fix the structures not self-sacrifice. Here, I'll give a specific example about how structural change works.

If we shape the room right, no one needs to be told to do *more*. We can design the room so we can do our best. When we actually allow each person to have their fair Share of Voice in a room, we stop limiting our best work.

Here are 10 practices that work.

1. **Do check-ins.** *Work happens through our interactions, so begin by connecting.* If someone's dealing with a hurricane, had a bad night's sleep, or just lost their cat, it's important to know. One minute for every two people means a five-minute check-in for a 10-person meeting. This way, we don't have to guess how people are—we ask so we can stay present to each other's humanity.
2. **Set clear agendas together.** Share agendas in advance. *Invite input at the top of the meeting by asking, What is the best use of our time together today?* This ensures that everyone has a chance to shape what we do together, not just those with power or authority. Also, this helps us all get our heads in the game.
3. **Rotate facilitators.** *Everyone shares responsibility for how the work gets done.*

4. **Set a speaking order.** Start by asking for volunteers. But after the first volunteer, we can make sure everyone has a chance to speak or weigh in on the topic. *Ask for input using a "round-robin with a pass" option.* Anyone can "pass" and choose not to speak, but we use this method to ensure that new people, introverts, women, people of color, and others who may otherwise be silent or ignored are socially and structurally enabled, included.

5. **Be additive.** Use the "+1 approach," because if something's been said, it's been said (but do use snaps, handclaps, and nods to signal unity and support for another's idea). That said, if you act as if no one *will* care to hear your ideas, no one *can* care. *Fill that space that is yours.*

6. **Do some silent work.** Do some brainstorming via silent writing. Let everyone reflect some and *then* jot down their thoughts. Then share/build. *Tap into the introverts.*

7. **Call out asshat behavior.**[11] We can define asshat behavior as being superior, dominating, entitled, racist, sexist, et cetera. *If you see asshat behavior happening, name it and ask for a change.* "Hey Joe, it seems that you're telling us all what to think, and we've agreed that many points of view are equally valid."

8. **Be present.** If you're planning to participate, don't do email/slack/texts or whatever else while participating. We can all feel it energetically. People are like heaters; *we warm each other with our presence.* You RSVP'd for a reason; don't half-heartedly show up to your own life. (That said, we get it if, say, you have a newborn and need to turn the cam off to nurse. Join as best you can.)

9. **Don't offer unsolicited advice.** Giving advice demonstrates a desire to be in control of another person or a sense of self-importance. You can ask clarifying questions, like "What have you already considered?" or "Is this the first time something like this has happened?" You can tell your own story if you've faced something similar, to say you've

gone through it and share some lessons you learned. But in general, stop trying to solve everyone's problems as a way to be helpful. *Someone can design their own best solution if they can hear their own question well*; help them do that.

10. **Wrap it up.** Don't keep talking until the very end of your allocated time and then run out. Leave enough time to thank everyone for showing up and participating. Point out key next steps. Remind people that we can be here for each other, even be accountability partners. *Wrap up meetings like you're wrapping a gift.* And do some checks to hear what you're not hearing. Use tools like surveys for anonymous input to get candid feedback, to always get better.

If—or, rather, *when*—we shape the room right, we are ready for the future, ready to innovate. No one needs to be told what to do, because they were present for the conversation, and decided together the right next steps.

By knowing how to manage and measure the Share of Voice, we can guarantee balanced contributions—so no one dominates the conversation, and no voice is drowned out. This is how to set the scaffolding for success. We're not asking individuals to do the work of change when it's not possible for them to effect change through their private actions. No, we're setting the organizational norms that allow us to do our best work. These aren't abstract concepts; they are actionable practices, steps with clear guidelines, measurable outcomes, and accountability mechanisms.

When we shape the social spaces so we can create value, we do our best work.

The future demands that we serve Progress, not Power.

INNOVATION PRACTICE
Share of Voice

Goal: Apply Share of Voice strategies at your next meeting.

- Pick a Share of Voice strategy you'll practice first.
- Write a note to the team sharing why you're excited to try it out.

"To make our work time together even better, I want to take more responsibility for changing our meetings' social norms. It's important that everyone's voice is heard. This is how we'll grow, and learn, and build what comes next. I'd like to start by practicing ABC [name it, sharing a description of how it works]. Let's integrate it into our standing ABC meeting, moving forward. You'll see me trying it out, and I might not get it 'right' at first, but I hope you'll jump into the pool with me to learn a new approach together."

With a colleague, do a walk-and-talk, to debrief/discuss.

- Celebrate what worked (include that you tried something new)!
- Ask how you can build on that.
- Identify one small insight you'll practice for the next time.

7

There Are Limits to Logic

Limiting Norm: Be Rational
Leading Indicator: Build Intelligence

The product was a flop, customers were bailing, and competition was driving down prices. The company's survival was in question. All the internal teams had put their best minds on the problem. Some of the big consulting teams had even come and gone without fixing the problem. People were anxious, even freaked out, about how bad things were. When my team and I were brought in, we were asked to do the Hail Mary pass, to save the game in the final seconds.

I understood that the situation was dire, so I looked the CEO—that freaked-out person trying so hard not to act freaked out—in the eye and told him exactly what to do.

"I need you to send an email to every single person in this company."

He nodded and picked up a pen like he was taking dictation. The CFO hovered nearby nervously, waiting for whatever hammer I was about to drop on the company through this email.

I took a deep breath. "The subject line should read as follows," I said. "Invitation to Play."

That wording is why some of the world's most powerful CEOs have tried to fire me.

It's not that I didn't respect the gravity of the company's situation or understand that they were desperate and in need of a solution yesterday.

Just the opposite.

I believed in his people. I believed that they were doing their best. I certainly didn't think I was there because I was smarter than them. I believed that the reason the company was stuck, the reason that the greatest corporate consulting intelligence hadn't solved the problem was that we, collectively, didn't yet know what the problem *was*.

And that's why I wanted to access all the intelligence we could.

The invitation to play was a way to open the doors to new ideas, to have a conversation about what we were missing, and to listen for what we didn't yet know. And the only way to hear what wasn't working was to tap the people who lived the problem every day. Those not in the corner offices but on the front lines. We needed to hear from customer service about the customer's lived experience and why the buyer was calling to complain. We needed to hear from the sales rep who was emotionally overwrought because they couldn't make their quarterly quota. Or the admin who always knew what the infighting was about.

Intelligence comes in every shape, from every place.

The CEO wasn't happy at what felt to him like a waste of time—he didn't want a kumbaya gathering where everyone shared rambling stories about their work experience. But then something happened as we were all gathered together, when a customer service rep shared her third story about what she was hearing daily from customers.

"When you hear the same thing over and over again," she said, "I'm pretty sure that's the real problem. People are mad that we haven't updated the product to fit their needs now. I hear it every day in call after call."

She didn't sling the lingo, she wasn't a trained expert, and her delivery was tentative, but those words sent a spark around the room. Everyone sat up a little straighter, those previously not paying attention looked directly at her, and even the CFO, who had been pacing in the corner, stopped pacing.

Intelligence is like that. It takes two (or more) to think.[1]

It's not what *this person* or *that person* knows. It's what *we* know.

Intelligence emerges in conversation.

It is not a private act but a social one, a shared act of meaning-making.

It isn't about finding a fact as if we're looking for a missing button but built together, from understanding the situation fully, including perspectives often ignored. The shared processing of facts and information is how we start to create change. It is why conversation is the single unit of change: We "make sense" together. Which is perhaps obvious but worth stating explicitly, a relational process. And while AI does a good job at imitating relational aspects, it will never actually be a relationship. It will never be human. It can only imitate, or be artificial. Hence the name "artificial intelligence." It cannot do what we can. Which is why we must.

Yet leaders nearly always shut down intelligence creation, not realizing how it's costing them their company's future.

A Narrow Definition

Our modern definition of "intelligence" is shaped by a narrow lineage—one that has long excluded other ways of knowing. In ancient Greece, Socrates, Plato, and Aristotle set the stage for how we define "smart" today. They valued "knowledge," whether it was practical wisdom (phronesis) or theoretical understanding (episteme).[2] Later, European philosophers like Descartes, with his famous "I think, therefore I am," framed intelligence as critical reasoning.

Immanuel Kant's work, still taught in most educational curricula, reinforced this ideal, tying it to his Eurocentric lineage. In his 1764 work, *Observations on the Feeling of the Beautiful and Sublime*, he wrote, "The Negroes of Africa have by nature no feeling that rises above the trifling."[3] In this chilling statement, Kant wasn't just reflecting the awful prejudices of his time, he was building a framework that tied intelligence and moral worth to his own European—that is, white—heritage.

Today, we see echoes of his thinking in systems that still prioritize certain kinds of intelligence—often those aligned with white, Western ideals—while dismissing others. The result? A persistent inequality. And a limited understanding of what human capacity truly is.

Then came the idea that intelligence is genetic. While Charles Darwin believed that intelligence was about the ability to adapt to one's environment— a definition that I think serves us well—he tied those adaptative capacities to genetics. Which is what allowed Darwin's take on intelligence to become twisted by his racist cousin Francis Galton into a belief in genetic superiority. We can hear those ideas spouted when a leader says, "We only want the *best* people," when really what they mean is the people who look the part because that particular profile is all we've seen. Galton's views, by the way, are the foundation for today's IQ tests, further cemented by Charles Spearman's early-20th-century concept of "g" (general intelligence), the so-called measure of all cognitive abilities.

That is *quite* a lineage.

The Greeks lived within a patriarchal society that largely excluded women and non-Greek peoples from intellectual life. The Enlightenment folks valued reason most, and certainly had a bias about who mattered in terms of class, gender, and race. And the evolutionist thinking led to the false idea of a superior class of humans. Even Howard Gardner, whom I loved reading in my early 20s for his suggestion that the definition of "smart" could be broader—including linguistic, logical-mathematical, spatial, musical, bodily-kinesthetic, interpersonal, intrapersonal, and naturalistic intelligence[4]—emerged from and spoke to intelligence within a predominantly white, Western, elite context.

When only a narrow group defines intelligence, we get a narrow definition.

The modern definition of "smart" or "intelligent" is tightly bound to logic, reason, and detachment—qualities often epitomized by characters like Spock from *Star Trek*. And one can see the appeal. Spock oozed scientific authority, which suggests an objectivity and fairness. He also embodied traditionally masculine ideals, being stoic, analytical, detached. People turn to rational thinking for the same reasons the captain of the starship *Enterprise* did: Spock symbolized control over chaos—his own and the universe's. That's comforting, a theme we keep seeing in what limits our best work. In times of crisis, comfort is what we reach for. No wonder we value rationality.

When we define intelligence as purely rational, severed from emotion; as strictly intellectual, detached from intuition; as objective in a way that denies the truths of lived experience, we don't just narrow the definition. We narrow ourselves. We strip intelligence of its full power, reducing it to something cold, calculable, and incomplete. And in doing so, we all lose—because the wisdom that could guide us, the insight that could move us, the understanding that could connect us, is left outside the frame.

This shows up in management.

Management as we understand it today was first designed for *hands*. For those doing production on an assembly line. It's been adapted over time for *minds*, and the ways in which ideas drive our economy. But management isn't yet addressing the fullness of how people create value, because of how intelligence is understood.

And that limitation affects everything.

It constrains our capacity, of course. And our economy.

Limiting our best work.

We see it in our everyday interactions. Research shows that just *saying* that someone is "emotional" means their ideas get discounted. And worse, it leads them to discount themselves.[5] This accusation holds power because we're told that emotions are the opposite of rationality, and therefore the opposite of "smart."

Only when we see intelligence as being as rich and as varied as every one of us will the brightest minds even recognize their own brilliance.

Sounding Smart

Sonia was leading a brand creative team responsible for creating a major Super Bowl ad under a tight deadline. After a tense meeting, she noticed that her team was tapped out. Tones were sharp. Energy brittle.

Instead of pushing her team to dive back into the grind, she paused. Trusting her gut—an intuitive sense that something needed to shift— she invited her team to step away from their fluorescent-lit conference room and take a quick walk outside.

They grumbled. It felt silly. But they went.

Outside, Sonia guided them through a few simple breathing exercises, encouraging them to focus on their breath and lower their shoulders away from their ears. The team slowly began to relax, their breathing becoming more even and their steps less hurried. Sonia then asked them to silently observe their surroundings for just one minute—the rustling leaves, the cool breeze, and the warmth of the rare British sun.

The whole walk-and-talk took about 15 minutes. Including the elevator ride.

Laughter returned.

The silliness was necessary.

When we define intelligence as purely rational, severed from emotion; as strictly intellectual, detached from intuition; as objective in a way that denies the truths of lived experience, we don't just narrow the definition. We narrow ourselves.

Back at their desks, the team was sturdy again. This previously scattered and fried group of people started to line up, ready to be resourceful and creative, coming together like firefighters who could pass the bucket of water and extinguish a fire in record time. Sonia had just transformed her team's energy and, thus, the team's ability to create value.

Because no one does their best work under stress or duress.[6]

Sonia didn't have a name for what she'd accomplished. But she was using her somatic intelligence—her ability to sense and respond to her team's physical and emotional state—to make this small but significant intervention that benefitted . . . well, everything.

She did something amazing.

And yet even she didn't see it.

In her next one-on-one, Sonia's supervisor told her she wasn't that "strategic."

She nodded.

Why?

Not because she hadn't made the right call.

Not because her team hadn't recovered.

But because her kind of intelligence didn't look or *sound* like what they expected.

No, what the boss was saying and Sonia was agreeing with was that there is a certain way to *sound* strategic. Which we all know. We've been in the rooms. We've heard it. We've all used it at times. Sonia didn't signal her smarts by speaking the jargon and lingo that is the measuring stick of corporate intelligence. And because no one (including her) valued a broader range of intelligence, it was easy to think she had fallen short.

Because here's what gets recognized instead:

"Let's take a data-driven approach." This emphasizes the importance of decisions being backed by quantitative analysis, making people sound analytical, rigorous, and precise. That sounds smart. Sure. Until you realize that not all problems have data. If we are working to invent the future, there has yet to be relevant data. Quantitative data is inherently backward-looking; to build what comes next, we must explore the quality of ideas to develop insights and tap our imagination. If you require solid, confirmable data to decide things, every new idea will be killed because there's no quantitative data to back it up.

And then there's this:

"We need to capture the low-hanging fruit for quick wins to move the needle." Referring to easy wins or opportunities that can be quickly and easily achieved, this shows a pragmatic approach to problem-solving. Which is a good thing. But the shadow side is less obvious. How the search for "quick wins" can lead teams toward things that could look good, or make money right away. This, too, *sounds* smart, but it nearly always means doing *something*, not doing the *right* things. Often, it's used by teams who don't know their values so they do something, anything, toward the optics of creating value.

As we covered in chapter 3, "Disrupting Value."

Oh, and then there's this one:

"Let's consider the 80/20 rule." Referring to the Pareto principle, this suggests that 80% of results come from 20% of efforts. The goal in bringing it up is to signal a focus on maximizing efficiency and effectiveness. While it is true that focusing on a few things can often result in efficiency, innovation and creating value are rarely, *if ever*, about efficiency. *Efficiency* and *disruption* are words used to sound like one is doing something interesting, but these abstract words often distract from value getting created; they sure sound like something important, but they can easily be decoys for the real thing. True innovation requires connecting seemingly disparate dots, which frequently involves wandering around and following some false paths to explore options and, therefore, is inefficient by design.

There's a big difference between *sounding* smart and *being* smart.

Sonia *was* smart, and she showed it every day in how she managed her team, in how she built value for the company. But if you see "smart" as a kind of calculus problem with inputs and outputs, of data and information vs. insights, of efficiency rather than innovation, well, we all miss out.

A lot of what we are told is smart will have us do what we've already done.

Which isn't the way forward.

Don't we need to tap into a wider and fresher way of working? Don't we want to access local and lived knowledge? Don't we want to listen to the body, not just a body of knowledge? Don't we need to trust our intuition? Don't we need to see smart not as a calculus problem but as a calculation? What did Sonia's boss and all the CEOs who wanted to fire me need to know?

We need to risk sounding unsmart to get smarter.
We need to not know for long enough to know.
We need to lean on one another to augment our own
    perspectives.
We need to include every type of intelligence.
We need to build a shared understanding.

Intelligence cannot be scored, compared, or ranked. It is broadly available. It is something we access when we are calm and creative, not limited by stress and duress. It is something we create as we relate to each other, and are open to creating together. Intelligence isn't a fixed measure; it's a journey—a shared journey we take.

I like knowing the roots of words, the field of etymology. It started because English was either my fourth or fifth language depending on how you count, and then immigrating to a country where English was the primary language meant I had (and sometimes still have) some trauma around saying something "wrong" and not sounding "smart."

That's why I know that the root of *intelligence* in Latin means "to understand."

I love that word, *understand,* don't you? It makes sense to me that understanding is what we're seeking more than being "smart." This is what we need to be future-facing. It's so contrary to "being logical," "being rational," or "knowing stuff."

The goal of intelligence therefore isn't measured one person at a time but by how we create collective understanding. When *we* truly seek to understand, we strive to understand the situation, one another, the past, and what we truly desire. It's in seeking understanding that we become smarter—not by how we *compare,* but by how we *connect.* Intelligence grows not in our obsession with being rational but in our willingness to *explore.* It thrives in our quest to understand.

Intelligence is created in an interaction, not by facts alone.

And that is why we collectively need to move beyond the traditional understanding of what is smart and toward its true essence: a living, breathing dance between us. It is a dynamic play where we connect, build, and shape our collective intelligence.

We come to play.

Leadership or management is often described as herding cats, describing the difficult, if not impossible, task of organizing a group of people to get work done. But it's not actually like herding cats; it's more like herding butterflies,⁷ which is, by definition, impossible.

Because butterflies go where the right plants are; it's emergent. Particular types of butterflies relate to particular kinds of plants. So if you want to herd butterflies, you must plant the right plants in the right soil and climate at the right time. Butterflies arrive as a result of relational factors.

So, too, does intelligence.

Management's job, then, is to build the relational conditions to enable our best work. How do you build the context for people to explore, connect, and discover?

The Art of Cultivation

Intelligence and its related value-creation don't sprout from thin air. Just like in nature, where butterflies go where they thrive, intelligence needs a healthy context to emerge. And you can play a crucial role in creating this environment—much like how a gardener carefully cultivates a garden, which is to say there are things you can do, but it's not all about you.

Know what to plan(t). Gardens don't thrive when they have only one type of plant. In nature, biodiversity is key to a healthy, resilient ecosystem. Having a variety of plants creates balance because each species plays a unique role in the environment—some plants fix nitrogen in the soil, others attract pollinators, and some provide shade or help retain moisture. This diversity allows the garden to be more adaptable and resistant to diseases, pests, and changes in weather conditions. Monocultures at work or in gardens are vulnerable. If a pest or disease affects that type of plant, the entire garden can suffer. Without variety, the ecosystem lacks the natural checks and balances that help regulate its health. Variation in a garden creates interdependence, where different plants support each other's growth in ways that a single species cannot.

This mirrors how leaders need to put together a mix of perspectives, experiences, and skills.

Generative ideation—the process of creating multiple, novel ideas—flourishes when various perspectives come together. Research shows that teams are more innovative than individuals because they approach problems from different angles,[8] much like how varied plant species contribute to a healthier, more resilient ecosystem. So whenever you are gathering teams, your job is to ask *who is interested in helping with a problem* and involve them. There is no one right type of person (the expert, the experienced one, the person whose job it is) who can help. What makes someone "right" is their interest in participating. And, then, perhaps obvious but important to say, *let* those who show up help you. It will seem chaotic for those unused to it, but that's just another view on and for emergent creativity.

Nurture the soil—enable nascent ideas to become robust enough to grow into solutions. Just as soil is the foundation of any thriving plant—providing the nutrients necessary for growth—organizational "soil" is the safety people feel in being able to share information, expertise, and feedback freely.

No one has done more to clarify this need than Harvard professor Amy Edmondson, with her construct of "psychological safety."[9] Her work says that none of us build on each other's ideas if we don't feel safe ourselves. We won't take risks, voice ideas, or admit mistakes if doing so comes with fear of punishment or ridicule. Psychological safety is essential for fostering innovation, learning, and effective collaboration, because it encourages individuals to engage in open dialogue, ask questions, and challenge the status quo.

And again, this isn't something you "manage" or "lead" or "direct." But you can support it, sustain it, nurture it. How? By what you encourage, and by what you embody. If you talk shamefully about trying something new and having it fail, the team will know it's not okay to make mistakes. Yet if you say, "I tried something new and it didn't go as planned; I am struggling to digest what it means for XYZ and am curious what you see that we might learn from"—if you make trying something new *safe* for you—you *show* it's safe for them.

Create the right "climate"—the favorable conditions for effective decision-making.

No matter how nutrient-rich the soil or how varied the plants, they won't grow in the wrong climate. Just as plants need the right combination of sunlight, water, and favorable temperatures, teams need the right environment to make trade-offs and choices. This is where discovery comes in—decisions are made not by planning cycles, facts, or static assumptions, but by learning in real time what is needed now. It is getting to a decision crossroad and asking, *What is the next right thing?* When decision-making is grounded in this kind of discovery, teams become more adaptable and resilient, much like plants that thrive in dynamic environments.

Cultivate the context, and intelligence will follow.

Ideas will rise up the way wildflowers grow in cracks in the pavement, always growing toward the light. We will lean on each other, learn from each other, and help each other grow, raising up each other's performance.

The job of those leading isn't to make something happen.

After all, you don't make a flower grow by building it cell by cell[10] but by knowing that every seed has within it all that it needs; your job is to set the conditions for growth.

That's intelligence-making.

Let's cultivate it.

Get Emotional

There's a strength in seeing the world through the lens of rational logic, of right and wrong. It sharpens conviction, fuels moral courage, and gives people the clarity to act when others hesitate. Those who think this way often become the backbone of teams, the ones who speak out, take risks, and stand firm. As Aaron Sorkin wrote in *The West Wing*, "Every once in a while, there's . . . an absolute right and an absolute wrong"—and it's in those moments that this kind of certainty becomes not just useful but essential.

But those are the rare exceptions.

Most days, the world is nuanced, and we need things like emotions.

Because our fullness adds value. Because we are not automatons. To believe anything less is to deny our worth. And our humanity. Let's change this, shall we?

If someone calls us *emotional*, let's celebrate that.

We'll celebrate the things that are good even though we are told they are not.

We get to be fully human and bring all of ourselves to the game.

We'll even laugh when they say it, because being emotional is not an insult but integral to who we are.

We'll know it's not right or wrong, it just is.

INNOVATION PRACTICE
Invitation to Play

Goal: Learn to set the stage that enables intelligence.

Solving complex problems is not about finding an answer as if looking for an object. Solving tough problems is about people joining together to create the intelligence necessary to solve them. And we do that by creating an invitation to play. When you're at play, you're present, open, calm, and creative. When you're playing, you're being generative. This playful space is what you aim to create.

Draft Your Invitation (20 Minutes)

- Choose a project that needs the intelligence of many.
- Remind everyone that they are welcome to bring their own ideas, big or small. State that no "expertise" is required—just curiosity and a willingness to engage.
- Signal that you're casting a wide net here, because you're excited to see what you discover together.
- Trust that whoever shows up is the "right" person.
- Don't tell them everything you will do when you get together; you don't know that yet. Name the goal as a direction, not a route.
- Ask a buddy at work to take a look at this note for you.
- Revise as needed before you hit Send.

8

Go Out Beyond Absolutes

Limiting Norm: The Right Answer
Leading Indicator: What Is Right for Us

We want rightness. It feels clear. It feels comforting. But it doesn't work.

That's because the world is not fixed—it's dynamic, complex, and full of nuance. Life doesn't fit into rigid categories of always or never, good or bad, right or wrong. The moment we try to impose absolutes, we erase context, flexibility, and the ability to adapt.

Take leadership: A leader who always takes charge may miss moments when stepping back is the right move. Or decision-making—if a company never changes its strategy, it becomes obsolete. Even in ethics, absolutism ignores the complexity of real-world choices where competing values often exist.

Absolutes simplify, but they also limit. They create rules instead of understanding. They stop curiosity, questioning, and the ability to respond to the actual situation rather than a predetermined ideal. Life isn't a formula; it's an unfolding process. And unfolding is slow and iterative—and ridiculously unclear.

And yet we crave rightness. It feels safe.

We want so badly to be on a right path—believing we're the right people, who went to the right (or right-enough) schools, who have done the right preparations and will come up with right answers.

But what if there is no single right?

Making Choices

That's the kind of question a young engineer faced when she had to decide where to begin her career.

Today, we know the outcome—Marissa Mayer took a major role at one of the world's most successful companies, Google. But back then, the choice wasn't obvious. The company she was considering had no revenue, no clear path, and just a dozen employees working out of a dusty garage in Palo Alto. It was one of many early-stage tech startups—promising, sure, but uncertain.

She did what many of us do: tried to logic her way through the decision. Built a spreadsheet. Weighed the options—salary, trajectory, even a "happiness factor." Each metric neatly organized.

And still, she wasn't sure.

At midnight, she called a friend, hoping for clarity. Instead, her friend said something that changed everything: *You think there's one right choice and 13 wrong ones. But actually, there are 14 very good choices. The difference isn't in picking the perfect one—it's in committing to the one you choose and making it right for you.*[1]

This is where most of us get stuck. We treat decisions like moral absolutes, as if the wrong choice will ruin everything.

This is the perfectionist's trap. Perfectionism—the disposition to regard anything short of perfect as unacceptable—is so commonplace, most don't question it. It is what Kant was saying: There's an attainable ideal.

But perfectionism isn't clarity. It's a trauma response.

It often develops as a way to cope with feelings of insecurity, fear, or past experiences of criticism, neglect, or unpredictability. If someone grows up in an environment where love or approval is conditional—based on performance, achievement, or avoiding mistakes—perfectionism becomes a survival strategy. It creates the illusion of control and safety: "If I do everything perfectly, I won't be rejected, shamed, or hurt."

And like many trauma responses, what once served to protect can easily become a cage.

At work, it does.

Perfectionism is how we chronically deny our own truth as we stifle creativity and growth.

Because the goal isn't to be perfect; it's to be fully ourselves.

Isn't that the tension?

We seek perfection at the expense of our own humanity. Yet the future requires us to be fully alive.

Which begs the question of whether we even know how to tap into our own desires, to know what matters to us. If not, we can easily let others define success for us.

Useful Until Unfamiliar

Mary and I were strangers on a plane when our first project started.

Her big company had just acquired another, and to make the deal work, each side's sales teams had to start selling each other's products. She and I needed to create a multichannel sales model—figuring out who would sell what, and what incentives would drive sales. Mary had no background in this kind of work, so she hired me to help her design the business model.

On the flight to Toronto, she looked distant, melancholy. I asked, "Is something missing from your incredible life?"

She sighed. "I don't see my husband enough. He's the CEO of a public company working out of Asia. I'm the VP of another. Our schedules are . . . intense."

"The classic power couple dilemma," I said lightly.

The next morning in the hotel lobby, she stopped me. "Can you join me for breakfast?" I figured we'd prep for the day. Instead, she said, "Your question kept me up all night. I called my husband right after we landed and again this morning. You're the second person to know—I want a baby."

I was touched by her vulnerability. "How can I support you?"

She didn't know yet. But a few months later, she did.

"I got my CEO's blessing. We can hire you to cover all my projects while I travel with my husband. I need support to get pregnant without quitting my job."

That conversation was the result of weeks of back-and-forth. At first, Mary saw her options in stark terms: Either she would get pregnant, or she would keep her executive job. But I challenged that binary. I saw a VP who loved her work, with positional power, a strong track record, and an employer with something to lose. Why not ask for what she needed instead of assuming it was impossible? Maybe we could design something that worked for everyone. Maybe is the opposite of certainty—or comfort—but it's also the birthplace of what may be.

And it did work. Not easily, but she got and stayed pregnant and had a beautiful boy.

If this were a made-for-TV drama, this is where the background music would change.

Five years later, I went to her first with *my* big news: Kiddo needed me. I was shuttering my company to be there for him. I didn't know what I'd do next, but I thought that by continuing some public speaking, I could still add *some* value—and be the kind of parent I hadn't had.

She had once trusted me to restructure her entire company's business model. Trusted me to carry her VP role while she stepped away. Trusted me to witness her desire for a child.

And now I was asking for the same: for her to witness and support my struggle.

But I didn't get that support. I got answers; I got advice.

Her response? "So . . . you'll become a talking head?"

Her tone wasn't cruel, but it was clear. Emphatic. As if there was only one right answer, and I was getting it wrong—as if I were abandoning real work for something hollow. She would say she was just objectively analyzing the situation, but objectivity is the idea that we can stand outside ourselves and see the world exactly as it is. We cling to it because it promises certainty: clean answers, solid ground, a way out of the tangle of perspective and power. But it isn't real. Every truth is filtered through the eyes that see it, the questions that frame it, the structures that decide which voices count.

To be sure, the reason her comment hurt was that it echoed my own anxiety about the future. What did I know about how it would work out? Nothing. Maybe I *would* be a useless talking head. Who could know? I felt like one big shrug emoji.

But this is how searching for "right" answers hurts us all. It gives us the comfort of believing in facts—but every truth carries the fingerprints of its teller.

She didn't mean harm, I'm sure of it. She probably thought she was nudging me just as I had nudged her. Or that she was helping me make the "right" call. But what she said in support didn't feel so supportive.

I was crushed.

Because if she was right, then I was wrong.

So, so wrong.

Commit to What Matters

Before we can choose what works for us, we have to stop letting others define success for us.

This is where most decision-making advice fails. It assumes that we all want the same things: status, money, external validation.

But as these stories show, what's right depends on what we value:

- Maybe what matters is building things that solve real problems—not chasing a big salary.
- Maybe working in small teams is more energizing than joining a big-name brand.
- Maybe stepping away from the corporate life allows for something new to emerge.

This is one's own work—which is to say, yours—to do.

No one else stands in that spot in the world where you do, shaped by your history and experiences, your ideas, your aspirations. Naming what matters is about tuning in to that. What do you crave? What energizes you? What is something you would do even if no one were paying you?

Oftentimes what comes to mind looks too easy or too simple and is discarded because it's so obvious to you. If something feels obvious to you, you assume it can't be that important. When in fact, the opposite is true. The thing that is so obvious to you is nearly always the foundation of who you are.

So before you build a spreadsheet or list your options, ask:

- What do I always want, independent of what others expect?
- What would I pursue if I weren't afraid of making the wrong choice?
- What, when I imagine doing it, feels like home?

And also ask a friend, *What lights me up?* It's as if we were all born with a certain shade of light bulb on top of our head, illuminating everything around us. It could be tangerine orange or cobalt blue. But you can't tell what it is. Because it's all you've ever seen. However, when you enter a room, others immediately perceive the change, exclaiming, "Wow, it just got cobalt in here!" None of us can see our distinct attributes, as these qualities are so intrinsic to our being that they become almost invisible to us. But our friends can be helpful if they can reflect back to us: *What you always seem to care about is this.*

We often think right decisions create success.

In reality, our *commitment* to a path creates success.

The best option isn't the one that comes pre-validated—it's the one you choose and then make right for you.

This is the shift we need: away from "Is this right or wrong?" toward "How does it work for me?"

We don't *find* the perfect path.

We *build* it. By showing up. And chasing down the thing that matters to us.

And even if we get something "wrong," that isn't the end. It's just another step. You go, *Whoops, that didn't work. Let's try another way.*

Perfect in Theory

We think figuring out the right answer will prevent us from making the wrong choice. At work we say things like:

I wish you understood the situation correctly.

That's not how things work; let me explain.

It'll never work that way.

If we want to succeed, then we need to do it this way . . .

That's not right.

We were taught this. In the 18th century, our friend Immanuel Kant argued that for something to be right, it had to be right in *all* situations. No exceptions.

But *wow*. That's some serious hubris.

To believe in absolutes is to disconnect from the lived human experience. It erases context. It denies nuance.

Kant's version of the world is neat, while humans are not.

And yet Kant is still revered—taught in nearly every philosophy course—because his theory gives the illusion of an orderly universe.

But that illusion holds only if you ignore reality. Even science evolves; we once thought the world was flat. The illusion also assumes that human beings—flawed, messy, brilliant—don't exist.

This matters in small and large ways.

Take the work of Karim R. Lakhani, a Harvard innovation professor.

He and his colleagues asked scientists to identify previously unsolved problems, sourcing from over 26 firms and over 80,000 scientists worldwide to find 166 unsolvable problems. These were problems the "right" people from the "right" schools had already failed to crack. The scientists were skeptical, but they let Lakhani and team do the research.[2]

And people showed up. Women who loved science but left the field when they encountered sexual harassment, young people who had been told they didn't know enough, and citizen scientists who cared about solving tough problems but hated the insular nature of the science field or lacked the resources to go to college.

Within a year, nearly one-third of the 166 *unsolvable* problems were *solved*.

One-third.

By people the system had dismissed.

Nearly 100% of the solution-creators came from undervalued groups—what the researchers called "left field" but we could just call . . . human.

This didn't happen *despite* their difference. It happened *because* of it. Instead of the "right people" having the "right answers," this research revealed something profound: The most valuable thing we have is variance in points of view. Rooted in that power of place where each of us stands. The distinct view each of us holds.

And right/wrong thinking kills that.

Because it narrows the range of who gets to contribute, what is heard, and how information is processed. The more tightly we cling to "rightness," the more creativity, economic growth, and truth we shut out.

Does It Work for Us?

In a world of right and wrong, *only* one side can be right.

That's what right/wrong architectures do. It's like a teeter-totter in an old, desolate playground, its rusted hinges groaning under the weight of our choices. Each decision we argue slams down on one side, jolting the other into the air with a harsh thud. In this relentless binary, when one is up, the other is down. A meeting in the middle might happen but offers no pleasure. That's not how the game works.

And let's name the dynamic of two people having this exchange.

The most valuable thing we have is variance in points of view.

Someone who argues that they are right and you are wrong is actively showing you that they are not interested in working *with* you. By definition, they do not show up to create a solution that *also* works for you; they "win" only by having you adopt their ideas as your own. The person who believes in right/wrong answers isn't interested in the validity of your point of view, only in telling you how to think "correctly." Equally, they do not want to respect your worldview; they want more than anything for you to become an emissary of theirs.

A conversation about who or what is right *might* sound like people attempting to collaborate, but it is *always* about controlling the narrative, controlling another.

Blech. (Also, *shudder!*)

I've been in plenty of relationships where the other party believed firmly in right and wrong. We all have. Whether it's with a spouse, or with our parents, or with a boss. To them, this is a contest of wills, of coming out on top.

The challenge is always how to redirect the conversation to something more fruitful.

Instead of asking, "Who is right?," try: "Does this work for us?"

After all, isn't that the point? If it works for only one of us, it doesn't really work. Period. When we ask what works for us, we shift the goal. It's no longer about winning the teeter-totter game. We stand on the same lever. We move together.

Research shows that when people want to cooperate (vs. win an argument), they admit that truth is subjective.[3] We can see a variety of needs and then create solutions that best meet those needs. Together, moving away from right/wrong moves from judgment to generative solutions, including solutions for the many ways we can add and create value.

Out beyond ideas of wrongdoing and rightdoing, there is a field, Rumi said.

I'll meet you there.

Observe and Interrupt

The best way to shut down judgment is to *observe* the judgmental behavior without adding your reaction and judgment into the mix.[4] Isn't that interesting? That's also the key.

To break the right/wrong dynamic, don't argue. Just observe it. Name what you see—calmly, clearly. That's how you interrupt the pattern. Say:

"It sounds like you believe you're the only one who knows how things work."

"It seems like you believe there's only one right way for things to work."

"It sounds like you believe there is only one way to succeed."

I used to engage. In life. In marriage. At work. I'd empathize. Offer facts. Manage my emotions. Listen harder. Try to validate the other person's point of view.

Until I realized that the moment I stepped into the right/wrong debate, I had already lost.

Because in that framework, someone always *has* to lose. Observation isn't about changing others. It's about refusing to play their game. You're not the mouse to someone else's cat. You're not picking up the rope in a tug-of-war. You say you don't buy into their binary right or wrong. You say you believe there are more solutions than their limited imagination allows.

That's how you choose freedom.

That's how you co-create what comes next.

(You're welcome.)

The leading indicator of great work is when we relate *with* each other, connect the pieces, and collaborate toward shared goals. We do that by having effective, two-way conversations. The hard part is that it can *look* like we're exchanging ideas while really we're tussling over the "right" and "wrong" perspectives.

Now, some of you will say that by not engaging, I'm not following my own basic edict. That all change happens in conversation, that conversations are the smallest unit of change. Let me explain the difference. When there is a back-and-forth where we build up ideas together, adding bits and pieces to each other's perspective and knowledge set, the conversation changes us. Rather, we are *allowing* the conversation to change us. We can, of course, attend meetings and just talk *at* each other. In that case, we're just "alone together," as my good friend, author of a book with that title, and MIT sociologist Sherry Turkle would say.[5]

Arguing right/wrong isn't a conversation.

It's a battlefield.

And none of us do our best work by going to war.

INNOVATION PRACTICE
MurderBoarding

Goal: Figure out what works for us.

We're often quite good at generating ideas and options but not as strong at figuring out what choice is the best for us. From options development through selection, how do we know what makes something more "right" than other options? Luckily, there's a method to determine this: MurderBoarding.[6] Created as a counterpoint to traditional brainstorming methods, this is a method to kill options so that we end up with one unifying, clear answer for what matters to us and why.

Pick a challenge and discuss these four questions:

1. Are we choosing something because it looks good on paper or because it's meaningful? How is it meaningful to each of us?

2. Are we making this choice out of fear (of failure, judgment, uncertainty) rather than genuine curiosity? Explore.

3. If we say yes to this, what are we saying no to—and is that a trade-off we want to make? What are we willing to risk?

4. Is this a solution that works for all of us? Whose needs are not being met?

The goal isn't to be left with a single perfect option. It's to clarify what *doesn't* fit so you can see what does. A friend of mine, Alex, always asks me the same lighthearted question whenever we're doing my wardrobe cleanout: *Would you fight me for that?* And that usually gets me clear on what I really care about. We can choose what works for us as we get clear on what we're standing for.

9

End Rank and Yank

Limiting Norm: Judgment
Leading Indicator: Encouragement

How we handle giving feedback at work—annual performance reviews—sucks.

No one likes them—not the person being reviewed nor the reviewer, the HR person, or the managers overseeing the process.

There are plenty of good reasons to hate reviews. For one, they happen only once or twice a year—way too seldom for feedback to be helpful. Another is that they're historical, documenting the past rather than focusing on the future. Reviews are also closely tied to raises, making it feel like we're all dogs performing tricks to get a treat. Nearly always, there's a summary assessment of what is supposedly *true* (as if there is one single truth, which there is not); the reviewer's job is to prove a point, as if they need to get a conviction in court. And if you're a team leader? You're nearly always told how many of your people are allowed to receive great reviews—forcing you to distort the situation, ration praise, and limit recognition. Instead of offering useful feedback, the review process often compares people to their teammates, turning feedback into a competition.

At their best, performance reviews are meant to motivate people to use their strengths, but they quickly become a way to scrutinize, inspect, criticize, rate, and appraise.

Reviews, in short, are ways to judge others.

Reviews aren't just judgy; they're expensive. When people receive an unfair review—a mismatch between how people see themselves and how they are seen—85% are inclined to quit.[1] The ones most likely to walk away are the ones who can. So the cost is attrition and the loss of our most valuable people. Like Dana.

Only Way to Improve

"Judgment day," Dana muttered, the words heavy as she steeled herself for her upcoming performance review.

She knew that she had delivered—hell, she'd overdelivered in a tough turnaround. But she also knew the review would bring odd questions. Like whether she bruised some people's egos while pushing for results, and whether her team saw her as "likable."[2] It would also measure how comfortable the boss felt when working with her, which, given her history of raising difficult questions, was bound to be tricky. She was often the only one courageous enough to speak the truth, while those who shared her views stayed quiet, too afraid of being branded as divisive. And no doubt, the review would point out what had been left undone while she focused on what was necessary for the business to survive, never mind that it was chronic under-resourcing from management that had set her up to fail.

She had braced herself for the review for days, if not weeks, even months, experiencing sleepless nights as her mind buzzed. Eager to showcase her achievements, she rehearsed what she might say to frame her contributions in the best light. She thought of how to remind her boss how her work made a difference. Preparing for the inevitable critique, she was trying to anticipate whatever shortcomings might be named so she could offer a rebuttal or at least be less vulnerable to what was said.

When I asked her how many hours she had put into this review cycle, she paused, then admitted, "Way too many!"

I nodded.

"But what choice do I have?" she added. "I can't act sad or mad or upset. If I come across as defensive, then I'm showing that I'm not open to growth."

Dana knew that being judged as "not open to growth" was the kiss of death in a performance review.

There are so many intangible costs to performance reviews:

- Lost energy.
- Lost time.
- Lost authenticity.
- Lost connection with one's team.
- Lost opportunity with one's boss.

Dana's company, like many others, did what is called "stack ranking," a management norm first inspired by Jack Welch, the legendary chief executive of General Electric who is often referred to as "the greatest CEO of all time." From 1981 to 2001, Welch turned GE into the most valuable company in the world and groomed a flock of protégés who went on to run other big companies like 3M and Home Depot. Welch supported stack ranking, a process by which he made managers sort their workers into what he called A-, B-, and C-players—20% were always deemed to be top performers, 70% had to be labeled average, and 10% subpar. The bottom 10% were systematically let go each year. Stack ranking—commonly called "rank and yank"—amounted to a heartless management edict, ensuring that no matter how well GE might be doing, tens of thousands of its employees would be shown the door, year after year.[3] It left workers afraid for their jobs, colleagues in competition with one another, and teams out of sync.

Let's be clear. The stack and rank wasn't about increasing the quality of work, the actual *performance*. No, Welch needed a method to sort and fire people because he was managing shareholder *perceptions*. He used this method, among others, to make it look like GE was growing when there wasn't any growth.

When optics take precedence over substance, it creates a façade of success while gradually gutting the organization. This applies in any context—politics, business, technology, education. Look up and around and you'll see Welch's impact everywhere.

Stack ranking has been tempered since the early 2000s, no longer leading to the automatic firing of 10% of one's team. Yet Netflix, long known for its good corporate culture, has an 8% involuntary exit rate,[4] showing how much that norm continues to drive today's business.

Rank and yank lives on in the bones of nearly every organization.

And in our bodies.

I tried to get Dana to detach, arguing that reviews were just a corporate tool, not one that she needed to invest so much in. But Dana didn't buy my take.

She believed that getting critical feedback was the only way to improve.

"Feedback is good," she argued. "How do we grow if we don't get critiqued?"

Let that sink in.

Do you really need someone else to judge you so you can grow?

Thoroughbreds Run; People Grow

I used to think like Dana. Earlier in my career, I was at a Hoffman Institute seminar with 39 others discussing this exact topic.

I interrupted the instructor with an observation: "I *love* being challenged," I said, my voice full of conviction. "It makes me stronger. And when others judge me, it's a sign that I'm not surrounded by yes people. Criticism forces me to raise my game; it makes me better."

Then the instructor asked me the same question I just asked you: "Do you really think you need to be judged to grow?"

And before I could answer, everyone else in the room burst into laughter. I was surprised. And embarrassed. Was I the only one who felt this way? Was it wrong to feel this way? Was I missing something? Yet I answered truthfully, though hesitantly, "Well, yes."

And then he said something that has never left me.

"Thoroughbreds don't run because they're whipped," he said. "They run because that's their nature; they have the gifts to race. Birds don't need instructions to fly—they spread their wings and soar because it's in their nature. Flowers don't bloom because someone demands it—they burst forth in color because they are meant to."

I felt something shift.

Maybe growth wasn't about being judged at all.

I grew up, like so many of us, being told what to do and how to do it. Judgment was how I knew I was on the "right" path, even if it was someone else's. I saw judgment as a sign of caring, a form of connection. A manager's judgment told me how to succeed, a boss's judgment told me how not to get fired, a peer's judgment told me how to be liked.

I viewed judgment as a way to stay connected. Maybe *the* way to stay connected. I thought that I needed it, that without it, I was lost.

It took me years to realize that by accepting others' judgment as necessary, I made myself a punching bag. Because I know now that growth doesn't come from surviving the toughest blows; growth comes from being encouraged to develop that distinct gift that each of us has, that special something of value we each offer the world.

To create growth, creativity, and innovation, we don't need judgment. We need safety, encouragement, and positivity. People thrive when they are seen/supported/believed.

There is, of course, research behind that. B. F. Skinner's research on operant conditioning laid the foundation: Positive reinforcement increases the likelihood of repeated desired behavior.[5] In a work setting, this translates to encouraging growth through recognition, praise, and support. A Gallup meta-analysis across 198 organizations showed that employees who receive regular recognition and encouragement are more productive, engaged, and loyal.[6] Then there's Stanford professor Carol Dweck's iconic work on growth mindset vs. fixed mindset; she taught us that "when managers believe in people's potential to grow and give feedback in an encouraging way, employees are more likely to take on challenges, persist after failure, and grow."[7] And I've already mentioned Amy Edmondson's iconic work on psychologically safe environments (which emphasize encouragement over judgment), where people learn faster, take more initiative, and innovate more freely.[8]

Under judgment, we retreat. With encouragement, we reach.

We've all been Dana. We've all been trained to be there. From how we are raised and educated and in our workplaces; this is the norm, the default, the standard.

And it's not about negativity or criticism. Even positive comments can harm. Those of us who seek other people's approval—people-pleasing is one form of it—are just finding another way to be judged. Whether we're taking in someone's judgment for good or bad, it's someone else's take on who we should be.

As if someone can and should assess our value.

As if our value isn't inherent.

The Bold Switch

When the very same people who hated getting reviews become managers, they turn around and say, "But we can't do away with them." As team leads, they'll ask, "Aren't we responsible for others? And isn't it our job to guide them?" Performance, they'll argue, needs to be assessed. Decisions about pay and promotions have to be made. If we don't make it clear to people what we need from them, they'll never be able to succeed.

This logic, however common, infantilizes people.

The real question is how to shift the focus from performance *reviews* to *developing* performance.[9]

Donna Morris, then head of HR at Adobe, faced that very question after noticing firsthand the inherent inefficiencies of performance reviews. How projects that had been completed long ago were being reviewed as if they were still fresh, and the time spent on preparation by all involved was draining. It was like a "dreaded dental appointment.[10] More importantly, it just wasn't helping us," Morris said. "We were a company that thrived on creativity and innovation, and the [review] system felt like the exact opposite of that."[11,12]

Rather than patch up a broken system, Morris and her team decided to build something entirely new.

In place of annual reviews, Adobe introduced the "check-in," a system focused on regular, ongoing feedback rather than once-a-year evaluations. The idea was simple. "The check-in system was designed to provide real-time feedback, encourage open dialogue, and focus on growth and development," Morris said. The goal wasn't just to *review* performance—it was to *encourage* it, in real time. Managers were coached to hold these conversations as often as needed, with a focus on coaching rather than critiquing.

The shift from annual reviews to continuous feedback didn't just change the conversation—it also saved an enormous amount of time. Adobe's management team calculated that eliminating performance reviews freed up approximately 80,000 hours of managers' time every year. That's the equivalent of roughly 38 full-time employees freed up to focus on something other than the bureaucratic grind of performance reviews.[13]

And that was just the managers.

Countless hours of employee time were also reclaimed, time that had been spent preparing self-evaluations or rehearsing for performance reviews. Or sleepless nights that rolled into crappy days. But the time savings weren't the only measure of success. Adobe's new approach had an immediate impact on retention. Voluntary turnover dropped by 30%[14] in the first few years of the check-in system, a significant reduction that pointed to a deeper sense of employee engagement and satisfaction. Employees who once dreaded the annual review now saw their performance discussions as part of a continuous growth journey rather than a onetime critique. Studies show that replacing an employee can cost a company between one-half and two times that employee's annual salary[15]—so a 30% reduction in turnover represented millions in savings annually. By retaining talent, the company also ensured that it was maintaining institutional knowledge and reducing disruptions to teams and projects.

Moving to this model, though, required some training.

First to insist that people didn't use the lack of bureaucracy as a reason to stop doing the work of managing people. But also to teach people how to coach vs. criticize. It wasn't just a change in *process* but a change in *practice*. As Morris succinctly put it, "Our goal was never to make things easier—it was to make things better."

And some companies have borrowed Adobe's leadership in this space (Adobe white-labeled it, meaning they shared what works so others can use it without having to reinvent the wheel.)

But just as many companies haven't.

Because it requires seeing the world in a different way.

Encouraged, Not Judged

As she did for many people, Oprah Winfrey helped raise me.

On one occasion, the writer Toni Morrison told Oprah how children feel when their parents are happy to see them. "When my children used to walk in the room, when they were little," Morrison reflected, "I looked at them to see if they had buckled their trousers, or if their hair was combed, or if their socks were up."[16]

To be future-facing is to desire for someone what they truly want for themself.

Morrison noticed that her children internalized that critical eye and looked down at their own bodies to figure out *What did I do wrong?* Morrison realized that as much as you care as a parent and want to guide your loved ones well by checking if their belt is buckled, you're not doing what needs to be done to show them they matter.

So what does matter? Oprah prompted.

And Morrison answered that it is how you notice someone. And what question did Morrison use to assess that?

Does your face light up?

Morrison was saying that people need to be *encouraged*, not *judged*.

After all, people are not machines.

What makes machines work better is identifying where they are broken or not working properly. But doing a "root cause analysis" on people is to analyze them rather than witness them.

To see and improve human performance is never mechanical.

Our future work? It's not about defining the best *for* others but bringing out the best *of* them.

There Is No One Best Way

Putting one person in judgment over another, as we do in reviews, doesn't just feel icky—it's harmful. Reviews assume that the boss is in a position to judge whether work meets a certain standard.

But how true is that?

There are at least 250 different ways to wash dishes.[17] Not metaphorically. Literally. The sequence, the tools, the soap, the water temperature, the drying method are all variables. What looks like a simple routine task turns out to involve a plethora of choices. And if something this mundane can be done 250 ways, imagine how many different ways there are to solve complex problems. Just as there's no one right way to wash dishes, there are countless ways to do just about anything. But often, we only understand what we've already done.

Those who review others may believe *their* way is the gold standard. That's supremacy in a nutshell—pretending that there's a universal "best" way and that those in power get to tell those "below" what that is. The push for people to accept this top-down judgment is about enforcing standards and order. And just remember, standards and order serve those in power. The implicit expectation in reviews is that everyone should accept and conform to someone else's standard, that acceptance is the only path forward. Yet those standards are almost always arbitrary, exclusionary, and designed to support the past. That's why performance reviews suck at the deepest level; they teach us to do what has already been done by those who have already done things. Great for order, not great for growth and innovation. Which is ironic because that's supposed to be the reason for performance reviews in the first place.

What we lose by imposing standards is the most valuable asset in modern times: the originality of approaches, the ingenuity of ideas. Each of us stands in a distinct spot in the world, shaped by our history, experiences, visions, and hopes. From that singular position, we offer something no one else can.

Where judgment limits, encouragement liberates. When we encourage people, they rise. Not just to meet our expectations, but to surpass their own, creating something we can't yet imagine.

To *regard* someone is *to look upon them*. With your face lit up, as Toni Morrison so beautifully put it. Not through the lens of what you want for them. Which is judgmental. Not to create a certain performance, which is demanding. As if you are the superior person they perform for. Or as if there is one best answer (there isn't).

To be future-facing is to desire for someone what they truly want for themself.

To say, *I want nothing for you except what you want for yourself.*

This is how we get the bloom, the rise, the run that each of us has to offer.

This is the future of work. So we can do our best work.

INNOVATION PRACTICE
Mirror Mirror

Goal: Help people grow via peer coaching.

Instead of traditional external reviews, we can encourage each other to self-determine the right next steps.[18] The Mirror Mirror practice isn't about ranking or measuring but about encouraging growth from within, helping someone to take responsibility for their growth and development by identifying their own needs, what's working, and how to build on that momentum to grow. Through this encouraging reflection, people step up and into their fullness.

PERSON 1 ASKS	PERSON 2 SHARES THEIR ANSWERS
1. What is your best hope here?	
2. What are you doing well that you're pleased about?	
3. Suppose that continues, what *difference* would it make?	
4. Suppose you get *support* from others, what would get better?	
5. What is a small next step(s) for you/your team/work?	

This Mirror Mirror exercise is a way to reflect on the work, goals, and gaps without asking for external judgment and instead build on one's strengths, resources, and capabilities. Through this reflection and conversation, people can see their own assets, and their own next steps. When someone is adding the value they want to add, and that capacity grows, it feeds an aliveness in the person, the team, and ultimately the outcomes.

10

Never Fake It

Limiting Norm: Confidence
Leading Indicator: Competence

Pretend to be someone you're not—that's the unspoken rule of success.

Of course, we don't hear those exact words. Instead, we're told, "fake it till you make it." Which is the same idea, just packaged differently. We're told that the goal is to project confidence, step outside our comfort zone, copy the behaviors of success—all while ignoring our self-doubt.

Emulating what already exists isn't necessarily bad. After all, imitation is our inheritance. Humans take longer than any other mammal to grow up. We're born into a conversation that started long before us: how to make fire, how to speak in our native tongue, how to advance the wheel. We inherit what works, improve what doesn't, and pass along something richer. We don't want to have to start from scratch; we want to imitate to leverage the history of who came before us. It's our collective way of learning.

But faking it operates by completely different rules. Where imitation says, "I want to learn this so I can build on it," faking it says, "I need to perform this so no one notices that I can't already do it." Imitation assumes that you have something distinct to contribute. Faking it assumes that you don't.

What's rarely discussed is the cost of this façade.

Cover It Up

Seo-jun stood in his boss Megan's office, clutching the project brief against his chest. Around them, every wall held a whiteboard, and every whiteboard was covered in scribbled ideas, reflecting the chaotic energy of their startup.

"So, Seo-jun, you're leading the next product launch," Megan said, her tone serious. "We need this to be perfect, especially with investors watching."

Seo-jun hesitated. "I appreciate the opportunity, but I'm not sure I'm ready. There are some things I'm unsure about."

Megan dismissed his concerns with a wave. "Don't worry. No one's ever fully prepared. Just fake it till you make it," she told him enthusiastically. "Act like you have it all under control. If you hit a snag, keep moving. The team doesn't need to know your uncertainties."

"Fake it?" Seo-jun asked, puzzled.

"Exactly," Megan replied. "Keep moving forward, even if you're unsure. If you question everything, you'll slow the team down."

"But what if I miss something important?" Seo-jun asked plaintively.

"In a fast-paced environment like ours, you need to make decisions quickly," Megan told him. "If you hesitate, you'll hold everyone back. Trust yourself."

Later, he called me from a phone booth—a small soundproof room—at the startup.

Faking it felt wrong, he shared.

While encouraging at some level, Megan's message just didn't feel right to him. He knew that if he made a big enough mistake, it would negatively affect his company's funding round. A mistake could also risk his job and associated green card. A lot was on the line. He didn't have anyone to turn to for the lowdown—most of the team had been with the startup since its inception, and they all seemed to know the ropes far better than he did. He worried about the little things that still tripped him up at times and the cultural nuances that felt just out of reach, given that he'd gone to school in the UK.

From the phone booth, Seo-jun described his other team members, all engrossed in their work. He wondered if any of them were also faking it as they hustled, pretending to be confident and covering up their concerns.

What was he supposed to do now? he asked me.

On the surface, a boss's advice to "fake it till you make it" builds confidence and encourages growth. But in actuality, it does just the opposite.

"Fake it" guidance often prioritizes appearances over substance, suggesting it's better to conceal what one doesn't know than risk exposing weaknesses. This approach can lead to dangerous oversights, favoring image over understanding and optics over substance.

Moreover, hiding discomfort means hiding one's true Self. By telling someone to fake it, we imply that who they are isn't enough for the work ahead. This not only undermines their actual confidence but also damages their psychological well-being. Together, these forces sabotage our best work.

I told Seo-jun to trust his instincts. To admit when he had questions, to show his thinking, and to ask others for help when he needed support. Ultimately, this would lead to the project working, and his team knowing what he needed. Instead of being the new one who felt disconnected, he could lean on them to get it done.

Telling Seo-jun to embrace his reality wasn't something rooted in theory; it was born from my own messy, nerve-racking experience. The first time I chose to stop hiding the reality of my life—to own my insecurities as part and parcel of who I was—it felt like I was stumbling through the darkness, desperately looking for a light switch.

I'm Nobody

Standing in a circle at my friend Nancy Duarte's book launch party, I struggled to hear the conversation over the crowd's din. Then I realized that everyone was introducing themselves: "Todd LeGrange, from Apple." "Glen Lubbert, CEO of Mojo Interactive." "Harry Max, adviser at Google."

I panicked, thinking, *Is it too late to walk away? Should I pretend my phone buzzed?*

Before I could decide, the question and their eyes turned to me.

And who are you?

What to say?

I had just shut down the company where I'd been the CEO, so I was no longer that. While I had written a few super small checks for entrepreneurs I believed in, I wasn't an investor by any stretch. And while I taught a course on innovation once in a while, I wasn't a professor.

As I searched for an answer, I wondered, *What do I do all day long?* I could talk about that. The highlight of my day was walking Kiddo to school every morning and returning in the afternoon to walk him home. But I didn't want to say that to these tech executives. I had once been one of them. Plus, that didn't feel like my identity. So who was I when I lacked a title, or job, or personal brand?

"I'm nobody," I blurted out.

A second that felt like a million seconds of awkward silence followed. Then people in that circle, people who knew me, stepped in. *She's run divisions in significant tech companies, been a VP of a hot startup, been a founder and CEO, and written a book on collaborative management.*

While all of that was true, they were also talking about my past. And my present felt profoundly disconnected from that history. Given that I had just quit my job to be present for my kid, I was deeply aware that my career could be "over."

So of course, at that moment, I lacked confidence.

And because "faking it" didn't seem right, I was doing the very opposite: shrinking.

What neither my friends who were encouraging me nor I, who was feeling defeated, realized was that this in-between stage between what we've done and who we're becoming is a signpost of growth.

Think about something you've mastered; can you remember when it felt challenging? Maybe managing people is now second nature, or a specialized skill that once seemed daunting has become routine. Or perhaps a relationship that once required constant effort now flows effortlessly, where understanding each other's needs feels almost instinctive.

We all want to be ready for big things from the get-go. But life doesn't work that way.

It would be like moving into a new home that is painted and decorated with all your favorite things on day one. It would be like expecting, as we end one relationship, to be in love again right away without allowing for some transition to process what didn't work and how we contributed to it so that we can make different and better choices. Or starting a new job and wanting to immediately have the confidence of the people who have been there for a while.

Becoming who we are *next?* It is a process. And even once we "arrive," we evolve and change into the next. In that way, we are all, always, unfinished.

According to researcher and London Business School professor Herminia Ibarra, we grow our identity by first creating "girders and spans" to build that authentic sense of Self.[1]

What Ibarra means is that we grow into a new job, a new skill, or a new experience, much like constructing a room in a house. First, we raise the girders and spans—the skeletal framework of our next thing. Next come the sturdy two-by-fours, forming the shape and boundaries of the space. Then we add the drywall, transforming that open expanse into defined, functional areas. Finally, we bring in paint and decoration, infusing the room with our personal touch, making it truly ours. Yet unlike a static space, the people and contexts around us shape our new work roles, skills, and experiences, making the process unpredictable and nonlinear. Ofttimes, we find ourselves taking down one "girder" as we change the shape of what we're creating. Growth is never all in one direction. Becoming who we are is a messy construction project full of missteps and do-overs. So while we might plan for girders and spans, the reality of transformation is often more haphazard, and full of uncertainty, and sometimes we don't even know what we are building until it all takes shape. We—our identities, our *selves*, that is—are created this way.

If you want to become more *whole*, you gotta let yourself be *partial*.

It's in doing the work that we build ourselves—brick by brick. Practice by practice.

That's how we create value: by becoming more capable.

This is competence; competence isn't granted, or faked. It's earned. It grows through applying effort, learning, having experiences, failing, and working with others. And from doing those things, we gain something more lasting: the ability to trust our own judgment and make our own choices, and the strength to face the next challenge.

Competence is the only way you create genuine, sturdy, and consistent confidence. The kind that won't fall apart at the first "tremor" but will withstand the full-on 9.0 earthquakes of life, because the girders and spans hold up.

We create competence by not being afraid to be seen trying.

Interestingly, and yet completely unsurprisingly, it does not come from faking it.

If you want to become more *whole*, you gotta let yourself be *partial*.

By understanding the steps to building competence, you learn to trust yourself. Not that things will always work, but when things happen, when things go wrong, and when you don't know what to do next, you know *how* to find your way. You build yourself not by creating a façade but by tuning your frequency. Every time you speak your truth, make decisions from your truth, connect in your truth, you reduce the distance between you and your goal.

A Sinking Feeling

Stacy London built her career on transformation. Literally.

As a co-host of *What Not to Wear*, she guided people through dramatic makeovers, showing them that a new look could be the key to a new life. She was the expert, the authority, the woman who knew exactly what to do.

Television has a way of making everything feel permanent. For a decade, *What Not to Wear* was a staple, and London was its beating heart. But when the show wrapped in 2013, she wasn't just losing a job. She was losing her sense of Self.

"I had wrapped my identity up so tightly with the show that when it ended, I felt like I had disappeared," she told me. "I really felt like I didn't know who I was anymore. I thought, *I'm either going to lie down and not get up again, or I'm going to figure out another purpose for my life.*"

But how exactly does one do that?

At first, she kept up appearances, accepting the occasional hosting gig, making public appearances, giving interviews. But behind the scenes, she was sinking. The loss of the show triggered a deep depression. Her confidence, once so unwavering, began to crack. By this point, she had already had several career transitions. Once an editor at *Mademoiselle* magazine, she was fired when a new editor in chief arrived on the scene. So she had gotten through big changes before. But this one felt different. It was more public, for one. But also, the economics of the situation only made things worse. A long-running TV show provides stability, but it also creates a lifestyle. The money had been good, but without a steady income, her run rate of expenses loomed larger.

London also noted that being on television doesn't necessarily guarantee financial security. "I wasn't just almost broke, I was broken."[2]

Like a lot of people, she spent money to keep her confidence up. Haircuts, jewelry, an outfit to help her feel special. Each hardship—a breakup, the sudden death of a friend, the loss of her father, painful back surgery—was a new reason to spend. As someone who had spent her career helping others define their worth, she was now questioning her own.

She could have just jumped into another makeover show, kept playing the role she had already perfected. But something in her resisted. Instead of forcing a reinvention, she let herself sit in the discomfort of not knowing.

It was messy, and therefore . . . terrifying.

She pulled back from the public eye. She struggled with her mental health. And then, slowly, she began to listen—to herself, to her body, to the changes happening inside her. She started to notice the way society treated women as they aged, the way menopause was a whispered secret rather than a shared experience.

"Nobody was talking about menopause in a way that felt real, and I thought, *Why aren't we normalizing this? Why are we ashamed of something that happens to half the population?*" she reflected.

It wasn't an obvious next step, but it was a real one. She had spent years helping people feel comfortable in their skin. Now she had to do the same for herself.

In 2020, London co-founded State of Menopause, a company focused on wellness products for women navigating aging. This wasn't just a business venture; it was deeply personal. She was pouring herself into something new, using her platform to start a conversation that was long overdue.

Running a company, though, was different from running a TV show. The financial realities were stark. Raising capital, managing operations, overseeing production—it was a crash course in entrepreneurship, and it came with enormous pressure.

"I thought my name would be enough to carry this, but the reality of running a business is so different. I had to learn everything from the ground up, and it was overwhelming," she revealed.

There were moments when she wondered if she had made a mistake. It would have been easier to put her name on a product, cash in on her fame, and let someone else do the heavy lifting. But that wasn't who she was. Who she wanted to be. She had taken this leap because she believed in it.

And yet belief wasn't enough. The company struggled to gain traction. The market was difficult, the challenges compounded by the pandemic. The company wasn't earning enough to pay her. Eventually, she made the painful decision to shut it down.

"It was one of the hardest decisions I've ever made. I had put so much into this, and it didn't work out the way I'd hoped. But I also knew forcing it to continue wouldn't be honest," she said.

She wasn't interested in the fake, but in the real.

This could have been yet another breaking point. But something had changed in London. She had spent years learning how to live in uncertainty, and now she understood its power. She didn't see the closure of State of Menopause as a failure; she saw it as part of the process.

The process of becoming who she would be next.

She didn't pretend everything was fine. Instead, she allowed herself to be fully inside the messiness of transformation. And because of that, she had found something deeper than success—she found her own integrity.

"I've learned that reinvention isn't about pretending you've got it all figured out. It's about owning the fact that you don't—and being okay with that," she reflected.

Today, Stacy London is a voice for aging, for reinvention, for embracing what's real rather than what's expected. And at the time of this writing, she has a new show called *Wear Whatever the F You Want*. Which, interestingly, shows her shift from criticizing wardrobe choices to encouraging people to be fully themselves. Work she has done from the inside out. Her story isn't a perfect arc, even though it has a beginning and an end and wraps up nicely. From TV show to TV show. That's because we're seeing Stacy's story looking backward. In the moment, in any moment, the fact is that real transformation isn't about finding a new label. It's about stripping everything away until what's left is true.

And it helps to know what to center. When going through change, it's so easy to fake it or to look outside oneself for what to do next.

But as Stacy says, "When you are lost, don't look out. You gotta look in."[3]

Over-Indexed on Appearances

After that unsettling experience at Nancy's party and before my current career landed, well-meaning friends advised me to manufacture a façade of success—suggesting I invent a new company name, seek an honorary board title, or even volunteer to work for a prestigious institution just to borrow its sheen. What they were really advising me to do was to create an illusion of "success," as if wearing the right title could substitute for the hard-earned authority that comes only from doing the work. Stacy's friends did the same for her.

Before you do the same for someone else, you've gotta know how bad that advice is.

So let's net out the cost.

- **People-pleasing and approval-seeking behavior.** On a personal level, faking it can be about doing what others want, a form of people-pleasing that leads us away from our true selves. When you mask who you truly are to fit in, you're denying

the unique distinctions that make you, you. Over time,
this can make us deeply lonely, not because we're alone but
because even in a crowd, no one truly sees us. They can't. The
façade gets in the way. And with that, we walk away from the
intrinsic power that comes from standing firmly in that spot
in the world that is ours. Some people hate criticism but love
approval from others. But criticism and approval come from
the same place: they both allow someone else to judge you, not
invite them to see you.

- **Performative behavior.** On a team level, and as Megan the boss
was encouraging, we're told our job is to always be winning.
Not only does work demand it but social media amplifies
the idea that we owe others an image of success. When you
mimic what is socially accepted, you are not winning—you are
conforming. The only person we owe anything to is ourselves;
we need to stand in the space only we can occupy, bringing
our unique perspective and value to the world, not performing
for others.

- **Fraud.** Faking is the very definition of fraud: a person or thing
intended to *deceive* others, typically by unjustifiably *claiming*
or being credited with accomplishments or qualities. Think
about it. When you fake confidence, you're lying to yourself
and others. When you fake something, you're avoiding the
commitment to truly learn it. When the social connections
you build as part of work are built on a false foundation,
they lack the relational support needed to shape ideas into
reality. Fraud is not the basis of value creation. To create value,
we must accept every stage of ourselves, including those
unmoored and wandering moments in between who we've
been and who we are becoming. By celebrating learning,
we grow our capabilities. By celebrating fraud and hustle,
we ensure that whatever value is created is transitory at best.

Pretending is an homage to those in charge, like the practice of courtiers imitating the behavior and style of influential figures at the royal

courts of Europe. In the 16th and 17th centuries, for instance, French courtiers would mimic the mannerisms, speech, and fashion of the king or other powerful nobles to gain favor. This imitation was a way of signaling loyalty and competence, effectively pretending to be someone they were not to align themself with the perceived standards of success. In the court of Louis XIV, courtiers would meticulously copy the king's behavior, down to how he walked, spoke, and dressed. This behavior wasn't just about exuding confidence; it was a strategic move to elevate their status and secure their position in a highly competitive environment.

Today's "fake it" practice echoes all of that. Individuals are encouraged to emulate the traits and behaviors of those deemed successful. When people emulate those people, it perpetuates this seemingly "leaderly" behavior. It makes our workplaces over-index on false confidence rather than build the context to create more competence.

Faking it has us following the existing template of what is good, and what is valuable. But that is to suggest there is one way to be "best." This is perfectionism and superiority blended into one toxic way of being.

INNOVATION PRACTICE
Cairning

Goal: Normalize trying.

Don't wait until it's perfect. Leave a trail as you go.

Just as backpackers leave cairns—those carefully stacked stones that mark the path for fellow travelers—this practice involves leaving markers of your learning journey for your teammates.

Once a week, share something you're actively working through—where you're stuck, what you're trying, what you're learning. Post it in Slack, Discord, or whatever space your team uses to talk shop.

This is not about having the answer. It's about showing your work so others can see the process—your curiosity, your confusion, your growth. When you leave cairns, you give others permission to follow your path, to offer help, or to feel less alone in their own journey.

Start by modeling it:

- Name what you're figuring out.

- Ask for input, insight, or examples.

- Reflect out loud as you make progress.

Cairning builds trust. It rewards the effort over the illusion of perfection. And it creates a culture where learning is both visible—and valued.

11

Strategy and Execution
Are One and the Same

Limiting Norm: Separation
Leading Indicator: Integration

There are two camps in any organization.

One camp belongs to the strategists—the visionaries who sketch the future before it's built. They set the course, dream up what's next, and anticipate the turns ahead. They're fueled by foresight, drawn to complexity, and energized by possibility. This is the boss with a telescope, not a to-do list. You'll find them leading innovation teams, steering R&D, shaping policy, forecasting revenue, and designing people strategies. Strategic thinkers celebrate deep research, incisive analysis, and the kind of insight that rewrites the playbook. To them, strategy isn't just planning; it's propulsion.

The second camp belongs to the implementers—the builders, the practitioners, the ones who translate vision into action. It's the test engineers, program managers, and accountants. Some argue that *this* is the group that truly matters. That without execution, strategy is just a dream. It's not about taking orders; it's about taking ownership. Execution people know that precision, timing, and adaptability are what brings plans to life. They're fueled by their deep knowledge, clarity, and the quiet thrill of getting it right. They hold everything together. And yet for all their impact, execution folks often find themselves fighting for recognition. In a culture that celebrates plans over action, doing the work is never enough.

So even those who take pride in execution begin to wonder, *Do I need to be more strategic?*

Most of us straddle both roles, integrating the two. But the system tells us we don't.

So we try to live in the binary. Blaming the other when plans fail. Wanting to show one's value *over* the other.

The strategist patronizes with, "You're not thinking strategically enough."

The executor fires back with, "Vision without execution is just a hallucination."

There's also the familiar "That needs more intellectual rigor."

And equally, "That's not how the world works."

These put-downs, while fun to list, reveal something deep. As long as we see these camps as separate, as long as there is a gap between the two, we limit our best work.

The biggest wins I've seen have come not from brilliant strategy or flawless execution but from refusing to separate the two.

Thinking Topples the Competition

"If she were that good, I'd have already heard of her," Katie Keating said of me.

Dismissive—even though Adobe had just brought me in as a consultant because of my expertise in growing revenue in the education market.

By then, I had been involved in designing four major education programs: for the State of California, where I was appointed by the governor to help community colleges feed into four-year universities through a bill called AB1725; at Apple, where I helped shape their education team's approach; as VP of GoLive, where I built the education program for the first WYSIWYG web authoring software; and at Autodesk, where I ran and expanded their $38 million annual global educational program.

I didn't just *know* the education space, I had *lived* it.

Which is why I also knew that Adobe's weakness was its education program. One of its main competitors, Macromedia, had been so successful in higher education that design students were coming out of college using—and preferring—Macromedia tools, not Adobe's. This was a strategic vulnerability.

As I started researching, I wondered . . . how much of Macromedia's unit sales were education-specific?

I mentioned it casually to Katie in the hallway.

Her eyes lit up. "That is such an interesting question; what would you guess?"

From my experience in tech firms, I knew the number could range from 20 to 40%.

In the weeds of publicly available data, I uncovered that Macromedia was at 50%. Half their sales coming from education.

That one fact changed everything.

Katie was ecstatic. "If Adobe could beat Macromedia in education, it would be a strategic hit to our biggest competitor."

Suddenly, the stakes went up.

Product teams were consulted: Could an upcoming product release still be influenced? *Maybe.* Education sales representatives brainstormed with their customers: If one or two killer features were added, could Adobe better compete with Macromedia? *If.* Senior leadership invited representatives of the top design schools to the corporate office to preview the upcoming product release, to ask: Would they then utilize Adobe? *Then.*

Maybe.

If.

Then.

Conversation by conversation, a new direction emerged.

Katie brought the insight up to her boss, the CMO, and together they took it Bruce Chizen, Adobe's CEO at the time. The executive team gave us the green light and budget to rebuild Adobe's global education program. We partnered region by region, adapting to local needs, co-creating the plans.

Within a year, Adobe began to win the education market. Macromedia became vulnerable.

Around then, Bruce got fired up about a book, *Execution,* by Larry Bossidy and Ram Charan. He bought thousands of copies—handing them out like he was a one-man book club. I was already aware of the book, but now I had to read it closely to understand what he was so excited about.

To build a *culture of execution*, the book advised:

1. Be clear about what results are needed.
2. Coach your team to achieve them.
3. Reward success.
4. Remove or reassign underperformers.

It made sense. Until it didn't. Something nagged at me: Only one side seemed to be doing the thinking. "Execution" felt like code for "Do what I say."

Our actual success was coming from something different. What moved the needle wasn't direction from above with execution on the ground. It was hundreds of minds, iterating the idea forward—thinking together.

Bruce had supported us, unquestionably.

But by handing out *Execution*, he was signaling that his people needed to "execute better" as if they weren't *already executing at a highest level*. We would create one of the biggest wins in the industry, not because *he told us what to do* but because *we shared with him* what might work.

Unreal.

Proof of how seductive the two-camps model is—leaders as thinkers, everyone else as doers. This wasn't malice. But simply that he, like so many of us, had internalized a false divide.

The Air Sandwich

When strategy and execution are two camps—what the book *Execution* was reinforcing—it signals a crucial absence. Instead of substance, there's just emptiness. This phenomenon is an organizational "Air Sandwich"[1]— like a PB&J without all the essential and delicious filling.

To avoid an Air Sandwich, we must do the simplest, hardest thing: think together.

Not by dividing strategy from execution, but by building a shared understanding—surfacing assumptions, naming risks, and shaping what's next. Without that, even clear direction and capable individuals aren't enough. Also, most of us do not even know what we are thinking until we express it to someone else, either in writing or speech. Our thinking partners can offer new directions of thought, expose flaws, or point out supporting or contradictory evidence that we may have overlooked. As we engage in conversation, we get clearer in what we originally thought. And we add to others' thinking, have the debates that flush out assumptions and risks until we gain shared understanding.

Without this, we leave just air. And air is empty of reality.

As I said earlier, an estimated 77% of all jobs (60% in the US and 80% worldwide) require little to no creativity, decision-making, or independent judgment. These jobs are designed to be nonthinking jobs.[2]

Just sit with that.

Jobs are designed to be "nonthinking."

As if a body can be *severed* from the brain.

As if we need only *part* of a person.

As if any of us *could* be nonthinking.

This limiting norm creates a subclass of people directed to do as they are told, rather than be trusted to think for themselves or with others. Designing jobs this way turns people into cogs—expendable, interchangeable, and disconnected from the meaning of their work. It stifles the fullest expression of every doer, not just at the bottom but at every level. And doing so props up a fiction: that those in charge are more capable, worthier, or more essential.

The subjugation of one group by the other is not a side effect, it is intentional. This scaffolding holds up the illusion of superiority.

We've seen this story before. In chattel slavery, the body was prized while the mind was denied—enslaved people were treated as muscle, not mind, forced into labor while their intelligence, creativity, and will were systematically erased. In modern-day warehouses, workers are reduced to hands, each motion timed and measured to serve a machine designed by someone else.

Today, even top-tier professionals are being told to adopt AI "for efficiency." *The Guardian* recently cut 100 journalists—then signed a syndication deal with OpenAI. British journalist Carole Cadwalladr likened it to "marrying one's rapist."[3]

The shape changes, but the logic remains: extract value, deny humanity, and call it progress.

Gross.

When I talk about this, I often hear—and sometimes even catch myself agreeing with—things like "I don't need my accountant, content creator, or cafeteria worker to think; I just need them to do their job." I've also nodded along when bosses tell us that execution will be interminably delayed if they involve "too many" or the "wrong" people or if the sheer volume of people would "complicate decisions."

I used to hear these ideas as pragmatism. But now I hear the hierarchy inside: a hierarchy of thought, leadership, and knowledge.

Many of us still uphold it. We scramble to make our work "more strategic," hoping it's importance will be understood. And who hasn't daydreamed out loud that we would love to "just" get an assignment that we can "simply do." Either way, we reinforce strategy and execution as two camps.

We have internalized an age-old hierarchy. We've inherited an old lie.

Believing that some *think* while the rest *do* limits our best work.

When thinking is reserved for the few, everyone's work suffers. We miss insight, creativity, and care. But it's more than that. When we split the mind from the body, we fracture our work—and ourselves.

We need to seek wholeness.

What if the entire strategist vs. executor thing is a false choice? What if the truth is we're already both? We just don't name it that way. Most people are thinking ahead, solving for what's next, trying to make something better. That's strategy. It's not some distant, opaque, rarefied thing. It's deciding what should happen. And execution? That's not the opposite. It's what happens when we sit with someone, troubleshoot, adapt, and bring the idea to life. Nobody gets to live in one mode only. We think, we build, we think again. Maybe the horizons are different—some of us are planning for next year, others for next week—but the shape of the work is the same. We're all in the mix. The real work isn't choosing a side—it's integrating the wholeness we're already living.

Integration, not separation, is how we create anything worth keeping.

When the goal of work is integration, then the team you build sets the rhythm for how that takes shape. Hiring then isn't just about finding those that match job descriptions—it's about shaping how we invite people to think together, to grow, and to challenge one another. It's the very first step. The foundation. The blueprint.

Often, getting that step right means trusting that every role requires thinking.

Hired to Think

I could tell from the tone of his voice that the VP of engineering wasn't happy. He practically growled. He had just finished interviewing a candidate I'd referred—Anand Chandrasekaran—and was calling to say it was a hard pass.

I was stunned.

Just a few minutes earlier, Anand had called me, elated.

He thought the interview had gone *great*. He'd spent the day in back-to-back meetings with different leaders and felt energized by the conversations. He'd asked more questions than usual—curious about the company's strategy, its weak points, the complexity of what it was really trying to build. He was thoughtful, even generous, in his assessment of the team. He thought he'd found his people. And a problem worth solving.

But the VP's version? Starkly different. He said Anand had asked "a ton of super annoying questions" and was therefore a "bad fit."

A promising candidate, being screened out.

Not because he lacked skill. But because he was thinking aloud.

Integration, not separation, is how we create anything worth keeping.

Most of us have had this happen to us. We just don't usually get to hear it. We hear only the silence. The call that never comes. The opportunity that quietly disappears. And we wonder what we did wrong, when all we did was show up whole.

I asked the VP what was missing. Did Anand lack the right skills or right attitude?

"No," he said. "He's done the work. But he kept asking us things we didn't know the answers to."

Let's pause. This is the moment to pay attention to.

What this VP was really saying, whether he realized it or not, was *I don't want to feel uncomfortable.*

Anand, by asking smart questions no one on the team had yet considered, made him feel exactly that.

Running from discomfort is what creates an Air Sandwich—a gap between high-level strategy and day-to-day execution that nobody names. And when it comes to hiring, that gap gets baked in from the very start. We interview for answers instead of inquiry. For track records instead of co-creation. For pattern-matching instead of possibility.

Work asks: "Have you done X or Y or Z before?"

Instead of: "How would you approach X or Y or Z with us?"

It's a small shift. But it changes everything. The first question filters for people who've seen and done your exact moves before. So they just have to imitate the past. The second filters for people who can help you create a new move. And thereby invent the future.

And that distinction matters. A lot.

Most leaders believe they're choosing from the best candidates. But most don't realize that their hiring process is fundamentally flawed. According to recent research, 75% of qualified résumés are screened out by applicant tracking systems before a human ever sees them.[4] And more recently, among the 6 in 10 managers who use AI tools, 94% of them use it to make decisions about raises (78%), promotions (77%), layoffs (66%), and even terminations (64%).[5]

Why does this deny our best work?

Because those systems are built to reward pattern matchers.

Not originality.

Not collaborators.

Not emergent problem-solvers.

And yet modern work demands that we build what hasn't existed before. AI can already answer known questions. What we need are people who can help us ask better ones.

What to Ask Instead

Let's return to Anand.

The only thing he did "wrong" was ask questions that revealed what the team didn't yet understand. That's not a red flag—it's a skill. And, if the team doesn't already have that skill, a necessary addition. Innovation, after all, requires *not knowing* long enough to *learn* and then invent new things. How can you build something new if you aren't okay with not already knowing the answer? Leaders need to build teams that can both *define* the right questions and then *discover* new answers.

So what should we be looking for?

First, seek capabilities, not experience.

Instead of asking whether someone has done a task before, ask how they'd approach it now. This uncovers capabilities—how they frame problems, surface assumptions, and seek input. It shows you how they think, not just what they've done. You do this because you believe insights can come from anyone, anywhere. And if you're in the interview hot seat, when someone asks for your experience, turn it around and say, "What matters is what I can add to the team; let me tell you about those capabilities."

When job descriptions ask for 10-plus years' experience doing the next big thing that no one's ever done before, that's just jargon for "Don't surprise me." But innovation *is* surprise. And if your candidate isn't asking questions that make you pause, they aren't adding enough to the team. Which is why when you're the candidate, be ready to ask and explore where you are interested in adding value, not to prove yourself.

Second, test for co-creation. When I ask teams why their last major strategy effort failed, they don't say, "We didn't get along." They say, "We weren't on the same page." That's the Air Sandwich at work: a silent, invisible gap no one names until the project is way off-track.

To avoid that, ask candidates:

"What do you do when you see a gap no one else is naming?"
"How do you move between roles when the project requires it?"
"Can you share a time when you helped a team reframe its goal?"

These questions help you see if the person knows how to play and think with others. You want someone who's fluid, not fixed—someone who is good at the assist, not just their part.

Third, uncover what someone loves to work on.

Innovation doesn't come from robots—it comes from people who care. People who are lit up by a question, not just proficient in a skill. Ask:

"What kinds of problems light you up?"
"What made that project meaningful to you?"
"What success are you proud of—and why?"

Their answers—our answers—will tell you where their purpose lies. The hiring team's job is to connect that purpose to their own. That's how we create alignment—and find our place in the circle of things—and how we create teams that build things that matter.

In the end, the VP did hire Anand. And the organization achieved great big things. It took effort, but over time, the VP came to value exactly what he had first resisted—someone who could name what others overlooked. Someone who could think with him, not just execute under him. Someone who filled the Air Sandwich, didn't widen it. That's the kind of talent every leader knows they need. But to get it, we need to stop screening for comfort. And especially to stop hiring for someone to "do" what we ask of them.

We need to hire for co-creation, the integration of strategy and execution.

And this changes our own work, too.

It's easy to believe that our job is to know all the things, that the more we know, the more valuable we are. But AI is going to be able to get us known information faster and easier. So our value isn't in knowing all the things. (It never was.) Our value is in knowing how to figure out *what* to know, to *challenge* existing patterns, and then build a team to invent the next big thing by figuring things out together.

Engaging the Divide

Philip Roth once wrote, "Life is, and."[6]

He meant that life is complex and nonlinear.

We live with many things at once: strategy and execution, theory and practice, research and reality. Everything is connected to everything, even if it's hard to see.

While there are countless ways to *create* value, there are only a few ways to *destroy* it. The Air Sandwich—allowing a gap between us by failing to think together—is on the shortlist of destructive ways. And believing that strategy and execution are two discrete things is one of the primary ways we perpetuate that gap.

Wherever we are, and regardless of how much we believe we need to just "do" what others ask of us, we can insist on adding ourselves into the mix. To think. To add. To build.

When we do what Roth suggested—what *is, and*—we fill the space between us.

Divisions are not superficial, or academic or theoretical. They are fissures, tears, and disconnection. Only in the healing of division are we made whole. This is everything. Because we are not meant to be divided or separated but connected. Within ourselves. And with each other.

We build value through the craft of thinking together. It's appealing to think of work as predictable and linear: first strategy, then execution. But nothing you or I have ever done works this way in real life.

This means we need a new, integrated way of working. One where thinking is something that each of us does. One where we celebrate "what is, and."

Fill the Air Sandwich

Goal: Create the spaciousness to think and execute together.

What gets lost in between—our roles, assumptions, silences, or doubts—can sink even the best plans. This practice is bridging that gap.

1. **Gather a project team.** Request an hour. Frame the session as an exploration—not into what's right/wrong, but into what might be missing.

2. **Surface the gaps.** What's one truth we're avoiding? What're we missing?

3. **Think.** Ask everyone to write privately for one to two minutes. Get introverts engaged.

4. **Share.** Ask each person to share one insight. No cross-talk. No fixing. Just listen.

5. **Discuss.** After everyone has shared, open the floor for a discussion. However, set the rule that the goal is to *explore* the ideas presented, not to *critique* or *debate* them. This keeps the space *spacious*. Ask people to focus on what *surprised* them.

6. **Close the loop.** As a group, integrate the thinking: Share shifts. What's clearer now?

12

Trust the Present, Not the Past

Limiting Norm: Trust Me, I Know
Leading Indicator: Trust What We Know Now

Trust but verify.

Actions speak louder than words.

Trust is earned, not given.

Trust takes years to build, seconds to break, and forever to repair.

Trust is built with consistency.

We've all heard the adages. All pointing to the same truth: Trust isn't declared but demonstrated. And yet leaders often turn to their teams and say (or silently signal) *Trust me, I know.* And more often than not, we do trust them. We fall in line, following, acquiescing to those who ask.

It's tempting to think the ones who trust too easily are naïve. That's not us, we think. We're sharper. More discerning. Always vigilant.

And maybe you've already decided, *I simply won't ever trust the boss.*

But what if the issue isn't about being careful or guarded enough?

What if the real danger of trust isn't *whom* we give it to, but *why* we give it in the first place?

How Our Brains Trick Us

About 15 years into her career, Rubina joined a consulting services company. She was thrilled to find a company that so fully shared her values. The company was known for creating "human-centered work."

Its website's home page said, "Don't just talk transformation; live it." The founder gave keynote speeches about being people-first, citing client stories that inspired her and the world.

"You can't talk this specifically about collaboration if you aren't already living, breathing, doing these ideas," Rubina said.

"So true," I agreed.

Yet no one helped her when she first got to the firm; there was no onboarding process or person to orient her and get her up to speed on projects. When she took the initiative to fix a super broken client process, she wasn't appreciated but told she was overstepping her bounds. Although she was a member of a small team, her leadership waited until her annual review cycle to give her some needed feedback, allowing the team dynamics to get funky instead of helping everyone work well together from the start. She was promised stock shares that never came.

But Rubina didn't see any of it as mistreatment. "This is my dream job, with an amazing founder and company doing my dream work."

Just a few weeks after having a baby, she learned her role had been eliminated. Throughout the next year, three other women who had gotten pregnant were also let go. It was likely illegal. And financially hard. But it especially hurt because it went against everything the company founder talked about.

"But how could they do this if they cared?" she asked me, the question heavy with longing.

It crushed Rubina's dream.

She had previously seen the gaps between her founder's words and actions, but instead of viewing this as a reason to distrust, she saw it as an "opportunity" to fix what needed fixing, to add value, and to build things collaboratively. *After all, isn't that what it means to collaborate?* she'd say.

As we were sitting in a Vietnamese snack shop talking about her experience, she sighed, "It turns out it was just really great marketing." But then she added, "Or maybe they *want* it to be true. Their messaging is who they want to be, but they just can't do the work to get there."

As I listened, I wondered why she was *still* trying to find a way to believe in the firm and its founder. Why the disconnect?

According to a study by NYU researchers who examined why we choose to trust despite the evidence, "Whom we trust reflects not only *who is trustworthy* but also *who we think we are.*"[1]

That explains why Rubina responded the way she did. She had been studying this firm from the outside for nearly a decade before she joined. She was smart, savvy, and analytical. Using her skills, she developed insight into what the firm was like, carefully evaluated it, and determined it was "the best."

She had made a smart decision. So her first response to the firing was not *gullibility*—just the opposite.

What she was experiencing was "confirmation bias." Confirmation bias is how we seek out, interpret, and remember information confirming our existing beliefs while ignoring or discounting information that contradicts them. Biases aren't bad in and of themselves. They are just the shortcuts our brains take so they don't have to consider or reconsider things—not because we aren't *being smart,* but because we *are already smart.* Bias can prevent us from having a fresh perspective or taking in new data. For someone like Rubina, a strong researcher and intuitive leader, confirmation bias tricked her into believing she'd done the due diligence already and was, therefore, "done."

Once our brains decide something is settled, they signal that there is no need to rethink these things.

But notice something important.

The question about trust isn't whether you trust *them,* but whether you still trust *yourself.*

In the Present State, What Do You Know?

Evidence shows that we all double down on past decisions instead of seeing what's true now. Once we trust, we stop thinking. That's how we find ourselves enduring hard situations—telling ourselves stories to help us stay where we are. Some version of the inner script runs:

It's not so bad. It's just a misunderstanding. Don't be so demanding. Be patient. It'll change soon. We can live with it. Tough it out. They mean well. It doesn't hurt that much. It's just one part of my life. Maybe this is an opportunity to grow. Let's give them every chance. They want to do better. We're here to fix what needs fixing; that's leadership.

And on and on.

We want to believe. We want to trust that we're smart, diligent, good at reading people, or whatever self-image we hold. And so we ignore what contradicts it. And justify our earlier decision.

Rubina's version was "How could this have happened, given that this was my dream job?"

From the outside, it's obvious: If management treats you poorly, it's not your dream job. Firing women for becoming mothers is not the future of work.

But to see that, Rubina would have had to re-see herself. Not as the savvy person who made a great choice but as someone who, like all of us do, misjudged the earlier situation. Only then would she be able to take in new data.

This takes work—mental, emotional, and personal work. It takes pausing, reorienting, and asking one important question:

What do I know now?

And that's what people who want you to trust them are counting on you *not* to do.

They don't want you to pause.

They want you to skip straight to belief.

They want you to trust yourself, but specifically your *past* Self. It's not because anyone has malintent but because it benefits them. Everyone's job is to advance their agenda.

But this nudge? This push to your prior Self? It's a form of bullying.

It pulls you out of the current moment.

And it uses your bias against you.

The question about trust isn't whether you trust *them*, but whether you still trust *yourself.*

And this is why when someone you respect says, "Trust me," your knee-jerk instinct is likely "Of course." Because in that moment, you're not just validating them. In that moment, you're being asked to validate *yourself.*

Rubina eventually got another gig. This time, she refused to romanticize it. She was no longer looking for a "dream job," just a place to work. This was a protective move: lower expectations, avoid disappointment. It's what so many of us do to avoid being burned again.

But there's another way to operate.

Learn to trust yourself. Now. And always.

That starts by seeing clearly what's happening now, as it *is* in the present. When we truly see what's happening and live in the present, we notice when and if words match actions. If what's being promised is being lived. Trust is not a future vision or a polished story, nor something we decide based on a burnished reputation.

It is a present-tense test.

Trust is linked to strategy and execution, from chapter 11, because it is also about thinking in real time. But trust takes that one step further. Trust is not a feeling we summon or a promise we make—it's the opportunity to *rethink.* When people think and rethink in real time—when their present observations matter—that's when trust, strategy, and execution align. All three are one thing: a live, unfolding integration of people, ideas, and action.

This scaffolding—that quiet architecture we cannot see but that directs our flow—changes the outcome. When we give people the space to think, trust happens. Not because you tell people what to believe, but because you give them enough space to decide for themselves. So we can decide: *What is it we can count on now?*

In the experience of living—in the present—we decide whom and what we trust. And only then can we trust ourselves to choose the next right thing.

We Trust Based on Our Experience of Things

"What should we do?" The team had gathered to determine how to spend some unexpected revenue, with many voices proposing rapid-fire solutions.

"All right, folks. We need to decide how to spend this money quickly.

Opening it up to a wider group will just lead to tons of cycles, costing the company everyone's time," one guy said.

"Hold on a second. Why is this even a discussion? We should just invest in things that have already proven successful. We've got early results from the first half of the year. Let's double down on what's working. We can't afford to gamble on uncertain ventures," another added.

"Well, instead of putting all our eggs in one or two baskets, why don't we allocate the $2 million proportionately to existing budgets? That way, everyone gets a piece of the pie," said a third leader.

Each proposed a solution they felt comfortable with. Each in a tone that said, *Trust me, I know!*

As I listened to the exchange, I stared out the corporate tower window and noticed how the sizzling heat of summer had transformed the view of the streets below into blurred waves of pedestrians and city architecture. Having extra money to invest in future growth is good, if not great, news. But being asked to put our trust in someone's specific and narrow solution felt like an equally big hot mess as the streets below.

I got up from my cushy chair and walked to the whiteboard.

Without interrupting the conversation or saying anything, I started to write out what I understood everyone was saying—what mattered to them.

- A process for spending the money quickly
- Investing to yield the highest results
- Involving everyone/broadly accessible

I faced the team when I was done, taking time to ensure that my handwriting was legible. By then, the talk was dying down.

"Are there any other criteria?" I asked. "Is anything missing? Is revenue growth, for instance, more important than cost savings?"

The group swiftly concluded that the three key points precisely encapsulated their objectives: fast, impactful, and benefitting a broad group.

However, they couldn't imagine a way to do all three simultaneously. They started talking again, not listening to one another but proposing we follow whatever specific solution they each individually trusted.

But we already know that trust isn't something you can just ask for. You earn trust through your actions. More importantly, trust happens when we experience those actions in real-time.

As their innovation adviser, I proposed an approach: *How about a hackathon for ideas, an idea-a-thon?* We could ask anyone—quite possibly everyone—in the firm to surface a new idea for how best to invest this money. My team could design a process that met our criteria.

Once we got the green light, I wrote an email that was sent company-wide explaining the situation, creating that invitation to play. We had an unexpected opportunity to invest in new things and asked for three things within three weeks.

- First, we asked people to form teams. Collaboration enhances innovation, I wrote. So we asked employees to unite and submit ideas. This would save us from having 38 far-too-similar suggestions and strengthen related ideas. We explicitly said no one had to work in the domain they had an idea about. For example, if someone in finance had an idea related to sales or a product, that was welcome.
- Next, we told them to size and scale each idea's impact. Ideas could be revenue-generating, market-growing, or cost-saving. Teams could get help from their finance business analysts to avoid just making up the numbers.
- Finally, we asked the teams to explain why their idea mattered to the business. Then we set a date and sign-up slots.

Crew by crew, employees pitched their ideas in the corporate amphi-theater space. Creativity came from the most unexpected corners. And by calling it "unexpected," I am not doing it justice.

One analyst from market research—think button-down white shirt, generic khaki pants, a timid demeanor, someone who carried an armload of folders to every meeting—had this super creative proposal. Her name was Julie, and she suggested reinventing how the company fed people in the in-house cafeteria. Unbeknownst to nearly all of the company, she was a "foodie," watching almost every *Top Chef, Good Eats,* and *Great*

British Bake Off series. She loved making new recipes every night and presenting tasty and healthy meals to her family.

She had found others at work with the same interests, and together, they went to the on-site food service team to ask if they could conduct an experiment or two. Within weeks, they had ideas. Their first suggestion was to flip the cafeteria design to present healthy foods before less healthy ones. Another was putting signs near the elevators to encourage people to use the stairs at lunchtime. Then, they did another creative thing: To size the project, they called the company's insurance firm. Implementing these proposals could reduce insurance payments by nearly 20%. The team's changes would cost very little but create so much intangible *and* tangible value.

The executives meeting in that tower conference room were genuinely surprised by this.

They hadn't trusted that their team's intrinsic desire to contribute would cause them to create so much value together.

But trust works exactly like this.

After all, trust is a by-product of *how we interact*. Trust is built in the "how": how we share authority, take turns leading, and center problem-solving on the situation and what it demands of each of us. And how we interact is always changing. This means that trust is fluid, not static. Trust is never one and done; we always have an opportunity to be like glue or a solvent at any given moment.

Until we experience something *ourselves*, we can't believe in it. We can't trust it. Everyone grew to trust the solutions created because they experienced them unfold. The teams signed off on the criteria initially, participated in the decision-making, and then saw the results. So they experienced a change in themselves as they were collectively working. They trusted what came out of it because they lived it—in the moment.

The question about trust is not whether to believe facts or words. It's whether we can stay present to the experience in front of us rather than let those who want us to do what they want time-shift us into the past.

To be present. In the moment. And make decisions about what we know now.

When Trust Is a Promise, Not a Practice

When Uber first emerged, it was a beacon of possibility.

A revolution for drivers; a solution for riders. It promised the freedom to be your own boss, set your own hours, and earn a living on your own terms. The company pitched itself as a game-changer in the transportation industry, offering an app that would connect drivers and riders with unparalleled ease. The message was clear: Uber wasn't just a ride-sharing service—it was an opportunity for independence, empowerment, and a better way of working.

Imagine being one of those drivers, believing you were finally free—only to realize the boss you left behind had been replaced by an algorithm that watched you more, paid you less, and never once looked you in the eye.

Uber was a master class in overpromising and underdelivering.

In 2014, after privacy scandals and accusations of a toxic culture, then CEO Travis Kalanick said Uber would become "a smarter and more humble company."[2] Five years later, after a string of lawsuits and regulatory battles, his successor Dara Khosrowshahi appeared in a nationwide ad campaign promising that Uber was "moving forward"— asking consumers to trust the company again.[3]

But in both cases, the appeal was emotional, not structural. Uber didn't change its business model. It didn't stop underpaying drivers. It didn't start acting with more transparency. It simply asked us to believe in its evolution. To trust that it had learned. Meanwhile, drivers continued to make below minimum wage in many cities. Uber spent hundreds of millions lobbying against laws that would have granted the drivers employee status.[4] The company counted on the power of its promise to outshine the facts.

Even when the truth was in plain sight.

In 2014, investor Peter Sims hopped into an Uber in New York. A few minutes into his ride, his phone lit up with texts from someone at a launch party in Chicago. They were watching his car move—live—on a big screen. Uber was using real people's rides as a party trick. Sims hadn't agreed to this. He hadn't even known about it. The company had already promised not to misuse customer data. And here it was, turning him into a prop.[5]

This wasn't a one-off.[6] Uber had built an internal tool called "God View," which let employees track the whereabouts of anyone using the app—celebrities, exes, journalists. The promise was privacy. The practice was surveillance.

That's not trustworthy behavior.[7] That's a bait and switch.

Trust.

That's the word Frances Frei—the former Uber VP of leadership and strategy and now a Harvard Business School professor—built her TED Talk around.[8] She offered a tidy triangle of how to build and rebuild trust: authenticity, logic, empathy. But somehow, she skipped the one thing that matters most when trust is broken: conduct. What the company actually *does.* Like whistling past the graveyard, she skipped over the mess. Ignored the lawsuits, the manipulation of surge pricing, the worker exploitation.

It's not that her trust triangle is wrong. It's just incomplete in the most glaring way.

And presented as if we wouldn't notice.

But maybe she and Uber were counting on how our brains work. How our brains use confirmation bias to make us stick with our early impressions, even when a newer reality contradicts them. Perhaps Uber banked on people clinging to the promise of being their own boss, even as that promise fell apart. And Frei might have crafted the only talk she could do at that moment without drawing attention to the fatal flaws of Uber.

But we now know better.

We know to pause and ask, *What is it I can count on right now?*

The takeaway?

We don't need better *frameworks* for trust. We need better *instincts* for what to trust.

And to do develop these, we start small.

Ask:

Who benefits if I believe this?

What's being left out?

What are you ignoring to make it seem okay?

What's the track record of behavior, not just the story?

Don't let the credentials do the seeing for you. Look again. And this time, notice what they're hoping you won't.

The Power of Reexamination

We are always doing the best we can.

In the early 1600s, the British arrived in India with a few boats and limited power. Yet without force or much bloodshed, they convinced leaders to relinquish an entire nation—and its wealth. Before this plunder, India held nearly 30% of the world's economy; today, it's at a mere 3%.[9]

How did the British achieve this astounding conquest?

With a convincing display of trustworthiness.

Trust is the linchpin of power, the quiet force behind everything. It's not just what makes collaboration possible; it's what makes it worthwhile. When trust lives in a room, people bring more of themselves. They say the hard thing. They try the riskier idea. They stop holding their breath. Trust doesn't guarantee results but makes great results possible. But when trust is brittle, or misplaced, everything cracks. People start editing themselves. They cover. The boldness disappears. Not because they don't care, but because it's just not worth the exposure. Collaboration becomes an act of choreography, not creation. That's the thing about trust; it's invisible, yet it shifts everything.

As trust goes, so goes everything.

Trust can be the binding power that builds value or the solvent that disintegrates it.

Consider the Indian leaders whom the British approached. At first, the British East India Company entered into fair agreements to trade the most valuable spices in the world, building a solid reputation for being reliable, respectable. But when the Mughal regime began to disintegrate, and the center no longer held, local Indian leaders needed help coordinating across regions. The British stepped in, offering "help" by saying, "You don't need to worry about all that complexity. We'll handle it, and you can focus on leading your territory."

I picture a local ruler, seated in silk, wanting to believe the promises and so signing a treaty with steady hands while his gut whispered what history would one day confirm: This partnership was not an alliance—it was a surrender.

Giving them the benefit of the doubt, perhaps each British leader genuinely believed they could honor that promise, and someone at the top of East India Company let them think so.

And so trust extended—from trade to governance.

What began as a partnership became a conquest. The same trust that built bridges was now used to burn them. Trust transferred without a rethinking can lead to subjugation.

And over time, it became easier to acquiesce than to resist an increasingly powerful force. Decisions to trust in the absence of data—Could the trust transfer from trade to governance?—became the default patterns. Decisions made in good faith were doubled down on until the East India Company wasn't a guest, it was the ruler.

Trust without reexamination transfers the way tides rise: gradually, then completely.

This exemplifies how confirmation bias hurts us. We all make decisions based on what we know. We trust what's worked before. But the hardest time to reexamine our trust is when we've already given so much of it. But that's exactly when we must.

We've all trusted the wrong thing at some point—a leader, a system, a story we wanted to believe. And the hardest part isn't walking away. It's facing what that trust once said about us. What we got wrong.

The moment we stop looking backward for clarity, and start listening inward for what's true right now—that's the moment we begin to trust again.

Not them.

Ourselves.

INNOVATION PRACTICE

Buzz the Bias

*Goal: Identify what you know at any moment
and assess what trust is warranted.*

Let's bring trust out of theory and into real time. Knowing to ask, "What can I count on them to do?" rather than accept the binary of trust or no trust.

🎥 Step 1: Pull up a TED Talk. Any talk. Hit Play. Watch the first minute.

🔔 Step 2: Buzz the Bias

- Notice your body. Are you nodding already? Feeling pulled in?

- Ask yourself: "Do I feel trust—or do I feel impressed?"

- If it's the latter: BUZZ. (Yes, actually say "buzz" in your head—or out loud if you're alone. It's weirdly satisfying.) That little jolt breaks the spell.

⏱ Step 3: Run the Trust Check

Press Play again, mid-talk, pause, and ask some questions:

- What do they gain if I believe this? (Track the money.)

- What's being left out, ignored, sidelined? (Look for convenient omissions.)

- Who gets hurt by this idea or by my following it? (Surface downstream consequences.)

- Would I be impressed if someone quieter had said it? (Charisma sells.)

- Do they want me to follow the idea, or follow them? (Spot manufactured dependence.)

- Do they live by this idea or just sell it? (Check for integrity.)

- Does this invite complexity or oversimplify? (Erasing nuance is dangerous.)

(cont.)

- What worldview does this enforce? (Individualism is often sold to us as "empowering.")

- Does this expand my agency or reduce it? (Even well-intended ideas can make us smaller.)

Learning to filter for trust isn't about judging the speaker or talk. It's about training yourself to see past style—and into substance. The point isn't to become a skeptic. Or to trust absolutely nothing. The point is to notice—and stay present to what you notice. Trust, after all, isn't earned in advance. It's earned in action. In context. In real time.

13

Don't Mistake Paternalism for Leadership

Limiting Norm: Servant Leadership
Leading Indicator: Situational Leadership

Step into any bookstore or scroll the leadership section online, and one message dominates: Caring for people is the gold standard of leadership.

And who could argue? Caring outshines *autocratic* leadership, where power flows top-down and leaders are obeyed, not questioned. It is certainly better than *transactional* leadership, where carrots or sticks replace real connection. And it's better than *bureaucratic* leadership, where good ideas get buried by rigid chains of command. Even *transformational* and *charismatic* leadership take a backseat to caring leadership—not because we don't want inspiration, but because what we truly crave is to be cared for.

It's not just a feel-good idea; it works. A study in the *Journal of Occupational Health and Psychology* found that when supervisors showed empathy, their employees were more satisfied and engaged at work.[1] Other studies show that when leaders protect employees' well-being, listen actively, and offer support, it builds trust and strengthens teams.[2]

No one questions it. From TED Talks to bestselling authors, from Simon Sinek to Brené Brown, the message is consistent. Leaders who care are the ones who succeed.

The archetype of caring leadership?

The *servant leader.*

As one AT&T executive concluded his illustrious career, he told us a true leader is a servant, someone who puts the growth and well-being of others over the pursuit of their own power or control.[3]

Or so the theory goes.

May It Please the Boss

Evan had been Jennifer's manager for 10 years, first as a colleague she helped hire, then as a leader who was promoted over her. After that, she managed most of his team. Evan focused on strategy; Jennifer made things happen. She led every major initiative, every turnaround, every win that Evan was credited with. While Evan managed five people, Jennifer managed nearly 1,000 people. She didn't just make his programs successful—she lined up operations, inspired teams, and kept the entire machine moving.

When Evan recruited Jennifer to his new startup, he promised the kind of collaboration they had always shared. "We're an unbeatable team," he said. And Jennifer believed it. She often raved to her friends about how her boss always had her back and created ways for her to shine. She felt lucky. He even offered her a title promotion—the icing on the caring cake.

But soon after joining the company, Jennifer found herself caught between Evan and the new CMO over resources.

The CMO had requested full operational support for a fast-tracked product launch—an all-hands marketing campaign, rushed logistics, and coordinated customer experience touchpoints. Jennifer knew the systems couldn't flex that fast. It was a setup for failure. Jennifer raised the issue with Evan, who was concerned this made his team look unprepared at a time when he was jockeying with the CMO about the role his team played in product launches. Instead of dealing with the resourcing (aka political) issues directly—with the CMO, or the executive team—he asked Jennifer to "handle it," knowing she'd make him look good.

Her loyalty to Evan was deep—he had always supported her. Her job had always been to back him. So she did so in this situation, too. At first, she feigned confusion about the CMO's ask. The next time, she redirected the conversation. The third time, she blamed some vague "limited resources."

"It wasn't just that I was trying to avoid accountability or discussing a messy topic," she explained. She felt the best way to handle corporate politics was to stay fully aligned with what her boss wanted her to do.

Doing what your boss wants you to do is *always* a winning strategy. Case study after case study teaches us that if you keep your boss or bosses happy, performance doesn't matter when it comes to whether you keep or lose your job.[4]

In the end, Jennifer was fired, and Evan told her he was unhappy because she wasn't "managing the business's needs." True enough. Jennifer had been managing *Evan's* needs. As he'd instructed her to do. And as she needed to do if she was going to keep her job.

So what do we do when we, like Jennifer, are caught between what the boss wants and what the work needs?

Who Made You King of Everything?

Evan and Jennifer needed to redirect their attention away from each other and toward the work. In their current dynamic, Jennifer's relationship to the work was filtered *through* Evan—by caring about what he valued. Evan's relationship to the work was about how to get others to do his bidding. This filter allowed only what served Evan's "vision." If she hadn't had to worry about pleasing Evan, Jennifer would have fully considered what the CMO requested—and figured out a way to make it work. Maybe that would have required the timeline to move, or a reallocation of dollars, or something, but they could have found a solution.

Overfocusing on the leader keeps us focused on what *they* want instead of what is needed.

While servant leadership is not the strong-arm leadership of the past, it doesn't need to be. When the people being led have internalized that someone *has to be in charge* and we have to *keep the boss happy*, we choose to be ruled.

Earlier, we discussed the role of benevolence and how it was "a priv-ilege" to serve power. Rulers have long found that being benevolent benefits them. Machiavelli himself warned that "a ruler must avoid any behavior that will lead to his being hated or held in contempt." In the long run, holding power through the niceties rather than by killing off one's subjects was cheaper, so this became the preeminent leadership mode—to be nice.

So "taking care" of others became a way to stay on top.

That logic is old. And dangerous.

To justify the enslavement of people over centuries, the ruling class argued that enslaved people were "like children who needed to be cared for."[5] Patriarchy regularly argues that some people require oversight be-cause they are incapable of caring for themselves.[6]

Let me repeat that. *Incapable of taking care of themselves.*

That's the same underlying assumption of servant leadership. This is not to equate servant leadership with the atrocities of the past, but to trace the logic that has long justified domination in the name of care.

This comparison is uncomfortable. And it should be. Because the logic that justifies control in the name of care hasn't disappeared; it's just evolved.

Caring *for* others—caretaking—can easily be a way to control them.

Which is how the Evans of the world keep winning. Either Evan gets to have the Jennifers of the world do his bidding, or he gets to sacrifice her to save himself. Servant leaders choose *how* and *when* to care. Care is on their terms. And theirs alone.

Which is all to say, servant leadership is deeply paternalistic.

Paternalism is when those in power take it upon themselves to care for their subordinates, assuming they know what's best. To be 100% clear, paternalism is the system, but any gender can participate in and uphold it. Women, too, can spend their energy reinforcing that someone must always be in charge.

Paternalism intangibly limits how much value is created. Even when well intentioned, it harms, because it centers control, not collaboration.

And it shows up everywhere.

Leaders are celebrated when they are "open to hearing concerns." In-stead of people determining their best path together, the social expectation is that the leader decides what is in everyone's best interest, as if "Father knows best."

Startups often offer policies like "wellness stipends" or "mental health days." These appear caring but serve as Band-Aids for burnout rather than addressing its root cause: an unhealthy culture addicted to constant productivity.

Company profiles proudly show the dinners provided for those working late as a way of caring for their people. But with food served at 7 p.m., it's more of a trap used to gain additional hours of labor, literal bait on a hook to lure people in.

When we celebrate servant leadership—whether in our boardrooms or in business books—we are participating in our own oppression. We break that cycle only when we are radically honest, radically transparent, and radically committed to building a workplace that cares about the work of leading, not the caring leader. We don't need care that looks like perks in exchange for loyalty. We need, in contrast, policies of care (healthcare, pay equity, etc.). We need the systems and scaffolding that allow each of us to lead.

How? It's a shift as simple as this:

Instead of *serving* your team, you work *with* your team.

Instead of working *for* your boss, you work *with someone.*

"*With*" changes the dynamic.

But let's be clear: This isn't about swapping out a preposition. You can say "with" all day and still build a cage around someone. You can say "with" and still be the one holding the key. "With" only matters when you mean it. It's not cosmetic—it's structural. It breaks the old trap: the idea that someone must always be beneath, behind, or beholden. To work with is to dismantle the hierarchy of humanity that holds people in place. To work with is to see each person not as a function but as a force—moving, choosing, shaping. Not a trapped being, but a co-creator, free and of the world.

When we insist that someone must always be in charge, we overlook the possibility that leadership doesn't have to rest with just one person. Leadership can be shared, with any of us stepping forward or stepping back, taking turns as the situation calls for.

Eliminating servant leadership doesn't mean that leadership disappears, but that it flexes.

Care, then, doesn't need to belong to a title or role. It's not a fixed identity. Rather, care is found in policies, in practices. It's a shared approach that we can all step into, like entering a room. It's not something we own or trade but how we move.

Instead of *directing another*, we let *our common goal* direct how we show up. When we don't understand this, we limit our best work.

Tough Choices

One of the scariest parts about being a human is having needs, something that has always made me feel far too vulnerable. What if I need people to care for me and they can't or don't show up? What if my needs are too demanding for those around me? For years—decades, really—I've tried to pretend that I didn't have any needs, thinking this would keep me protected, safe, and connected.

But having a health crisis—a multi-trajectory brain injury—forced me to ask for help. For care.

One of my best friends said she was happy to help in any way. We made plans to go to the grocery store on a Sunday, but I left a voice message canceling the day before, explaining that I needed to do my (neuromuscular) PT exercises instead.

For my recovery, my neurologist had directed me to do eight exercises daily. She didn't tell me that it would take me most of a day to do them, that each one would wipe me out, giving me such vertigo that I'd nearly throw up. After each exercise, I'd have to lie down, rest, and wait for the room to stop spinning to work up the capacity to do the next one. Though the neurologist had assigned this to me on Tuesday, I had yet to complete the full set. And it was now Saturday.

I knew that to get better, I had to prioritize these exercises.

My friend left me a return message. She shared her disappointment at my canceling our plans and said she had "many, many people" she could care for, and that she'd been "choosing" me.

Her words and the resentful tone that accompanied them really gave me pause. I was scared I was failing. Was I a terrible friend? Was I being ungrateful? Had I made a big mistake?

My brain was injured. I couldn't tell if my choices were wise or wrong. That made everything feel shakier. I wanted to recover, but I couldn't trust my instincts. I'd never want to hurt my friend of nearly 20 years. Should I choose her? Or the PT work?

The following Tuesday, she showed up and drove me to my neurologist. Before we got out of the car, my friend put her hand on mine and asked if we could talk first. *Of course*, I said. I felt a little trapped, but I also wanted to be the kind of friend who could always engage and be there for my people.

And then.

Her sobbing felt like a bass unit cranked high, shaking the air with raw emotion.

She told me that I was being ungrateful for not appreciating her efforts.

That's when it snapped into focus: Her care came with a contract I hadn't agreed to. I was supposed to reflect her goodness back to her. Care wasn't about what I needed; it was about how she needed to be needed. Her kindness had strings. And suddenly I was tied up in them.

At that moment, I realized that I had violated a code. The caretaker's job is to provide care. The person receiving care? Well, they owe appreciation for being cared for, like Jennifer did with Evan.

Caring *for* another then reflects on the *person* doing the care, not *the care* itself. It's a way a person affirms their goodness and value. When someone sees their value in caring, they need the other person to need them.

This form of "care" isn't an act of loving generosity; it is designed to create dependency—a tactic to increase a person's power or influence over another.

I expressed my concern about my friend's caretaking.

I said her resentment showed that she was caring beyond what was reasonable or healthy for her. She explained that she was doing this because of how much I "needed" her. I have needs, I agreed, but pointed out that she wasn't the only one who could address them. Eleven others were in my care circle. She claimed that they weren't stepping up. And I noticed how my bestie was body-blocking their involvement.

And I knew this conversation was about more than how we managed a care spreadsheet. And it wasn't about saying the wrong thing in a time of stress.[7]

When we insist that someone must always be in charge, we overlook the possibility that leadership doesn't have to rest with just one person.

Our conflict was that my friend was defining her worth and value *through* me.

I knew it wasn't right—for either of us. It was unhealthy. Whether done by a friend or a boss.

And I regret not seeing it earlier.

Needing help, comfort, love, understanding, support, friendship, positive reinforcement, someone who can care for us without expecting things in return, is the most ordinary yet extraordinary thing because it allows us to care for one another.

Having needs isn't bad. It's a chance to be fully human. So the issue is never whether we have needs and need care. The problem is who is served by the caring. It was hard for me to say that to my friend—hard to name it for what it was.

Just as it's hard to name servant leadership for what it truly is.

Servant leadership started with the right intentions, to care for people. But it centers on the wrong thing, which is *the person doing the caring*, not the *care* itself.

The net effect? It's the difference between caretaking and care.

- Caretaking undermines authority by stepping up/in, while care respects the autonomy of the other.
- Caretaking breeds dependence, while care supports self-trust.
- Caretaking prevents growth by rescuing or fixing, while care creates the space for one to grow.

- Caretaking comes from the place of control, while care is love.
- The caretaker needs to be needed, while care has no preconditions.

The difference between the two isn't about who leads, or how. It's about whether we're enabling free choice, not to *need* another but to *want* each other.

And yet it's so understandable why we cling to the servant leader model. Given that so many of us haven't been well cared for, it's no surprise that we are grateful to have someone—*anyone*—care, especially at work. We do not notice that, in an invisible way, we have become the object in someone else's story rather than the subject of our own.

Like my friend, a servant leader often claims the moral high ground— but it's just another way to stay in charge. To secure control by appearing selfless.

Let's stop calling it care when it's really well-packaged control.

The Law of the Situation

What if leadership wasn't about a *role* but about *responding* to what the moment calls for?

About 100 years ago, Mary Parker Follett, a pioneering management thinker, gave us a radical idea that still hasn't gotten its due. She called it *the Law of the Situation.*[8] At its core, the law says that no person should be "in charge" of another; instead, we are all in service to what the situation requires.

Instead of a person commanding authority, Follett argued for listening to the demands of the moment. The *situation* becomes the boss rather than a title, a hierarchy, or someone's ego or seniority. The work tells us what needs to happen next. And from that, leadership emerges—fluidly, functionally, and, often, collectively.

This idea reframes everything.

Rather than asking, "Who's the leader?," we ask, "What is needed now?"

In a world where complexity rules and no one person can know it all,

Follett's idea is more relevant than ever. And yet few teams today know how to apply it. Even fewer have the structures—or the shared norms—to make it real. So let's unpack that.

But before we do, let's be clear that what we're talking about isn't just a clever way to delegate. It's not a way to stay in charge while handing off the work.

The Law of the Situation is a different definition of leadership entirely. One rooted not in control or caretaking but in contribution. It makes leadership shared, not singular. It shifts the focus from roles to results. It asks us to replace status with usefulness. It's what makes distributed leadership not just possible but powerful.

So why don't we do this already?

Because we're still clinging to an old invisible norm: Leadership must live in a person. One decision-maker. One ultimate authority. One boss.

We're taught to believe that if everyone leads, no one does.

But, again, that's not future-facing. That's the oldest of old norms: patriarchy.

Beneath it all is fear: If power flows, who am I without it? If leadership rotates, what happens to my identity as "the leader"? If I step back, will anyone step forward?

So we grip harder, tighter. We over-care, over-function, over-own. We confuse being essential with being in charge and being needed with being valuable. And we reproduce the very hierarchies we claim to want to change.

To apply the Law of the Situation—to move from control to contribution— we need new norms. Not just new tools or structures but new agreements about how we show up and share responsibility.

We need to ask: What is the situation asking for? Who has the knowledge, experience, or relational trust to take the lead here?

Sometimes it's the manager. Sometimes the designer. Sometimes the person with the lived experience. Sometimes the one who knows what it's like to be on the margins. And sometimes, the best leader is the quietest voice in the room.

The key is not to flatten all roles, but to allow people's capacities to be called into use, to rotate who leads based on what is needed. We let people lead from their point of view—not their title. Just like we said with care: We must stop making someone the king of everything. Leadership is not a crown you wear. It's a capacity you lend. It is not being the leader, but leading.

This is Situational Leadership. Which is not a new term. In the 1960s, Hersey and Blanchard taught that the best leaders adapt their style to the competence of the follower. Useful, yes—but notice where all the power sits: with the singular leader. Everyone else is cast as the follower.

That model has outlived its usefulness. So let's call our version Situational Leadership for modern work. We do not place the person at the center. We do not make leadership a solo act, where one individual bends and flexes while the rest wait to be led.

The shift we need today is twofold. First, from person → work. Leadership is not about the traits of an individual but about what the work requires in the moment. Care should be embodied in policies, not in the thing we earn because of our relationship with the boss. Second, from singular → plural. Leadership is not held by one appointed figure but shared among many of us, depending on who is best positioned to lead in the moment.

Here's the contrast in plain terms:

- Old model: one leader adapting to the follower.
- New model: many leaders adapting to the work.

This is what I mean by reclaiming Situational Leadership. Not the leader changing style, but leadership itself shifting shape. Fluid. Collective. Future-facing. The situation decides, not the title. As Parker-Follett first suggested.

When we see it this way, leadership stops being a pedestal and becomes a practice—one any of us can step into when the work demands it.

INNOVATION PRACTICE
The Law of the Situation

Goal: Apply the Law of the Situation to a project.

Step 1: What Is the Situation Asking For? (10 Minutes)

As a team, respond to these questions together:

- What's the next goal here?
- What does this moment need most?

Write answers on sticky notes or a virtual board. Let everyone add what they see. Then cluster the insights into themes.

Step 2: What Roles Serve the Situation Best? (5 Minutes)

Ask: "If this is what the situation needs, what roles or energies are most useful right now?" Make a quick list together: e.g., Navigator, Connector, Builder, Challenger, Closer.

Step 3: Match People to Purpose (10 Minutes)

Invite team members to choose or be matched to the role where they can best serve the situation—not just based on title or skill but based on timing, energy, and interest. Be wary of the person assigning themselves to everything. The person who doesn't know themself can often try to do too much to "add value."

Step 4: Act → Learn → Adjust (Ongoing)

As the project unfolds, check back in regularly:

- Has the situation changed?
- Do our roles still fit?
- What needs to shift?

This is not about having rigid plans—it's about staying attuned to what the moment is asking for. Because the team is orienting around reality, not routine. Power flows from usefulness. That's the Law of the Situation.

14

Stop Fighting for the Emperor's Pleasure

Limiting Norm: Combatant
Leading Indicator: Detective

It's called the Gladiator Strategy.

The Swiss CEO of a shoe company stirred his espresso as he tried to convince me of his preferred way of working: "I think a battle of ideas is so important. It helps us fight things out, so the one idea left standing is the absolute best idea."

In Roman times, the best gladiators weren't necessarily the best athletes or the strongest physical performers but the ones who knew how to entertain the crowds in the way the emperor loved. Whatever, whoever amused the emperor was given the thumbs-up. The workplace parallel is perhaps obvious: People can "win" internal fights in those boardrooms by arguing for the ideas and perspectives that the boss already loves. So "fighting for the best idea" becomes a public way to endorse and validate the emperor's—er, boss's—opinions.

I asked, "You believe that putting people and their ideas under extreme pressure will yield diamonds?"

"Yes!" he answered enthusiastically, as if I was *finally* understanding him.

Some coffee spilled.

I really didn't want to burst his bubble, but I also knew that his beloved boardroom battles wouldn't fix the innovation problem he wanted solved.

While some people might respond well to ripping apart their colleague's ideas in a meeting, this is usually not the best way to bring out the best in people, I told him. Most will feel psychologically unsafe, which means they will hold back their ideas and questions. Fights in boardrooms mean people won't lean on each other; they won't work together. So your business performance suffers. Because in the end, we're talking about humans, not rocks, right?

I paused. That was a big thing to drop.

Would he ask about other options so we could find one that was better suited, or was he super committed to converting me to his worldview?

And then he said, "But Ray Dalio does it. Of Bridgewater."

Ugh. Hedge fund gazillionaire Ray Dalio. Dalio had given a legendary talk on "radical transparency" at a TED event. He also threatened legal action against a journalist who wrote a book about Bridgewater; so much for believing in radical transparency.[1]

I didn't want to have that debate, so I quickly calculated and redirected.

"A better example might be Microsoft's Steve Ballmer, who, like Dalio, is a big fan of a Gladiator Strategy."

Steve Ballmer is a 6-foot-5-inch-tall man with a booming voice. *Animated, crazy, wild, zany,* and *freakouts* were some words used in headlines to describe his legendary press events when he was CEO of Microsoft.[2] He would shout, run, and dance onstage at events. And because tech is a tiny little universe, it wasn't uncommon to hear many inside baseball stories about him that mirrored his external persona: throwing chairs, books, and coffee mugs at people in the office over the years. His boardroom fights to create a high-performance team were legendary. Yes, people felt inspired to perform, but they were also scared of him.

Under Ballmer's leadership, Microsoft grew revenue and made healthy profits. However, the stock price stayed flat nearly the whole time he led the company.

Then Satya Nadella showed up and took over as CEO.

Nadella was as soft-spoken as Ballmer was loud. And Nadella's leadership philosophy couldn't have been more different. He publicly shared that he wanted Microsoft to stop its know-it-all culture and step into a learn-it-all culture.[3] His boardroom meetings were so vastly different that they *weren't* talked about, whispered about, or gossiped about. What people would say was that Nadella encouraged rather than shamed. He listened rather than told. He didn't believe in right and wrong answers. When I would run into people at SXSW or other tech conferences, they would joke about how vastly different it felt to work at Microsoft, like being at a different company. One said it was the difference between working for Attila the Hun and Mahatma Gandhi.

I tracked what happened financially.

- Revenues grew.
- Profits grew.
- The stock market rewarded Nadella's leadership and the company with a 969% increase in stock price.[4] By the top of 2024, Microsoft had become the world's most valuable public company, claiming the crown that Apple had held for nearly a decade.[5]

A Team by Name or by Function

"It's not just that the stock price grew. It's what that stock price represents," I told the Swiss CEO.

Remember, 84% of the stock market's value is considered "intangible." This means the things we can measure—like intellectual IP, buildings, furniture, and payroll cost—account for only 16% of the stock value. That intangible metric captures what is happening within the company. It measures whether they are doing their best work, or not.

So a flat stock price is the market saying: We believe the company's value creation engine is the same as yesterday.

We've all been a part of teams. Some brought out the best in us, and some diminished us. Yet the same word, *team*, is used in both circumstances. It's worth digging deeper.

- Sometimes, *we call it a team when all we do is work next to each other.* Each person's contribution is simply added together to reach the final result. If person A contributed 2, person B contributed 5, and person C contributed 10, the total would be 17. Many of us work in this scenario: We each do our bit, and our bits add up. The collective gain is **additive**.

- Next, *we call it a team, but only because we have to.* The work produced by the team is less than what any of the individuals know is possible. Despite everyone giving their best effort individually, the result of the collective always feels like missed potential. Using math, it's as if every teammate gets hired for their contribution but performs less than they are capable of. Instead of 17, you get 10. We are collectively **diminished**.

- Finally, *we're not just a team in name; we work toward one objective.* We're willing to play our position as we help the whole team play their best. What is produced as a team is much more than any individual can do independently. Each person's contribution is raised by the collective. The math becomes exponential. Each party makes a specific contribution, but now it's magnified. Mathematically, it becomes . . . 2 x 5 x 10. Or 100. We are exponentially **raised**.

These scenarios—*additive, diminished,* or *raised*—describe how the relational intangibles shape what we create.

And fighting is central to how this plays out.

There are many ways to fight—unhelpful and helpful.

Unhelpful is when we see the other person as the issue. Fighting with each other never helps us figure out the issues. Fighting over right or wrong is domination. Fighting over resources is like a game of Hungry Hungry Hippos—a scramble to grab what's there rather than face what's missing or generate what's needed. And not fighting at all? That's just avoiding the topic, dodging the very conversation that helps us grow.

We often think fights divide us—that disagreement proves we can't get along or makes us cruel. But if we focus on *learning* instead of *winning,* fights can *unite* us.

So the question isn't whether to fight—it's what the fight serves. And how we show up to it—as a combatant or a detective. Yet work rarely makes this distinction.

Fight for and with Each Other

When we learn how to fight *for* and *with* each other, we build impactful ideas—and with them, growth and performance. Exchanging arguments and perspectives is a way we become strong—*we* being the operative word.

I told the CEO all of that. As best as I could.

The Swiss dude didn't ask any more questions, so maybe it landed. But I worried he would return to his office and continue attempting to prove what he'd tried to convince me of—that boardroom combat fights were valuable. I sensed that he wanted my approval and endorsement, not my input.

I should have said one more thing to him. Perhaps it could have made a difference.

The leaders who love gladiator strategies—the Steve Ballmers of the world—are being fooled. Those leaders argue that fighting it out in the boardroom is the way they'll win in the marketplace. But their people, those combatants—they know how to "win" in those conference room fights. Corporate boardroom fights can easily be "won" by telling the leader—the emperor—what the emperor is *known* to value, what they *already* believe to be true, and what they want *to be affirmed*. But that's not the same as winning in the marketplace.

So "boardroom fighting" doesn't turn out to be a battle of ideas; it ends up being a performance for the emperor's pleasure. *That's why the emperor loves it.*

Conflict is rooted in difference. Apart from natural disasters, most of the pain, destruction, waste, and neglect in human life is a result of our overreaction to difference.

Any of us, all of us, can have this overreaction. It's natural.

But the job is to pull up our adult pants and learn how to be more intentional.

When conflict happens, we wonder if we've done something wrong. Or we want to avoid losing face. And so we start to create a story where someone is the villain, or the victim, the perpetrator, or participant.

But we can find a new way of viewing this, a way that is more true.

When having a conflict, we can see ourselves as *the conflicted*.

The issue is rarely each other, but how we view the conflict. If we can teach ourselves to see "the conflict" similarly to the way we see "the situation," we can all deal with it better.

There doesn't need to be any pathology around being conflicted.

The Māori word for ADHD is *aroreretini*, which means "attention goes to many things," and the word for autism is *takiwatanga*, meaning "in their [or my] own time and space." There is no disorder, no pathology, no judgment, just description.[6]

Names change how we view a topic.

This is what we need to do with conflict.

Building this shared framework does not mean we agree on *how* to solve an issue; it says we agree on the problem. We can't fight for and with each other if we don't know what we're fighting about. It probably goes without saying, but doing this requires that everyone involved have a shared interest in learning and growing together. To believe in the validity of a multiplicity of views. To not make it about right and wrong.

The goal is to be able to say: "We are fighting about X, agreed? Yes. Okay, at least we got that conflict clear."

INNOVATION PRACTICE
Be the Conflicted

Goal: Build a shared framework to describe
a problem so all parties can agree.

First, **pick a current conflict** and understand that the conflict isn't something to be solved alone—it's something to be explored together. Think of it as a puzzle, not a battle.

Next, **become great detectives** to learn about each other and the issue at hand. It's so hard to table what we know to learn what we don't. Here are some prompts:

- What is the larger story here?
- Help me understand how you're seeing this.
- How is this bigger than the immediate moment? What is it bringing up from the past?
- What am I missing here? Do you want to hear what I think you're missing?
- What can I learn from you? What can we learn from this?

And then, **craft a narrative** where you become the conflicted. Now that you've explored and understood, the next step is to co-create the narrative of what is happening. This is the moment when you both name the issue, not as a division but as something shared. I find this works well if someone writes it down. Or, even better, if both parties write it down separately and then discuss it. This is the foundation for resolution, because only when we both agree on the nature of the problem can we co-create a solution. You'll know you have it when all parties can say, "Yep, that's what we're fighting about."

15

Labels Limit More than Liberate

Limiting Norm: Categorization
Leading Indicator: Curiosity

Imagine if I told you there was a way to know your strengths and weaknesses and how you could add value to the world. The same goes for your teammates; you'd know them and how best to work with them.

Sounds amazing, doesn't it? Who wouldn't want that kind of clarity?!

Enter the Myers-Briggs Type Indicator (MBTI). It's a test that measures personality, approaches, attitudes, and beliefs. The test promises to serve as "a powerful framework for building better relationships, driving positive change, harnessing innovation, and achieving excellence."[1] Most of the faithful think of it as a way to be known. It's used often in early adulthood as a tool for telling you your proper career choice. It's used later in one's employment, often in team-building workshops for teams to work together better. Once a person is scored, assessed, and labeled, bosses and HR use it to place people and assign projects.[2]

The Myers-Brigg test asks you to answer questions like "Do you find it easy to introduce yourself to other people?" with either a yes or no answer. After you've answered 90-ish questions, the test categorizes responses into four vectors. It then answers if you are extroverted or introverted (E or I), intuitive or sensing (N or S), feeling or thinking (F or T), and perceiving or judging (P or J).

Combining these four elements, 16 labels or quadrants define . . . everyone, which is a clue unto itself. There are 16 buckets for all 7 billion of us. Which is generic and simplistic. And wrong.

Let's dig into it.

Take the question *Do you find it easy to introduce yourself to other people?*

How would you answer?

People who easily introduce themselves to others have likely had it modeled to them. Maybe they've seen it in action more than others because they were only children and thus treated as adults early on. Or they might belong to a group whose members, through cultural coding, can expect to be well-received and valued, and thus can have fewer worries about introducing themselves.

Their answer to the question reflects *their* specific experience.

An immigrant speaking a foreign language, a latchkey child who rarely socialized, or someone raised not to speak unless spoken to might be worse at introducing themself to people.

And *their* answers to the question reflect *those* experiences.

But as people check yes or no, all the specifics are lost. This is how the MBTI test gives us a generic view of who we are, not a distinct view. It might help us understand what we have in common but never what is distinctly true to the individual.

The answer to the question might also change based on recent experiences. If you're at a venue with all new-to-you people, it might be easier to introduce yourself to others because you feel less tethered to how people know you versus being in a gathering of friends of friends. Equally, if you're between jobs (or gigs), it could be difficult to introduce yourself since so many of us define ourselves by our work. Any of us could find ourselves saying, *I'm nobody.*

Context changes everything. Yet the test doesn't account for that.

Over the years, I've noticed that many people could take the MBTI over different days with different results. It's easy to think we just suck at self-awareness; however, the management literature backs up our experience. Research shows that a personality type will change for 50% of individuals if they simply retake the test on the same day.[3] Add different days and circumstances and no test will capture us because—as the Walt Whitman poem says—we are large; we contain multitudes.

Yet the MBTI test wants us to compress ourselves into a single identity.

When someone says, "Porter is an ENTJ personality, always competitive and driven," they have categorized and pigeonholed someone. It could be that when Porter has finally gotten some much-needed therapy, he no longer feels the need to challenge others to prove his worth in every meeting. His more present demeanor is not a sign that he's not who he is, but a sign that he is more of who he is (less reactive and able to choose his responses).

But the MBTI signals a certainty, a static state of being.

Not only that, most of us take the test knowing our colleagues are going to hear the finding, so we can skew our answers, signaling not who we are but how we want to be seen. Many of those who have gotten different results over time pick the version of themselves they like most—often, the one that others are more likely to like—and share that as "true."

This only reinforces how much we collectively hide who we are at work.

Kenji Yoshino, an NYU professor, did iconic research to show that 60% of us "cover" at work.[4] Covering is why a female executive with a boorish husband might not bring him to a company event, worried that he won't use the right combination of forks and knives at the posh dinner. It's why so many of us don't talk about childcare or eldercare responsibilities; we don't want to appear anything less than fully committed to our jobs. Or why some people use hair relaxers to straighten their natural hair to appear more "professional." Or why someone doesn't reveal that they are heading to a doctor's appointment since they don't want people to think they're not up to the next big task. The thing about covering is that as we do it, we create a façade, a performance. Then the MBTI (and other tests like it) captures and reflects that covering performance as if it were true.

The cover story we tell about ourselves seems ever more true once it's in a test result.

And that's how we can submerge who we actually are. In that way, the MBTI test amplifies rather than addresses the "covering" that happens at work.

Whenever we are being categorized, we are not being seen as ourselves.

And then there's the fact that the test is focused on the individual rather than the team. Groups are comprised of individuals, yes. However, who surrounds us affects us. If we're surrounded by five people who diss us at every turn, we are one person, but in the presence of people who want us to thrive, we are another. We change based on whom we're with. Not because we're a chameleon but because humans are social beings, and we orient ourselves so we always belong. So why are we using a test that studies an isolated person instead of looking at how we collectively interact?

Personality tests promise to predict who will perform best at certain work. Colleges and universities worldwide use the MBTI test, as do 89 of the Fortune 100 companies, according to CPP, a company that administers the MBTI.[5] Similarly, the Social Styles personality test, which categorizes people into four communication styles—Driver, Expressive, Amiable, and Analytic—suggests that a "driver-driver" will be a great CEO, and an "analytic driver" will be a great marketer. Coaches pay to certify this material and then use it for their work. Once certified, test administrators become cheerleaders of these tests, ensuring that their use is perpetuated.

Yet when it comes to predicting job performance, personality tests mostly miss the mark. Even the best predictor—conscientiousness, measured by the Big Five personality test—correlates with job performance only between 20 and 30% of the time.[6] But the far more popular tools, the ones we've been focused on, don't even get you on the board; they have no reliable tie to how well someone will do their work.[7,8] If hiring or team assignments are based on these tests, it's the equivalent of throwing darts blindfolded, virtually guaranteed to miss the bull's-eye.

So what *does* predict job performance?

Job performance.

Not some personality test.

And what helps us know one another? Certainly, it is not a standard personality test: one that loses the person's specificity, doesn't address context or fluidity, creates a single story, reinforces our façades, isolates the individual, and doesn't predict performance. Being labeled creates the illusion of knowing one another and stops us from doing the work.

Because the way we know each other?

Through curiosity.

Shocker.

Every Individual Is an Exception to the Rule

We desperately want to be known. And valued. And able to add value. When we're young, we're dying for someone or something to reflect back where we can add our best work. When we're in a good workplace, our colleagues want to know us so we can work well together. Our best leaders want to know us so they can enable us to thrive. Our future-forward companies want to place us in the best role—to put us to optimal use.

And that's the appeal of tools like the MBTI.

It's why I once loved it. I loved "knowing" I was an ENTJ. I loved the seeming clarity. I felt like I understood myself better. I loved the write-up and its powerful language. I kept the description at my desk for years because I'd look to it for answers if a situation arose. What would an ENTJ do in certain situations? Oh, okay, then that's what I'll do.

Labels can feel good—sort of like being tucked into bed when you're really tired, everything snuggled around you. They can comfort us and help us feel clear about our place in the world.

Growing up, I was expected to have an arranged marriage. To some Westerners, it sounds outdated, but it was also comforting. Rigid external rules can be. Nearly anything that is non-nuanced can be comforting because it asserts that if we just follow the plan, things will work out. When we don't have to figure it all out by ourselves, we feel less alone, safer, and more cared for. In the arranged marriage, I hoped that those who loved me would know who I was and what I needed. The MBTI sells a similar hope—you don't have to do the messy work of self-discovery because someone else already has.

Labels give us certainty in a world of uncertainty.

So there are perfectly valid reasons why so many people want the MBTI and related tests to be useful.

We buy into these tests because we want clarity, insight, and validation for how we best work. It's like people who believe an astrological horoscope describes them well, even *after* they realize that they are reading the wrong one. We can see ourselves in anything if something is written with enough ambiguity. It's what is called the Barnum Effect.[9]

But here's how it limits our best work: By putting someone in a box, we stop noticing the distinctions that make each of us ourselves. This is the underlying thread in so many of these norms perpetuating power as it currently exists. People without power are seen through an abstraction, but people with power are seen as themselves. That is the issue. All personality tests, whether the MBTI, Enneagram, CliftonStrengths, DISC, or Keirsey Temperament Sorter, can be equally problematic because they categorize humans rather than encourage the curiosity to help us be known as our distinct selves.

Being seen through a label isn't the same as being seen—it's the kind of shallow visibility that actually deepens the ache we have to be seen. Modern loneliness is not a function of being alone in the world but a function of not being seen. These personality tests are not the solution but part of the problem. Carl Jung—on whose research the MBTI test is built—said it best when he wrote: "Every individual is an exception to the rule."[10] To find any person uncategorizable is to return to the mystery and awe of discovering one another, again and again.

Just a Middle-Aged White Guy

Garry introduced himself to me as "just a white, middle-aged guy in the chemical industry." He added, "I have nothing of particular value to offer."

I find moments like this so awkward. Because even though someone has told me something about themself, they've also told me nothing. If nearly half the population is male, how is that useful for knowing someone's capacity to add value? It's the same for race. Those labels are generic instead of specific, suggesting that race and gender form a single story.

"Tell me more," I asked.

And he did. He talked not only about his supercute dog but also about how deeply frustrated he was by the extractive industry he operated in. He talked not only about friends we had in common but also about why he loves to build community. And so on.

After about 20 minutes, I paused to reflect what I was hearing—what I had learned about Garry—back to him, using his exact language. I said, "I hear you saying that what you care about is X, Y, and Z." I connected his desire to build community with his desire to create change in his industry. I asked if he had ever considered mobilizing the people who cared about changing that extractive industry.

I didn't want to solve anything or direct him.

I wanted to witness him into being.

To say, *Garry, you have a particular point of view based entirely on that spot in the world where only you stand.*

That point of view wasn't *"nothing"* but *"everything."*

In our modern economy, the key to doing our best work isn't efficiency-based—the measure of the rate of return on capital. Rather, it's about utilizing distinct points of view.

Because here's what's changed: Those distinct perspectives, when combined, allow individuals to accomplish what once only large organizations could. Creativity requires both novelty and value—a new way of seeing that matters. And today, value gets created not by owning more assets but by reimagining how existing ones connect. Digitally enabled firms don't win by scale; they win by combining strategy, resources, and insight in novel ways.

And here's the trap: When we focus on abstractions—tests, labels, demographic checklists—we distract from that distinct POV. We reduce people to categories instead of unleashing their irreplaceable perspective. That's why the shift matters.

Because each of us is an *instrument* to be played. Our distinct POV *integral* to doing our best work.

Let's use Steve Jobs as an example again. Today, we know that Jobs is credited with inventing personal computing. But let's think of what formed his POV. Steve was born in Silicon Valley and exposed to early tech. During that era, DEC was the biggest computing technology firm out there, and the CEO once said, "There is no reason for any individual to have a computer in his home." Jobs studied design in college, loved calligraphy, and played with RadioShack kits because his friends did, too. His insight wasn't just technical. It was human. He believed tech could be beautiful. Easy. Personal. That was his distinct point of view—and it changed how the world works. (Not that he did it alone; he didn't.)

Let's add another example: Airbnb's founders initially received a lot of pushback because no one could see many people letting strangers use their homes. It was a novel POV from folks who regularly couch-surfed.

And one more. Filmmaker Ava DuVernay tells stories that shift systems by grounding them in how they're felt. In *Selma*, she doesn't just show us Martin Luther King Jr. the icon; she shows us the tension, the fatigue, the fear pulsing through a movement asking to be heard. In *13th*, she draws a straight line from slavery to modern mass incarceration, and makes you feel every link in the chain. With *When They See Us*, she takes what could've been a procedural about the Central Park Five and instead gives us a devastating, intimate portrait of stolen boyhood. Each work foregrounds human dignity while confronting structural inequality with emotional precision and political clarity. That's her distinct point of view—she doesn't just argue that the system is broken; she makes you feel how it breaks people.

That's what a distinct point of view does.

It adds value. Distinct value. By helping us see what's possible. What's broken. What needs fixing. And what matters to us.

Tests can't tell you that. Labels can't either.

They help us *sort*. But they don't help us *see*.

Garry and I have stayed in touch over the years. Recently, as we were catching up, he shared how he had helped a local Green political party grow its seats threefold.

And he said it before I did. He was using his POV to create change. "Who I am," he said, "isn't just about being a middle-aged white guy."

So true. And so freeing.

Because labels can't sum up a person. They can't offer what we most want and need: to be seen for who we truly are. Labels kill curiosity. And curiosity is what fuels insight. And that distinct insight each of us has? It's what fuels value.

That Spot on Which You Stand

This is not to say that race and gender do not shape us. They do. Of course they do. Race and gender are some of the identities we're born into. We also inherit where we are born, our native language, our family religion, and many other identity elements. We can call these *vertical identities*— who you are based on whom you were born to.

But identifying yourself primarily by your race or gender misses what you care about, the choices you've made about what to study or even *if* to study, the friends you choose, your hobbies and interests, what you choose to read, and so on—what we can call *horizontal identities*.

Combined, you stand in your distinct axis point in the world. Where only you stand. That specific combination of history, experiences, visions, and hopes makes up who you are, what you care about, and how you work and connect. And create value.

This *blend* of identities is what forms your point of view.

A perspective distinctly your own.

It's something that no test can or should capture in 4, 9, or 16 quadrants.

The stakes for why we need to get rid of standardized tests at work are high. The world of AI is coming faster than any of us can imagine, and it will be able to do the work that can be programmed and then help reprogram itself to do more. If we know how an ENTJ would do something, we can code that. If we know how an analytic person would process something, we can code that, too.

What is valuable in this AI-assisted world where machine learning tells us known things? It's the new and fresh points of view that we each come up with. That distinct point of view. Which is yours today and will evolve again tomorrow.

Curiosity Is the Killer App

There's one place where we don't want to reduce complexity. It's with people. Never with people.

People are not easy to understand, and—this is important—*they aren't meant to be.* We humans are specific, complex, and ever-changing. That is a good thing. We are meant to work at understanding ourselves and each other. That is work worth doing.

And when we see our perspective as distinct, we allow ourselves to see the uncommon, contrarian, or novel. With that perspective, one can add value.

This point of view is not one single thing but the accumulation of the many parts of you, your fullness of identity. If you are just doing what everyone else is, that's a commodity view—one you could find on the shelf of any big-box idea warehouse. When you have a commodity view, you are saying, "My opinion is replaceable by that of anyone else here." In comparison, a distinct point of view says, "I see what I see, and here's where I might change things, add things, and build things."

Labels kill curiosity.

Every industry, business, and team has orthodoxies that can and should be questioned. Uncommon or novel approaches can be the key to changing any of those. And we limit value creation by not believing that each of us has a POV to offer.

People sometimes ask me what we would do if we didn't have the MBTI test. I want to suggest a new protocol. It's a tool that is far more reliable in understanding human complexity, practically infallible, and surprisingly practical. It helps you understand and improve your relationships with people. It also helps you learn how to communicate better, especially in the face of conflict.

That tool? Curiosity.

And it's something AI doesn't have. By being curious, we pay attention. We come to know people. We allow ourselves to be surprised. We notice how someone may be different today than yesterday. We see how someone's point of view may change after a tough project or even after a good conversation.

Curiosity is a killer app, and I can tell you how to deploy it to maximize its impact.

It's with this single request: *Tell me more.*

And then we'll all listen to each other, and that's the point. Not only will we gain the benefit of the information but we will also increase our capability to have difficult conversations. Those ongoing conversations, not the assessments, will improve relationships and organizational results.

Don't Assign Work, Choose It

One of the most interesting organizations in America is W. L. Gore & Associates. Many know them because of Gore-Tex—the waterproof fabric.

But what I want to focus on is their insides, the way they organize work. It's really . . . different. And powerful.

At Gore, when they form teams, they do something that sounds simple but is actually pretty radical: They really, really pay attention to who people *are*. What they can do. What they want to do. Who they actually show up as—not just what's written on their résumé or what their job title says.

The whole company runs on what they call a "lattice structure"—no formal hierarchy, no bosses in the traditional sense. Instead, people connect directly with each other. You figure out what you need and build that team yourself. Equally, you self-assign to projects based on where you think you could add your distinct point of view, your interests, your passions. Even the person leading isn't determined until the team is assembled. Leadership is something you *do* when the situation matches one's contribution, not a role that's assigned to you.

Now, when you join Gore, you're hired for your capabilities and then you're paired with a sponsor—not a manager. A sponsor is someone whose job is to help you figure out where you fit, what you're good at, where you can make the biggest impact. They're there to *know* you, not to control you. Or, it's fairer to say, they are there to help you know yourself. Which means their job is to help you understand your skills, your aspirations, and where you need to grow—what they would call your learning edges. Sponsors help not by having a list of what you're *supposed* to be doing but by having an ongoing conversation about what you *could* be doing.

Then—and this is key—they don't get you assigned to projects. You *choose* them. You *commit* to them. You *connect your value to the value being created together*. And so you're signaling where you think you can most help, what part you want to be responsible for. It's a system that leans hard on agency and accountability. You're not hiding or getting behind orders from above.

You're making a choice. And choices have consequences.

Of course, this creates some tension. What happens if someone commits to a project but can't deliver? Or isn't a good fit for what the team needs? Gore has built a norm of peer feedback—people are expected to talk about the situation and conflicts directly. To be honest, respectful, but also urgent in naming what's going on. There's no manager to step in and fix it—it's on the team to surface issues, recalibrate roles, and make necessary changes.

It reminds me of a project I did in business school. In what's called the capstone class, you have to do a final project, in a group. That one paper determines most of your grade and is meant to synthesize all your learnings in the program. Because so much depends on this group project, most students pre-assemble their team, choosing whom they want to work with. Then they sign up for the class together, picking, for example, the 5:30 p.m. session in a certain quarter. I was part of a pre-assembled team. When a student joined the class at the last minute, the professor asked if one of the established groups would take him in. Mine did. And then we regretted it. He'd show up late, nearly at the last minute of study sessions. He'd turn in his assignments, but they were of such poor quality, we could tell he was just going through the motions.

My team and I gave him feedback that he needed to do better. But nothing changed.

Finally, one Saturday, we gathered at 9 a.m. for an all-day-long work session and the guy was MIA. I named it with the group and asked whether we were going to say something. Everyone saw the conflict: He wasn't adding to the team, but he was benefitting from our work. I left him a voicemail, saying how not okay it was that he was doing another no-show. Then I texted our professor. Would it be okay if we fired the guy? It would mean he wouldn't pass the class, right? The professor gave us the green light and told us it wasn't our job to manage who passed the class. Our job was to manage our performance.

When our supposed teammate showed up at noon, I took him aside and delivered the news. Later, the professor gave our group the highest grade he'd ever given, because we'd done the hardest thing involved in teamwork: created accountability.

Gore is doing the same. It's a very adult system. Which is to say it expects us all to be accountable. It expects a lot of self-awareness, a lot of conversation to connect, and a lot of curiosity to figure out what to fix. And if things get really stuck, they have HR systems in place—but even those are designed to coach and guide, not command. HR is trained to help teams work through performance dynamics early, before they fester into real problems. But the decisions are team-based.

There's another piece that I love: Gore builds in what they call "dabble time." Associates are *expected* to spend a portion of their time exploring new ideas—things outside their main job. It's like a company-sanctioned curiosity hour. And what that does is deepen skills, foster new interests, and build unexpected collaborations. Innovation doesn't come from sitting still. Or working from what we already know. Gore knows that. They've baked that into the rhythm of how people work.

The model assumes the best of people in three ways. First, that people *want* to contribute. Second, that people *know* what they can do (or can learn). And third, that *peer accountability*—not top-down authority—can drive alignment.

And it works.

Gore has stayed innovative for decades across wildly different industries—not because they find "perfect" people but because they build the systems and scaffolding that let people be fully, distinctively themselves, and then hold each other accountable for what they choose to do.

Some people will say they *can* do this because they're a privately held company. Or because their technology is *so* profitable. Or because of something else that makes Gore do what others deem impossible. All of that could be true. It could also be true that the reason their technology is so profitable is because they maximize creativity in their team assignments. Or that they can be privately held because they're clear on what they value. Chicken or egg. There's an argument to be made both ways. Gore's not a utopia outlier but a company that has figured out how to enable everyone to be seen in the messy—which is to say human—world of work.

It's a living example that organizations don't have to box up a person to utilize that person's capacities. That's the cage too many organizations impose, without meaning to.

A label is a container. It could hold a piece of who we are. It offers a way in. But because we're alive, we're always in motion—growing, shedding, becoming. And that's how labels sneak up on us. Slowly, we become trapped. None of us end where we begin. We're not meant to. That's the problem with labels: Categories freeze us in time and call it done. Curiosity does the opposite. It doesn't box us in—it points us forward. It reveals our interests, our questions, and our next Self.

When we give ourselves permission to learn who we are—to be curious rather than categorized—we reclaim the fullness of our identity. And that fullness isn't just vital to feeling alive; it's how we contribute something original and essential to the world—value that no one else can offer but everyone benefits from.

INNOVATION PRACTICE
The Five Stories

Goal: Learn how to witness someone into being.

Ask people to *tell you more.*

Specifically, find someone you work with and ask them to share a story of their life and how that story shaped who they are today. As you listen, notice not just what happened but what choices they made.

- Ask about those choices and why they made them.
- Ask what they would do if faced with the same situation tomorrow; anything differently?
- Invite them to tell you what they think it means to how they approach their work today.
- If you do this over five stories (over time), you'll have a sense of what matters to this person, and even more importantly, why. (This can be something you keep doing.)
- Repeat back what you hear so clarity is aligned. It's not about your interpretation but about their clarity.

When we understand what drives someone's distinct point of view, we can celebrate it, integrate it, and tap into it for the benefit of the whole.

16

You Are Not for Sale

Limiting Norm: Recognition

Leading Indicator: Relevance

It does something corrosive to the soul to be forced into selling itself—to have to tell others, "Hey, I matter."

Yet the pressure to package, polish, and position yourself is nonstop. It feels unnatural because your true Self doesn't want to be marketed. Your authentic Self, the part of you that knows you add value in your own distinct way, simply wants to be seen, recognized, and valued.

So why, then, do we all buy into personal branding?

We care about branding because our workplaces demand it, equating it with success. But let's confront the harsh truth: Workplaces use personal brands to match us to a scope of work and then put us "to use." We've become so accustomed to this that we fail to see how branding converts us into products—pitchable, marketable, and, ultimately, disposable. To productize a person is to flatten their complexity into a single, sellable narrative. Once you're branded, you're only as valuable as your continued "usefulness." And in a world that treats people like products, it becomes easier to downsize, right-size, or "optimize"—all euphemisms that mask the brutal truth of discarding human beings as if they were obsolete inventory.

Yet so many of us yearn to have a better brand.

A Brand Is the Exhaust Fume of the Engine of Life

"I've really been looking forward to picking your brain about becoming a thought leader," Joshua said as soon as we met. We did the double kiss that people do in Europe, even though both of us were Americans.

"Oh, well, then you might be disappointed." I had a feeling he wanted me to talk about how to get published, give talks, and shape a platform. And while I get why those things matter, this question of people wanting to be thought leaders represents so much of what is stopping us from doing the work that matters.

As we talked, Joshua shared specifics. He wanted to leave his day job in NYC because he was burned out and wanted to transition to a different field. He'd been doing advocacy work within the progressive movements but had a hard time earning money that way, so he had also been doing marketing campaigns for products he really didn't like. He hated managing people more than he could describe. And so on and so on.

He hoped I could tell him the secret of being a "thought leader." He wanted to become so well-known and recognized that he could pivot to do more meaningful work.

And I wondered, *Why the pit stop?*

Once you're branded, you're only as valuable as your continued "usefulness."

Branding is—at its best—about clarifying the relevance of something or someone so it can be recognized and seen. However, in its current use, personal branding is more about recognition and less about relevance. We talk about building the "brand called you" instead of creating the work you love to do. We discuss ways to be a "thought leader" without asking first, "What original thoughts do you have?" We are told by marketing gurus that "everyone now owns a media company," as if making noise in the market is itself the goal rather than a means to an end.

Marketing has become the default language—the lingua franca of the day—for describing the value of work, and it is distorting how we measure what matters.

And here was Joshua, the CEO of a media company, sharing how he wanted to publish a book, give a TED Talk, and be recognized as an influential thinker.

I suggested that he stop using marketing language to discuss meaning. I said: The brand follows the work. Your brand is the exhaust fumes created by the engine of your life. It is a by-product of what happens as you share what you are making and with whom you are creating. It is a sign, yes. Significant, yes. But the real signal comes from answering these three questions:

- What do you care about?
- Who else cares about that, too?
- How are you all doing the work?

That's how you can create real value. You do what you care about and find those who care about the same thing and, together, you make an impact.

Do I Have To?

While co-teaching a course at Stanford, I was swamped with students wanting one-on-one meetings. My assistant pointed out how they were devouring my schedule like locusts. She asked how many hours this group was allowed.

I had been trying to get into a regular exercise routine but was struggling. Between work, family, and everything else, self-care was always on the back burner. Around that same time, venture capitalist Heidi Roizen suggested we have a walking meeting. It was fantastic—we covered a lot, both literally and figuratively. Inspired by her, I decided that all student meetings would be walks. That way, I'd get my much-needed exercise while helping others.

This became my near-daily routine. Anyone wanting coaching, advice, or anything from me had to join me for a walk. I averaged 200 walking meetings a year. These walks turned out to be creative and connected times.

I started telling colleagues about these walking meetings and encouraging them to try them out. Some did and found them equally transformative. Those folks became evangelists, too, and word spread. Some of them worked at TED. One day, they apparently compared notes about how they had adopted this new habit.

When TED asked me to speak about my walking meetings, I thought they were joking. I had many ideas about improving work—couldn't I give a talk about that? But they were convinced this was an idea worth spreading. When I gave the talk, I had five years and nearly 1,000 walks under my belt. I didn't need or want recognition on this topic. In fact, it probably puzzled people—why was this strategist speaking on walking?

I almost said no because of my "brand"; I wanted to be seen as more serious or something. But I said yes because I could see the value of sharing what I cared about. If I had focused on the optics, I would have trapped myself in a smaller box, a productized version of me.

Boxing ourselves up limits who we are and who we can become; it limits our best work.

The talk—"Sitting Is the New Smoking"—definitely made me slightly better known, but the interesting part I pointed out to Joshua is that it added value. The Apple Watch has a stand feature and a 10,000-step feature because of those three minutes I spoke onstage. Some researchers from Stanford met with me and asked me to shape some research. That research was well circulated. And it led to the productization of stand-up desks and watch features and so on. Which is how all of us act differently.

So to Joshua, I said, Listen, I didn't *aim* to give that TED Talk; I did what mattered to my life, and the rest just took care of itself. Why not do that?

Branding is about gaining *attention*. Branding might increase the price one can charge for a product, but it doesn't lead to more value being created. Value creation is about *connection*—of ideas and of people around those ideas so that they become real. If value creation in the industrial era was about building things, value creation in the modern era is about connecting things, people, and ideas. This is not to say that branding doesn't matter; it does, but not as the prime directive. We should not forget that the real signal is the work itself, and social signaling is just its echo. One is the engine, the other the fumes.

That's why I find it untenable that workplaces promote personal branding. If you're not being valued enough, brand yourself better, says the company HR leader. This redirection on brand puts the onus on the person being undervalued rather than fixing the workplace to better notice the individual and distinct talents that each of us already has.

It hurts so many people in so many ways, but it is always in invisible and intangible ways so the people themselves can't see what has happened and what to change.

We Are All Maya

Maya was exceptional at promoting herself.

She had a super impressive résumé documenting what she had done and how she could do it for others. I was ready to hire her to help me with some communications work so I could focus on other things. But I always reference-check people, not by contacting the people someone gives me but by using my own independent sources. I figured out whom I knew who might also know this person to hear about their experience.

And I learned some things about Maya:

"She used to cry in a hallway closet before and after every meeting. She was so in over her head."

"Those numbers she's using on her résumé are off by a factor of 10."

"Someone actually good at leading wouldn't make the kinds of mistakes she makes."

I thought about just not hiring her.

I also wondered if the feedback about her was gendered or ageist; it could reflect the bias of the people giving me their perspective.

And as I thought about it, I also saw why Maya was doing what she was doing. What so many of us feel the need to do. Because we have to. Because of how much pressure there is to land a job, how HR encourages and rewards having a personal brand, how future bosses would compare her résumé to others', and how getting hired meant standing out. From the time she graduated, every passing of a business card relied on an unshaking, confident smile and a slew of larger-than-life career accomplishments. Thus, the cycle continued.

And we can lose ourselves in it.

When personal branding becomes more about creating a façade or projecting an image that doesn't align with who you are, it can lead to feelings of disconnection and emptiness. After a while, you don't even know yourself. So you push even harder on personal branding to signal you're okay to yourself. Until you are so lost that you can't find your way back to yourself, to that home that you always carry with you.

So I decided to ask Maya if she'd like some feedback on what I'd learned.

"Here's what I heard you say," I started, listing off what I believed she had conveyed to me about her capabilities. Maya was smiling and nodding, so happy to see that I had remembered so many details of the stories she had sent me or told me.

After I confirmed my understanding of what I'd heard from her, I shared what I had learned from her former clients, not those on the list she had given me but people I had sourced.

And her face grew still. Her lower chin hardened, probably because she was trying to hold it together. It's hard to be questioned about one's reputation. But there was a clear gap between what she said she could do and what others said.

I asked the hard question: *What do you think that gap is about?*

Her explanation was this: *I am a recognized expert in this area.* She listed the media events, placements, articles, ideas, and brands she was involved with. It took her a while to share the extent of her media profile.

I waited.

Then I shared my take, using her words: *recognized expert.* I pointed out that everything she had just told me was about *recognition*, and I was asking about *expertise*.

I wanted her to see that *recognition* without the underlying *relevance* was damaging.

And there was no answer.

She knew how to get attention for something that, in most cases, she didn't know enough about. And I said, "Hey, listen, come back to me when you're ready to learn and grow. You care about this stuff, I can tell, but you have to be willing not to know long enough to learn new things."

From that depth of knowing more, we get to figure out our distinct perspective on things—what works, what doesn't, what's missing, and what could be better. And that distinct point of view will lead you to build, create, and change things. And that's how you'll end up really being recognized for what you care about.

I said all of this to Maya.

What I didn't say then is something I say now.

It does something to the soul to have to sell itself. And it's the cause of market failures.

Branding Eats Truth

It started with a story.

Elizabeth Holmes didn't begin with fraud. She began with an aspiration—a sleek vision of a simpler future, where a single drop of blood could unlock early answers and save lives.

Holmes cultivated not just an idea but an identity. The deep voice, the black turtlenecks, the Steve Jobs comparisons—these weren't accidental. She understood something elemental about modern power: If you can craft a strong enough narrative, the facts might never catch up.

It wasn't just the product that investors were buying; it was her brand. To the tune of nearly a billion dollars.

She was what Silicon Valley, and the hustle culture, call "fundable."

And in a world where brand precedes substance, that was enough.

Holmes raised hundreds of millions of dollars not by proving that her technology worked but by telling a compelling story that it someday would. She borrowed language from Apple and promises from Edison. She even named her machine "Edison."

When challenged, she said things like: "First they think you're crazy, then they fight you, then you change the world."[1] This quote is a paraphrased

version of a saying often misattributed to Mahatma Gandhi: "First they ignore you, then they laugh at you, then they fight you, then you win." Holmes
adapted it to align with her narrative of being a misunderstood innovator
facing resistance while attempting to revolutionize healthcare.

As if she didn't deserve to be questioned.

It was disruptive. And efficient. And iconic. But it was never true.

As the world soon learned, the device didn't work.[2] Not early on, not
later. Theranos manipulated test results. It used commercial machines
behind the scenes. The company's blood tests gave dangerously inaccurate
results. But none of that stopped Holmes from raising hundreds of millions from investors or from signing deals with Walgreens and Safeway.

Because the story worked.

But here's where things get darker. What happened at Theranos
wasn't simply fraud. It was a feedback loop of deception and belief, of
how brand management becomes exaggeration becomes conviction. *Wall
Street Journal* reporter John Carreyrou framed it this way: "By positioning
Theranos as a tech company in the heart of the Valley, Holmes channeled
this fake-it-until-you-make-it culture, and she went to extreme lengths to
hide the fakery."

Startups often live in the gray area between ambition and reality,
promising what they hope to deliver later. Hyping your product to get
funding while concealing your true progress and hoping that reality will
eventually catch up to the hype is not only tolerated but encouraged in the
tech industry.

That's the part that hurts. It wasn't that Holmes was uniquely de-
ceptive. It's that she followed the script a little too well. She dressed the
part, she went to the right schools, she networked with the right people,
she used the perfect jargon, and she was passionate as she insisted—over
and over—that success was just around the corner. Eventually, even she
seemed to believe what she was saying. So that when her own employees
told her, "We've been fooling investors. We can't keep doing that," she
tried to have them fired for insubordination.[3]

And they kept fooling investors. Because once the brand machine is
turned on, it has to keep going. The persona is no longer tied to a person.
The vision is no longer tethered to reality.

That's where the cost of branding stuff grows. It's not just that a company failed, but that lives were endangered because the story took precedence over the science. People got test results they couldn't trust. Some were told they had cancer. Others were falsely cleared. This wasn't just a branding error. It was medical malpractice wrapped in marketing genius.

And yet when challenged, all Holmes had to do was say she was being resilient. At Stanford Business School, she once said: "I think the minute you have a backup plan, you've admitted you're not going to succeed."[4]

This is when grit and brand join together to form a delusion.

And yet Holmes kept going. Since I've met her, I can tell you that she wasn't evil in some comic-book way. Not in the least. She was more like a fragile doll. Speaking in a quiet voice, not her manly one; wearing colorful clothes, not the black turtleneck that was part of her façade; and cuddling with her part-wolf puppy. My sense as I talked with her was that she was so lost in the image making that she just couldn't find her true Self anymore. This is what "fake it till you make it" and "personal branding" lead you to. It's the collateral damage.

Theranos is what happens when branding eats the truth.

It's tempting to treat the Theranos situation as an outlier. A cautionary tale. A singular fraud. But that misses the point. Holmes is simply one node in a larger system that rewards narrative over nuance, confidence over competence, velocity over veracity. Her story is our story, too. It's about how much we care about the optics vs. reality and how intently we focus on gaining recognition vs. creating relevance.

When the brand becomes more powerful than the work, the consequences aren't just financial—they're moral. They're social. In the end, branding didn't just cover up the lie—it *was* the lie. And that's what made it so powerful.

And so fatal.

It does something to the soul to have to sell itself.

It's worth repeating.

We do not have to market ourselves; we need to be ourselves.

Wendell Berry once wrote, "We have replaced the old market on which people were sold with a new market on which people sell themselves."[5] That quote stays with me—because it names exactly what branding asks of us. The practice of branding is a little too reminiscent of humanity's worst practice, trading humans in a marketplace and documenting them on a balance sheet. According to those who have researched accounting for slavery, people were evaluated and assessed based on their productivity levels and fertility. An accounting ledger turned someone's humanity into a numerical value.[6] Worth was determined by the ruthless whims of supply and demand and by whether the person could do certain things.

Not too dissimilar from personal branding.

While a lot is different between someone earning $70K at a call center and another working in the field for no wages, the echoes are the same. The cold, indifferent pen strokes define someone's worth. When humans aren't commodities.

That's why personal branding is so harmful.

None of us are meant to be used.

We each deserve to be valued.

INNOVATION PRACTICE
Signal Without Selling

We all want to be seen for the work we care about. But in a world of personal branding, even our attempts to share can become performative. We shape posts, bios, and updates to prove our worth—not to create value. Even the best of us can smuggle in the ego's hunger to be admired. This practice helps you spot if you're signaling what matters . . . or if you're marketing yourself. (Pair up with someone.)

1. **Name it.** Before you post or share anything, say out loud what you're about to post and your intention behind it. What are you trying to shine a light on?

2. **Ask your partner:** "Is this adding value? Or is it trying to *sell* the idea that I *can* add value?"

3. **Rewrite or release.** If it's the latter, revise it—or don't post at all. Try creating something that doesn't need to prove anything.

4. **Document the discomfort.** Do morning pages to log the following: What did you want to say, and what did you actually say? What did it cost you to *not* posture? And if you postured, what did it feel like to be creating an image of yourself vs. showing yourself?

5. **Reflect.** At week's end, ask each other:

   Where did you feel the pull to prove?

   Where did the best contributions come from—and what made them feel true?

Do this practice for one week. You'll start to see how much of your communication is about being seen—and how to shift toward being understood.

17

Cease and Desist Bad Behavior

Limiting Norm: Whatever Happens, Happens
Leading Indicator: What We Allow Happens

We all want freedom—the kind that allows us to be fully alive at work, to matter, to make something true. But what most of us miss is that freedom doesn't—*cannot*—survive without limits. Rules and their consequences are the necessary container for freedom. They don't confine us—they steady us. They make it possible to show up, shape the work, and stay in the room when things get hard. Without consequences for bad behavior, our capacity to innovate—let alone excel—is stifled.

Alex Krasne found this out the hard way.

Usually the epitome of good humor, my friend was seething. She had devised a zany and creative marketing idea for her firm. Securing the budget, designing a content strategy, hiring a creative agency, and then doing all the related work had consumed Alex and her team for a full six months. This was on top of their already demanding jobs.

And then the unthinkable happened.

"Before the idea was announced, one of my coworkers, a PR guy, shared the idea—*my* idea—with the CEO and CMO." I watched her pace around my kitchen, her face getting redder and redder. "While he didn't *exactly say* he'd done the work himself, how he talked about it made it seem like it was all his."

"Did you tell anyone, go to your manager?" I asked.

Alex stopped her pacing. "I did, and he said, 'When you're creative, people will steal your ideas—you should just get used to that fact.'"

I sympathized, but I wasn't surprised.

As we talked, I could hear that under Alex's anger was something else—curiosity. About what this all meant. About what she *could* have, or *should* have, done differently.

Was *she* the problem?

Did she need to figure out how to play the game better?

Was the PR guy the issue?

Or her boss?

And if it was her boss, did she need to quit?

Those were the wrong questions, I told her.

It's not you or them. The problem lies in the norm of tolerating bad behavior.

When our workplaces say, "Creative ideas get stolen," it's the equivalent of "Boys will be boys." These excuses normalize bad behavior. Making harm a given, not a choice. Just as "Boys will be boys" permits everything from aggressive behavior to entitlement and even criminal acts against girls and women, "Creative ideas get stolen" validates aggressiveness and entitlement and harms the least powerful among us.

Ideas get stolen *because* there's no accountability.

To be clear, sometimes an idea is just in the air, and two or more people come to it around the same time. And oftentimes, we create ideas together. I'm not talking about those moments.

I'm talking about when it's fully apparent what is happening—idea theft, where one party gets or takes credit for the work of others—and how theft is tolerated. Research shows that knowledge workers are keenly aware of idea theft; nearly one-third report having had it happen to them.[1]

The Cost of Theft

Work says idea theft is no big deal.

It's as if one flower is being picked from an entire field of wildflowers. "Oh well, who cares who grew the flower . . . as long as the organization got it?"

This shows just how much work doesn't understand the implications:

- Integrity is lost when ideas are disconnected from their source. The depth of the concept or the completeness of the thinking is lost. Downstream decisions are made without the rootedness of the original inspiration. Idea integrity—the state of being whole and undivided—is necessary for the successful execution of any idea.

- Theft demotivates the next idea. When ideas are stolen regularly, idea generation shuts down because no one volunteers to be violated.
- It divides the team. Organizations often excuse this behavior by saying, "Ideas are a dime a dozen; execution is everything." This reaffirms the two camps model, an unnecessary division between those who do the thinking and those who do execution work. This separation hurts those who must work together to turn nascent ideas into new realities.
- Originality is denied. Allowing idea theft communicates that originality—that distinct point of view each of us has—doesn't matter or matters only if it comes bundled with power. Originality is rooted in each of us but stolen from only some. After all, no one steals Steve Jobs's or Sir Richard Branson's ideas. (Jobs, for what it's worth, is wrongly credited with the famous "Think Different" campaign when that couldn't be further from the truth.)[2] Thus, we limit the 70% of ideas from people who are traditionally powerless.
- The ultimate definition of success is the ability to repeat it. The next time work needs original ideas and creativity, they won't know how to find the source—that idea wildflower field that is Alex; they will instead seek out the idea thief. Allowing theft means they get just one winning shot rather than becoming a winning team over time.

The costs of idea theft are enormous.

The cost of bad behavior is even bigger. Bob Sutton, whom we've already mentioned, defined and wrote a book about asshole behavior. He developed the TCA ("Total Cost of Assholes"), a metric to show the cost to workplaces. He defined not only how to spot an asshole—how they are addicted to interruptions and insist on being right, while enjoying sarcastic jokes and "teasing" as an insult delivery system—but calculated the TCA. He created an economic measure to calculate the cost of individual bad behavior on the whole team—so that many companies today have instituted a "no asshole rule."[3]

We need to extend this calculation.

It's the Barrel

It's not just individuals who do bad things—a few "bad apples"—that harm. It's also the organizational norms—the barrel—that create rot and reinforce bad behavior.

- **Scarcity.** We often operate within a scarcity mindset, where the belief is that resources, recognition, and opportunities are limited and finite. This forces people into a cycle of self-preservation and competition. At Alex's workplace, this drove the competition to take credit for the few creative ideas.
- **Superiority.** The idea that some can just take what they want from others suggests a sense of superiority. In my experience—and based on all the self-help books one can read—this sense of superiority is rooted in insecurity. It's what drives someone like Jobs to take credit for an ad when he had *plenty* of other things he rightly could have taken credit for.
- **The lack of consequences.** The lack of accountability enables the harm. It's Alex's boss telling her to ignore it instead of fixing it.

This echoes history.

The colonization of the Americas had the same scarcity mindset, superiority, and lack of consequences. European settlers, driven by the belief that land and resources were limited, saw Indigenous peoples as obstacles to their survival and prosperity. Positioning themselves as superior and with no one to administer accountability, they justified the displacement, exploitation, and genocide of Indigenous communities to claim land and wealth for themselves. This ruthless behavior of colonization—the act of settling in a territory and exerting control over the people who live there as if some do not deserve sovereignty—has been behind centuries of violence and oppression. Those who funded this latest set of colonizers, primarily the French, Spanish, and British governments, felt no consequences for their prior theft of land and resources.

To them, it was "no big deal" that Native people were killed and their land stolen.

Today's corporate idea theft is part of that lineage.

And to be sure, Alex's boss *is* right about one thing: Alex will certainly create more ideas. People create when they feel safe enough to imagine something new. That—by definition—is why regulating bad behavior matters. And the boss's actions negate just how valuable Alex's contribution is. He assumes, too, that he and the work will continue to be the beneficiaries despite their treatment of Alex. That idea? The one stolen? It was one of the firm's most successful efforts that year. It inspired the company's next ad campaign and the related Super Bowl ad.

But they didn't have any follow-up to this one-off success.

Why?

Because they no longer had Alex.

Consequences Are Not a Private Act

I told Alex to leave. I could see the danger in her situation more clearly than she could. That's how it works, oftentimes. Like frogs in boiling water, we adjust to harm—until someone else names it out loud.

My moment came on St. Joseph's hiking trail, of all places.

"I locked my door last night," Kathleen said as the dust rose in soft puffs under our feet.

She explained how she had lain awake for hours replaying dinner. The reason? Hubster. He'd been drinking, and a conversation about politics had spiraled. He'd leaned in, red-faced, voice rising as if his volume could beat her expertise. Kathleen, who'd stood her ground in New York courtrooms and public town halls, had frozen.

She stopped mid-stride, in the shadow of an oak tree, and looked me in the eye.

"Now I believe you," she said quietly. "This is what you've been trying to tell me—he's rageful, irrational, nasty. And his so-called apology? No responsibility at all."

Her words named the norm.

I explained my experience: It seemed to me that his outbursts stemmed from fear, a desire to feel worthy of the conversation. How I had heard the story of how he had yelled at his eldest daughter before we married but hadn't believed it, hadn't believed her. I thought I had married someone who would never raise his voice. But then he did. Rarely, at first; he said he did it to "clear up misunderstandings." Now when he lost control, it was my fault. "I wouldn't yell if you didn't make me," he'd say.

I didn't tell Kathleen this, but I had started wearing sneakers whenever he was around.

I asked why she hadn't called him out in the moment. I thought it would be similar to my reason: What's the use in naming the fire to someone who's going to insist the smoke is your fault?

Her answer was clear: "It's not my job to fix him," she said. "His behavior was wrong—unacceptable—no matter what I did or didn't do. It wasn't yours to fix either."

Her certainty was solid, like the trail beneath us.

Mine wasn't.

For years, I'd told myself that if I yelled back, I'd forfeited the moral ground. That I was complicit by having participated in the dance. That's how these power dynamics work: Once you defend yourself with the same tools used to harm you, the clarity erodes.[4] From the outside, the harm looks mutual. Murkiness enables more harm and entraps the harmed.

Kathleen naming it—and setting a clear boundary—was a shift that gave me hope. I wasn't imagining it. I was no longer alone. And the problem wasn't mine to fix.

Later, in therapy, Hubster began yelling so close that some spit hit my face. The therapist, Harry, intervened. "You're allowed to feel anger, but not to harm others with it. That's not okay."

Someone had named it. Again. It's not okay.

This time, it was someone with authority. A boundary had been set. And it held.

Relief.

And I understood: This isn't work any of us do alone.

If bad behavior is tolerated, it grows. When it meets consequences, it stops. Bad behavior isn't mysterious—it's simply a crime of opportunity, repeated when no one intervenes.

This is not a personal problem. It's a social problem. It's up to those who see it to act—to create the consequences. Not just to protect the harmed, but to stop the harm from spreading.

If You Change the Rules, You Change the Game

We're taught to "be nice," not to "make a scene," and to "go along to get along." We're told it's "just the way things are"—the boss who belittles, the friend who crosses lines, the leader who abuses power. We learn early that staying quiet keeps the peace, that calling something out might cost us something we can't afford to lose—our job, our standing, our place in the room. And so, we hesitate. We wait. We hope it doesn't happen again. And of course, those who behave badly hide it *just enough* so they have plausible deniability. They act like a "good guy" with others. Then, privately, they tell us we imagined it, gaslighting us. As witnesses to someone's bad behavior, we might even question if we *should* do something; after all, we don't want to overstep and caretake another person and undermine their agency to take care of themselves.

Underneath all this, we hear the whisper: *What difference will calling it out make?*

Yet we all know that silence has a cost. It makes us complicit in what we ache to change.

When we enter any relationship, we agree on how to come together. Whether that agreement has accountability is what keeps it solid.

In sports, the rules shape everything. In soccer, the size of the field, the number of players, the offside call, the red card—none of it is incidental. It's the rules that create the game. A defender doesn't hold back out of personal virtue—they do it because a foul has consequences. A striker doesn't hover by the goal because the offside rule makes that move irrelevant. The flow, the drama, even the beauty of the game—they're all made possible by these social rules. The rules enable good play.

The same is true at work. What we allow is what happens.

- When we listen to the person who constantly interrupts, we reward dominance.
- When we let deadlines slide without consequences, we make reliability optional.
- When we allow people to steal ideas, we allow credit to eclipse contribution.

The norms aren't just background noise. They're the rules of our game. They quietly decide who gets ahead, who gets heard, and what kind of play is possible. And like in soccer, if we want a good game, we don't blame the players—we enforce the rules.

Commons-ing

When something harmful happens at work—when someone talks over a colleague, constantly launches into monologues, gets red-faced with anger when things aren't going their way, dismisses a contribution, or grabs credit that wasn't theirs—our instincts split: ignore it or wait for someone in charge to handle it. This is the bystander effect, a well-documented social phenomenon where the more people witness harm, the less likely any one of them is to act. It's not just about fear or apathy—it's about diffusion. Everyone assumes that someone else will do something. So no one does.

We've been taught to behave this way. Those in charge have sold us the idea that they are the best provisioners of care: well intentioned, competent, and uniquely qualified. It's why servant leadership gets so much praise. When we believe care flows from authority, that those in charge are the arbiters of care, we not only submit to their power, we rely on it.

The underlying assumption—the invisible norm—is that care isn't something we can give each other.

But what if that's wrong?

What if waiting for someone else to save us is exactly what keeps toxic dynamics alive?

There's a different model. And it doesn't require more rules, more leadership. It requires more ownership—by us.

This is where the work of political economist Elinor Ostrom becomes relevant. In 2009, she won the Nobel Prize in economics for proving something that went against decades of economic orthodoxy: that shared resources don't always need top-down regulation. Before her research, economists widely believed in the "tragedy of the commons"—the idea that when a resource, like a river or a fishery, is shared, individuals will overuse it, deplete it, and destroy it. The only fix, it was thought, was external control: private ownership or government regulation.

Ostrom proved otherwise. She showed that communities, left to their own devices, often devise highly sophisticated, self-governed systems of shared management. Systems where consequences don't come from a distant authority—they come from the group itself. The people who depend on each other can also hold each other accountable.

Her work wasn't about office politics. But it applies.

Every team shares something. It might not be water or grazing land. It might be trust. Energy. Credit. Voice. And just like natural resources, these intangible goods get depleted when people act only in their own interest at the cost of shared interest.

When a manager takes all the credit.

When someone interrupts constantly.

When emotional labor always falls on the same shoulders.

What Ostrom teaches us is that we don't have to live inside that dynamic. We can protect shared goods—not with permission from the top, but through practices we design ourselves. Through consequences we create and apply together.

Here's how to do that—a five-part framework for building consequences into the daily fabric of teamwork.

1. **Get clarity on what's acceptable and what's not.**
   Consequences work only when they're tied to something
   clearly defined. That starts with naming the behaviors that
   erode trust and fairness. Is it interrupting? Dismissing?
   Withholding information? Talking over someone? Taking
   credit? Most teams never do this explicitly. So people know
   something is wrong but feel too unsure or isolated to act.
   Clarity removes that confusion. It says: Here's what we
   expect of each other. And it's just as important to name
   what's welcome. Speaking up. Sharing credit. Holding
   space. These are behaviors that strengthen the commons.
   They deserve reinforcement, too. Any working group can
   define what matters to them. It requires no one's approval to
   create a social contract.

2. **Design for everyone's needs.** When people want boundaries,
   they design for what works for them. And far too often,
   workplace rules are shaped by whoever has the most power.
   That usually means norms protect those who already benefit
   from the system. But consequences build cooperation only
   when the system is seen as fair. Designing for everyone's
   needs means co-creating norms. It means involving people
   across levels and identities. It means checking for blind
   spots: Who bears the burden of keeping the peace? Who
   gets the benefit of the doubt? When people are heard and
   seen in the process of creating this social contract, they're
   more likely to trust the outcome—and to help uphold it. I've
   already shared that if it doesn't work for you, it doesn't work.
   But it's just as true that if it doesn't work for us, it doesn't
   work. That's because "us" includes you.

3. **Create consequences that are clear and escalating.**
   Accountability isn't the same as punishment. But it does
   mean that when boundaries are crossed, something
   happens. Not just once. Consistently. That doesn't mean
   a single offense gets someone fired. But it does mean that
   each offense has a consequence—one that fits the moment

and builds, if necessary. It starts with naming the behavior. Maybe it's saying, "Ouch" when someone delivers a subtle put-down. So that it doesn't go unnoticed. Maybe it's saying, "I don't think that's okay" or asking, "Did you mean it that way?," which interrupts behavior without escalation. Then there is the escalation: to conversation. Then a team reset. And, if needed, more formal steps. Each stage gives room for people to realign.

4. **Hold violators accountable.** Here's the hard truth: If someone consistently violates a group's values and faces no consequence, the values don't hold. That's how cultures rot from within. The accountability doesn't have to be harsh. But it has to be real. Often what matters most is that something happens—and that it's visible. When people see that the rules are enforced, they start believing in them. When they don't see the rules being enforced, they stop trying to follow them. This isn't about perfection. It's about consistency. A team's culture is not defined by words on the wall—it's defined by what happens when someone crosses the line. Disrupt the default silence of complicity and it will benefit not just workplace dynamics but family and friendships, too.

5. **Ensure that everyone—not just the harmed—reinforces the norms.** One of the most damaging norms at work is that it's the responsibility of the harmed to speak up. The junior person talked over in the meeting. The one whose idea was stolen. The Black person asked to educate the room. But the people best positioned to reinforce a norm are often the ones not directly affected by it. When a peer speaks up, it's seen as backing the team. When the harmed person has to do it, it's seen as acting in self-interest—or worse, defensiveness. Which creates murkiness. We pry the bars of the cage apart not with individual effort but with our relational support. When we pull together—when teammates reinforce the group's values even when they

aren't personally threatened—we shift the whole dynamic.
We say: This matters to all of us. It's an act of solidarity. But
also of design. The more we reinforce collectively, the less
we need to rely on any one person to carry the burden.

Work doesn't need to feel like a zero-sum power game. We don't need
to live inside a tragedy of the commons. But avoiding it takes more than
good intentions. It takes practice. Structure. Sanctions that feel fair and
visible. And a shared belief that our relationships are worth protecting.

The people who depend on each other can also hold each other accountable.

Elinor Ostrom's brilliance wasn't in proposing another hierarchy—
it was in showing that people, given the chance, can govern themselves.
And the economic implications for each of our teams are Nobel Prize-
worthy. Consequence-creation isn't the job of the powerful. It's the
responsibility of the collective.

End the Silence

Look. Bad behavior sucks.

And it's hard enough to deal with it, much less be responsible for fixing it. But nothing changes if nothing changes. When we say "whatever
happens, *happens*," we're saying that we have no power. But it's in that
abdication that the harmer gets *more* power to then create *more* harm.
Our future? It's knowing that what we allow happens.

Monica Lewinsky, dragged through the mud of a scandal she didn't
create alone, knows this in her bones. She calls on us to be *upstanders*[5]—
people who don't just stand *by*, but stand *up*. Who see cruelty and choose
courage. Who see public shaming and meet it with empathy.

She reminds us that the internet may have made cruelty easier to
scale, but it also gave us the power to reach across that void and say: *I
see you. You matter. I'm here.* That is what an upstander does. They resist

the easy slide into silence and instead say the thing that needs to be said. They become the one person who didn't look away. The one who says it's not okay.

When bystanders step in, bullying stops within seconds—proving that empowering peers to act can cut bad behavior in half.[6]

If you're looking for permission to be *that* person, consider *this* it.

End the silence. Not because it's easy. Not because it's clean. But because it makes it possible for everyone to do better, be better. Because silence with bad behavior is a slow-acting poison. And standing up—for others, for what's good for us—might just be the antidote.

You won't always get it right. You'll stumble. You'll speak when you're scared. But if you want to live in a world worth living in, you have to add your brick to it, to *build* it. With one choice. One word. One refusal to look away at a time.

When you do, you won't do it alone. Another person will join in. And then another. Until teams decide we can be clear, fair, and firm with each other. That our shared space is worth defending, protecting.

Let yourself run *toward* that danger, not away from it.

INNOVATION PRACTICE

Consequencing

*Goal: Design sanction(s) to regulate team
dynamics toward desired behavior.*

A Nobel Prize–winning economist taught us that we don't need top-down control to create consequences but rather group commitment to each other. We don't need to wait for someone to save us; we can save ourselves.

Practice Prompt

- **Name** one team behavior that shuts down originality in your company—like idea-stealing, interrupting, or defaulting to the loudest voice.

- Now **design** a *small* but *clear* set of consequences. Example: If someone claims credit for another's idea, they're first asked (gently) to clarify where it came from. Then, if the same person does this twice, they have to send a note to the team that says they didn't give credit to the right person, to publicly correct their mistake. The third time, it becomes an agenda item.

- Make the consequences known; **share** them widely.

- **Deputize** everyone: Anyone who spots the behavior can enforce the consequences. Remind the team: The goal *isn't* punishment—so no rubbing someone's nose in it. The goal of consequencing is to get back on track.

- **Celebrate** the first time you need to use the consequence. We're building the conditions where original thinking can thrive. Yeahs, balloons, clap emojis.

18

New Solutions Need New Questions

We are obsessed with answers.

We're trained—especially in business—to solve problems. To be decisive. To be quick. To know all the things.

But what if having all the answers inhibits real progress rather than enables it?

What if all progress starts with generating better, new, and more questions?

It was 1867 and George T. Downing, a New York–based restaurateur and Black activist in the Underground Railroad movement, asked a question at a meeting of the newly formed American Equal Rights Association.

"Is it the negro's hour or the women's hour?"

Imagine. That room. That moment.

If you were an abolitionist, you had *finally* ended the legal practice of chattel slavery, where Black people were considered property and treated as things. And while you were joyous at that progress, you knew that the practice of white people oppressing and dominating Black people since 1619 wasn't somehow just "over" because the Civil War was. It would take more than winning a war to rewrite the false narratives of hierarchy as a natural order. More than new procedures to enable access to equal resources. More than new laws to end the near-constant violence on the Black body.

If you were a white woman in that room, maybe even having fought as an abolitionist, you had witnessed this promise of equality coming into being. And you yearned for it, too. You were tired of being dominated. Tired of how, once you married, your own legal existence ceased and was consolidated into your husband's. Sickened by how the crime of rape was legal within a marriage. How if you worked, you got just half or one-third of what he earned. How you didn't even have the rights to the custody of your own darn children.

Downing's particular question at a meeting for *equal rights* not only ignored the intersectionality of Black women in the room, it also reeked of scarcity.

It signaled that freedom is a competitive sport.

That there is not enough freedom or power or liberty to go around.

And that we must each go through the turnstile of progress one at a time.

Which explains why the people in the room responded as they did.

"I'd be jealous," said Lucretia Mott, an abolitionist and Quaker who preached that the divine light of God lived in each of us, "if men got the vote and women did not."

"I would not trust [a Black man] with my rights," Elizabeth Cady Stanton said. She was angered at the idea of 2 million Black men being allowed the vote before women like her. She was spitting mad that she, "a native-born citizen, having the same religion, speaking the same language, equal in wealth and family and education," had been politically ostracized by her own countrymen, subjected to being governed by "barbarians" and "savages."

"If you will not give the whole loaf of suffrage to the entire people, give it to the most intelligent first," Susan B. Anthony famously said. Later, Anthony reported that when "colored" women came to ask for her help in forming a branch of the suffrage, she "declined" due to "expediency."

(Grrr.)

"With us, the matter is a question of life and death. When women, because they are women, are hunted down . . . when they are dragged from their houses and hung upon lamp-posts; when their children are torn from their arms . . . when their children are not allowed to enter schools; then they will have an urgency to obtain the ballot as equal to our own," was Frederick Douglass's response. This explains why he accepted the 15th Amendment, two years later. The 15th Amendment offered the vote to Black men first and formally split any potential coalition between Black people and women (but that amendment was deemed meaningless by poll taxes, literacy tests, and persistent violence).

Is it this or that? George T. Downing asked.

And four notable suffrage leaders answered. Some, *this*. And others, *that*.

The room responded to the question asked. As we all do.

Now, notably, two folks *did* challenge the very premise of the question. Francis Ellen Watkins Harper and Lucy Stone are both on record arguing that the very question of priority shouldn't even be considered. Harper added, "The rights of Black men, Black women, and white women are all bound up together."

But even as Harper and Stone *challenged* the validity of the question, in all my many readings I couldn't find anyone providing an alternative formulation, a better question.

Maybe they did and weren't heard in that room. Maybe it wasn't recorded. Or maybe everyone was carrying the ball just as far as they could . . . for that moment in history, on that day.

I don't know.

All I *do* know is that the question invisibly shaped the thinking of those in the room. The problem with the question is that it presupposes that our fates *could* be ranked.[1] It's rooted in white supremacy and the presumption that our destinies aren't linked, which is, by all evidence, a lie.

A lie with a very real cost.

This kind of jockeying for position explains why, after Black men got the vote, in 1870, the right to vote next went to white women, in 1920. Native Americans followed, in 1924 (and didn't actually get to vote in all the states until 1962). Then Asian American women, in 1952. Black women waited until 1965. Folks with disabilities waited until 1990. (And many others are still waiting. For example, Puerto Rico and DC.)

By focusing on answering the question being asked, the suffragists didn't ask the one that could have generated better possibilities.

That's why the room, more than 100 years later, remains relatively unchanged.

And we're all so susceptible to this behavior.

Me included.

False Dichotomies

Questions are like that toy wooden cube with shapes on all sides, the gizmo that toddlers play with as they learn how to match things up to know what fits where. The triangle 3D wooden block goes into the triangle outline on the box, not the rectangle or circle. (And the sippy cup won't fit at all.)

Questions frame and shape a conversation, inform what possibilities are even considered, and so direct our attention to what comes next. Ask a limiting question and everyone's attention is directed to limited ideas.

It happens when someone has an experience—takes a vacation, puts in their first day on a project, attends a conference.

You ask, "How was it?" This question, innocuous as it may seem, forces a good vs. bad judgment that the answerer may not be prepared to render.

Asking, "What was your experience like?" allows for raw description, for nuance, and provides knowledge that you could not have known to ask for. Partly because the person gets a chance to hear themselves.

Binary questions box us into false dichotomies. Yet ask a generative question and the possibilities open up wide.

Questions, in that way, can direct destiny.

Yet at work, most of us are taught to answer the questions we are asked smartly and crisply, and not enough time is spent teaching us how to ensure that we're clear on what the *actual question is.*

In bustling conference rooms and cozy coffee shops alike, we leap at the chance to solve problems for our colleagues and friends. It's instinctive, almost reflexive, for us to step up and offer our solutions, eager to add value by sharing our expertise. We effectively say, "Hey, I can fix that for you," without asking even one question. In the professional world, problem-solvers are hailed as heroes. Résumés boast this prized skill, and those who have it get hired and celebrated. After all, problem-solving is crucial. It drives innovation, fuels growth, and tackles obstacles head-on, leading to new policies and impactful changes.

Until we step outside our knowing to un-know, we can't create what comes next. Old questions rarely, if ever, lead to new solutions.

Explore It Fully

I sat in a meeting organized by Vistage, a monthly gathering of about a dozen leaders of small and midsize companies. We were what's known as a CEO peer group, a gathering of business owners who meet regularly in a confidential setting to discuss their challenges, share experiences, and provide each other with feedback and support. There are tons of these groups, and the CEOs pay a fee to fund the group management role. Ours was a guy named David Silber. He met with each of us one-on-one regularly as our executive coach. He also helped us as a group to have effective meetings.

A friend of mine, Glen, now the CEO of Stamina Lab, brought forward his problem, similar to one I had solved before.

My hand shot up. I wiggled my fingers a little, like a third grader dying to get the teacher's attention.

I knew that I knew the answer.

Isn't the answer such and such? I asked.

The group laughed. We all loved to do this, injecting our perspective into the conversation but posing it as a question, as if adding a slight inflection at the end of the sentence changed what we were doing.

David redirected me and us.

Explore more, he reminded us.

In fact, he had a protocol for how we ran these problem-solving exercises. If you brought a problem, you had to name whether it was a small, medium, or big problem. That defined how much time you were allocated. Then, two-thirds of that time was dedicated to questions and just one-third to solutions. So a medium-sized problem took 30 minutes, and the first 20 minutes had to be questions only. I normally abided by the protocol, but I was too impatient that day to follow the script. I wanted to solve the problem already and move along. Why were we wasting time? Hence posing an answer as a question.

Redirected, I joined the rest of the CEO group to come up with questions.

- Can you tell us when you first noticed this challenge?
- What solutions have you already tried?
- Is this a recurring problem? Has it happened to you before?
- What did you do the last time this problem came up, and why?

By the time we were done asking questions, we'd gotten to know the person in the hot seat better. We'd also explored the problem from multiple angles and understood the historical context and why this particular challenge had become so ingrained.

The presenting problem was rarely ever the real problem. We learned that only by asking questions.

And even more important? By exploring questions, Glen saw the problem more clearly—he understood himself and his situation better.

Before we went to the solution phase, Glen recapped his own dilemma with fresh eyes. There was no need to "solve the problem" for him; he already had the clarity to see the right next steps (and future answers) for himself. The rest of us would still offer resources and support, but that was backup for the capable person as he solved his own problems.

Our urge to solve others' problems keeps us from creating new value; we're just recycling what we already know. When we take over their problems, we're imposing our views, assuming that we know what's best for them—a power play, even if a subtle, likely well-intentioned one.

Listening Loudly

There's a Japanese manufacturing company that has quietly built an empire not by outcompeting rivals but by making them irrelevant. They've expanded into dozens of industries, created customized technologies, and transformed the way their customers do business. And they did it not by asking, "What's the solution?" but by asking, "What are we not seeing?"

Their name is Mayekawa. You've probably never heard of them. But their approach is one of the most radical, hopeful models of business I've come across.[2]

They once produced and sold industrial parts, things like compressors used in industrial refrigeration. As a supplier, they made generic parts that businesses regularly source for the lowest cost. Then, Mayekawa decided they wanted to transform who they were to be a solutions provider, to create innovations jointly with their customers.

This wasn't a tweak but a reinvention.

At first, Mayekawa partnered with Takaki Bakery, a respected Japanese bread maker. Takaki wanted to upgrade their freezing systems. Or so they thought.

But Mayekawa didn't offer a technical fix. Instead, they embedded their engineers on the bakery floor. Those engineers watched. And then asked questions. And listened to the workers grumble.

And slowly, everyone realized that the freezing system wasn't the issue.

The real issue? A breakdown between the company's identity and its business model. Takaki was known for its European-style, high-quality bread. But the wholesale market they were chasing demanded speed, volume, and uniformity. The product and the process were in conflict.

"We had to ask the fundamental question: 'What does Takaki want to be as a company?'" That question changed everything. The goal wasn't to optimize the system they had—it was to imagine a system that matched who they actually were.

This wasn't problem-solving. This was visioning work.

To reinvent, we have to listen loudly—not with certainty but with questions. Not with ego but with imagination.

And it worked. Together, Mayekawa and Takaki restructured how bread was made, shipped, and sold. They improved taste, cut waste, and aligned the company's operations with its values. But more importantly, they reframed the problem. They shifted from solving the problem as defined to figuring out how to do what was most needed.

They enabled something more than making; they reimagined the essence of what they wanted to create.

"Often, customers themselves don't know what they want . . . Only after we dwell in and around their shop floor do we come to understand them."

That phrase—*dwell in and around*—is worth pausing on. In most business relationships, the vendor drops in with a pitch deck. Mayekawa drops in with curiosity. They spend time. They feel the friction. They don't extract answers—they absorb the world.

Mayekawa's internal structure is also built for this kind of inquiry. They're divided into dozens of tiny companies called doppos. Each one is self-managed. Ten to 15 people. Fully responsible for their own strategy, sales, even hiring. But they're not isolated. These micro-companies collaborate and combine as needed. It's a living system—flexible, relational, interdependent.

It's similar to that of W. L. Gore, the company that brought us waterproof fabric, among other things, which works in a lattice model and focuses on teams that self-manage.

"A doppo is designed to be a self-sufficient organization. But when members think deeply about how they can exist as a doppo, they come to understand what they lack. Then they start thinking about how they should work together."

This isn't a traditional org chart. It's more like a coral reef—living, adaptable, shaped by context and relationships.

At the heart of this system is a process called kigyouka keikaku—literally, "enterprise creation planning." But it's not what you think. It's not data tables or three-year forecasts. It's a collective act of imagination.

Each team starts by asking: What are we feeling in the world around us? What kind of company do we want to become? What relationships will we need to change to make that real?

"It is not an image based on the present state of things but an image of the future pulling the present forward."

You don't predict the future by projecting from the past. You imagine the future and let it pull you to it.

This process often leads to surprising insights. In the bread factory, it wasn't the equipment that needed fixing—it was the story the company was telling itself. Once that became visible, everything could change.

This is a company that teaches us a profoundly different way of thinking about innovation. They remind us that problems don't live in isolation. They live in relationships. And relationships can't be fixed from the outside—they have to be reimagined from within.

"We are created in the relationship with the environment, rather than existing as an independent, isolated entity."

In a world obsessed with solutions, Mayekawa gives us permission to ask better questions.

Not: How do we fix this?
But: What are we not seeing?
What are we really trying to become?
What is this relationship asking of us now?

Their story is a quiet argument against the tyranny of the answer. And a powerful invitation: to live in the question a little longer.

Create New Answers

By asking questions, you can lead someone to their own answers.

Inquiry expands your understanding. If you never questioned anything, your perspectives would be limited. Asking questions—whether about yourself, your colleagues, or how the market functions—makes you ponder different angles. This encourages growth as it allows you to expand how you think today.

You don't predict the future by projecting from the past. You imagine the future and let it pull you to it.

When giving people answers to their problems, you could easily make them believe that they can't solve things themselves, that they are incapable or too inexperienced. Worse yet, you're giving answers to things *you've already solved*, so you're repeating existing solutions instead of generating new ones.

So instead of giving your best answer, ask others, *What is your question?* This is not to say we leave our people on their own.

We all have a part to play, but it is not to transfer our perspective to others. Instead, it's to do what we were being asked to do in that Vistage meeting: develop the other person's ability to think through an issue and feel confident in their own decision-making. So that they gain deeper self-understanding and trust themself. This is different from mentoring, where you pass along your wisdom. This is about getting everyone to be self-trusting, and generative. Instead of having one leader who "knows," we build up our collective capacity to understand.

Questions expand that capacity. Not knowing is how we grow. The psychological construct of "competence" describes the four stages of learning:[3]

- First, you don't even notice an issue. The technical term is "unconscious incompetence," since you don't even see anything amiss.
- Then you see that something's wrong but have no idea how to fix it. This is called "conscious incompetence" because at this stage you see the problem, the brokenness, and feel the pain of not knowing.
- Next, you start practicing new things, to grow. This stage is called "conscious competence" because you work (!) at new things and slowly but surely pull yourself out of that hole and into the future. You "get it right" through practice, and the rate of going up the curve (faster or slower) is based on your capacity to take actions, to do the work.
- Finally, one day you totally own what you once struggled to know. With this "unconscious competence," you've learned to do it automatically.

Questions are what start the journey. One of my favorite insights is something Harvard Business School professor Clay Christensen once said: "Without a question, there is no place for the answer to go." I take it one step further: Without new questions, we have no way to reach for new solutions.

The quality of our work depends on the quality of the questions asked. It's how we explore the unknown, the uncertain, and the uncomfortable. And we grow—in both economic and human ways—*because* we get okay being uncomfortable with uncertainty, with not knowing. None of us want to be unclear. We'd rather "know" and now. But think about it this way: A beautiful way to hold the unknowing is that you know what you don't know, and that is how you build the next whatever.

Questions paired with sanctions shape the flow of work. Just as sanctions (as discussed in chapter 17) signal what's in and out, questions direct our attention—toward possibility or toward blame, toward the future or toward the past. If sanctions are unclear or misapplied, people become hesitant or performative. If questions are narrow or backward-looking, people get stuck defending old decisions instead of making new ones. Generative questions create space for new answers, and sanctions create the safety for those answers to emerge. Together, they define the edges and the energy of work.

To know you don't know is to be discontent with the current situation. This discontent is you yearning for better. It is beautiful. Instead of pushing it away, pull it in. If we hold on to the answers that comfort us, we miss the riches of the questions that change us.

Question everything until there is nothing left but something you could never have imagined.

INNOVATION PRACTICE

Generative Questioning

Goal: Prepare to use meetings to surface
uncertainty by asking thoughtful questions.

Before Each Meeting, Ask Yourself:

- What do I genuinely not know that I am curious about? About the goal, the problem, the options, the other person's perspective, or the trade-offs?

- What are two or three generative questions I could ask? Generative questions open up the aperture to new possibilities—they don't demand answers but birth worlds. They are the cracks in certainty where light enters, the spaces between knowing and unknowing where wonder takes root. Unlike their cousins that seek to close loops, or find rightness, generative questions open doors that didn't exist before they were asked. Possible starters:

  - What might we be missing?

  - What assumption are we making? What happens if we flip the assumption?

  - What are we experiencing here?

  - What did I not ask that I should have?

  - What small experiment or pilot could we run to explore this further?

  - If we had unlimited resources, how else would we approach this challenge?

19

Stop Making It All About You

Limiting Norm: High-Impact Players
Leading Indicator: High-Impact Plays

I was hungry for the kind of challenge that scares most people off.

A colleague from Apple recruited me to Autodesk. He wooed me with the promise that I could work with Carol Bartz, the then CEO of the company, who was a shining star in tech at the time. She had been an executive at Sun Microsystems and later became Yahoo's CEO. A chance to work with Carol was exactly the kind of opportunity I wanted to advance my career.

When I got to Carol's office—with its big wall of windows overlooking the California hills, the kind of view you could only get as a CEO—she explained that the position I was interviewing for wasn't straightforward. She wanted to promote someone from within, but that leader lacked the deep operational knowledge needed for the role. So Carol wanted to create a "two peas in a pod" organizational design. I would join the team to run the internal operations of the $200M+ business, with the title Revenues Manager. So that the internal candidate could be promoted to VP and become the public face of the Americas.

Carol said, "You'll be part of my top leadership team, fix anything that can and will go wrong, and you can drive every new strategy for our market growth."

Perfect, I thought.

It was a hot shit role. Not just high visibility—high stakes. I wouldn't just work hard; I'd step into the gaps where leadership was missing and clarity was scarce. I'd handle what others avoided, navigate the unknown, and figure out where effort mattered most. This wasn't about staying in my lane but about making a difference. It was the very definition of being a high-impact player.

Of course I said yes.

Celebrating the Player, Not the Play

Business rewards being the exceptional player to the extreme.

We do not see how being the exception—which, by definition, means being an exception to and from everyone else—divides rather than connects. How it signals that only some of us can "make it." Or that it makes success a competition not just to excel but to beat out others.

These messages bombard us. Apple's initial "Think Different" campaign ad, which first aired in 1997, was called "Here's to the crazy ones" and featured icons like Albert Einstein, Muhammad Ali, Amelia Earhart, and Pablo Picasso. The ad didn't celebrate scientific discovery, athleticism, groundbreaking flight, or art. No, it celebrated the exceptional *player*, not the *play*.

Work has all sorts of names for this. Top performer, high achiever, game-changer, rock star, MVP, and trailblazer. All code for a high-impact player.

And the messaging lands.

Of *course* it does.

Because it makes each of us central to the story. We all want to be essential, valuable, and necessary. We all need to matter.

I wanted nothing more.

The Battle at Work

Carol's promise that I could fix problems turned out to be true. Anytime people didn't agree, I got called in. But I wasn't "the fixer" in a good Olivia Pope kind of way. Most days, Carol would call at 7 a.m. and start the conversation abruptly—no "Hello" or "Good morning," just an immediate "What the fuck is wrong with . . . ?"

Quite the way to wake up.

Let's say she expected a big deal to go through, but something happened and the sale didn't close. I was the one Carol called. I would get on the phone and later on a plane that same day to meet up with the regional leader, the sales rep, and the customer to get to the bottom of what happened. The next day, I'd fly back to the office to speak to the product manager about how to fix the problem. This happened so often, I had travel bags in the truck of my car, one for cold weather, the other for hot. Though I wasn't "in charge" of anything, I was responsible for solving whatever affected revenues.

Despite the intensity, I loved the job.

Until the day my role was put to the test.

While preparing a multiyear growth strategy that would ultimately go to the company's Board of Directors, I disagreed with the marketing lead about how the business would allocate marketing dollars. I wanted the budget to be spent more on new customer acquisition and less on existing programs. The marketing person believed it was more important to maintain existing programs while expanding.

First we disagreed privately and then publicly.

This was a messy problem, and I had a chance to be useful, necessary, smart, and valuable—just like high-impact players are told to be. So I lobbied the other corner offices, pointing out the flaws in my counterpart's argument. I presented facts and figures in a smart, results-oriented way to show the team how my take could make a difference (and, in turn, how our business could be more impactful).

The person I was disagreeing with, though? This was someone I had known for years. Back at Apple, we had spent long hours together training for marathons. When we both ran the California International Marathon, she was the kind of friend who, despite finishing ahead of me, doubled back to run me in. Not only that, she had the crowd yell my name. This one-person cheerleading team was the person I was now battling at work.

I had drunk the Kool-Aid of a capitalist system built on the celebration of the high-impact player. The title sounded noble—but it came with an invisible contract: prove your worth through outcomes, outperform your peers, and tie your identity to the value you create. There were high-impact players in one corner and everyone else in the other. It was a game. A hierarchy. A subtle war. I told myself I was rising, but I was really narrowing—folding my sense of self into whatever work rewarded. I'd watched others jockey for power like this, and now I had become one of them. It wasn't personal—I still liked my friend—but the exceptional mindset that had been instilled in me from my first days at Fortune 500 companies taught me that I had to be the *one* to make the case, the *one* who made it happen. I honestly didn't know another way. So I did whatever it took to get the job done right.

And get it done we did. The board approved the direction I supported, and the next day, Carol called me for a chat. I was psyched; I was sure I would get a pat on the back for my super heroic efforts because the board had noisily applauded the presentation.

And the conversation did start that way. Carol said she trusted my calls and knew I would "deliver." But, she pointed out, I had also "alienated" my team. I felt called out and confused.

I rationalized my actions to Carol, mentioning our tight timelines and my desire to ensure that budgets were spent well. She responded that how I went about winning meant the team would not trust me the next time. And ultimately, they might not execute the plan because of the way I'd created it.

Carol wasn't wrong, and I knew it. Neither was I, and she knew it.

But only one of us was going to win.

She initially offered to move me to another department, but I passed. I didn't want to look weak. Regardless of the title, I'd be taking a step backward from her leadership team, negatively impacting—if I can use that word in this context—my career. When I went home that night, I could hear the death knell of my time at Autodesk.

Within a week, I was fired.

Social Context Creates Stars

I thought I had done everything right. And yet clearly, I was missing something important. This put me on a quest to learn, using Carol's lingo, what the f*** was going on.

I started to pay deep attention to how new ideas became real.

Nothing new appears fully formed—newness first appears nascent and fledgling, like a baby bird unable to fly. Without a *safe* context, new ideas don't even make a sound. Without socialization and friction, ideas can't be *shaped* to be strong enough to matter. Without the *support* of people putting their shoulders behind it, newness never becomes real.

High-impact work is never the result of one player's actions—it's the result of collective play.

Research on Wall Street "stars" proves this: Boris Groysberg studied over a thousand "star" analysts—those who had outperformed their peers financially—at Wall Street investment banks, following their careers for many years.[1] When the analysts switched firms, their performance collapsed. For five years. Their earlier "star performance" depended heavily on their former firms' invisible context—the organizational norms, and networks. There were a few exceptions: the "stars" who moved with their teams and the stars who switched to far better firms, presumably those with better norms. Also, female stars perform better after changing jobs than their male counterparts. But most "stars" who switch firms turn out to be meteors, quickly flaming out in their new settings.

The invisible connections between us, not the singular talents of individual "stars" in our midst, create high performance. It's like the dark matter that holds the stars in the sky; the things we can't see but that connect us are what matter.

And that makes sense if you think about your own lived experience.

None of us do our best work alone.

So why do we believe we need high-impact players?

The gospel of the high-impact player doesn't spread because it creates value—it spreads because it flatters power. It promises CEOs clarity, control, and a hero to bet on. It seduces our egos, too—offering a fast track to mattering. It's in high demand; not because it's most *true* for good work but because it *sells* us what we want to buy.

The high-impact player ideology that promises to make you indispensable actually makes you exploitable. If you believe you need to be the One, you tend to do whatever you're asked to do. And then you end up using the language of being the One to describe your work to the next generation. So they, too, sign up and get on that hamster wheel.

Which is why we've gotta stop thinking in the singular.

Because all genius is a collaborative effort.

Shine a Bigger Light

Franklin Leonard, the creator of a hugely disruptive model in Hollywood, was twenty-something when he lost his job at McKinsey. As he thought about what to do next, he binge-watched movies all day on his couch. For. Days. On. End.

Somewhere in there, he realized that what he loved—I mean really, *really* loved—was great storytelling. And that's how he found himself going to Hollywood for an entry-level job.

Like most entry-level jobs, his was primarily administrative: answering phones, handling correspondence, setting up meetings for his boss and her clients, and even at times fetching coffee from Starbucks. But in Hollywood, it is also a junior person's job to read and vet scripts, writing up "coverage." Coverage is a recap of a story to highlight the plot points, characters, tone, and genre of a script.

When he read *The Hunger Games*, he was so excited and told his bosses, "We should buy this." But his bosses were like, "Franklin, come on. Female-driven action doesn't work."

Similarly, when he went to them to buy a film with a Black lead actor, they would say, "You can't sell Black actors abroad."

He would ask, "What about Will Smith?"

And their answer was, "*Well*, he's the exception that proves the rule." Franklin would challenge the fact that the movie *Coming to America* made $300 million abroad when it came out. And the bosses said, "Wellllll, *that* was Eddie Murphy, which is a different thing."

Franklin tried so hard to engage his bosses to select the best stories. But time after time, he found himself unable to do so. And he started to wonder (based on his bosses' responses) if maybe he wasn't that good at his job.

That's how he found himself sitting at his desk late one night, composing an email, asking for help.

First he gathered the email addresses of everyone he'd met during his first year in Hollywood. Then he created a new Gmail account because he thought his bosses would object to his reaching outside his firm's hierarchy. And the note he sent was simple:

"Send a list of up to 10 of your favorite scripts from this year that meet the following criteria:

1. You love the script.
2. You found out about the script this year.
3. It won't be in production by the end of this calendar year."

"It was a straightforward, quid pro quo transaction," he told me. He would get information and share that information. Though he wasn't counting on everybody's participating, pretty much everyone responded, and some even said, "Hey, I've also got a friend who would love to participate."

By the following day, 93 people had submitted responses.

Franklin collated all the input into a PDF file (putting his McKinsey skills to work).

He gave it the same title as his anonymous email address, the "Black List," in a cheeky nod to the political witch hunt against supposed communists that had ruined so many Hollywood careers in the 1950s. He wanted to do the opposite with his list: create careers with great storytelling.

After sending out the PDF and printing off some of the scripts to read, Franklin went on vacation. (This was back when we actually left our devices and went off the grid!)

In his absence, the Black List went viral. "By the time I got back from my break," Franklin said, "the PDF had been shared via email more than 100 times." And because he hadn't put his name on the list, no one knew that he was the creator.

He soon learned that many of the recipients—a fair number of whom were also "powerless peons" in Hollywood terms—took the list to their bosses and re-pitched scripts they hadn't been able to sell them on the first time, some of which were put into production.

The scripts hadn't changed. Not one iota. However, the bias in evaluating them had been overcome. That was because the Black List established an alternative social structure of power. As Franklin engaged with people that he expected would share his purpose to see more inventive and wider-ranging scripts produced, they collectively shifted the context for each individual pitching.

It changed things.

By 2024, of the approximately 1,500 scripts that appeared on the list, a third had been produced, earning over $30 billion worldwide. They've collectively received 267 Academy Award nominations and 54 Oscar wins, including four Best Picture wins, for *Slumdog Millionaire*, *The King's Speech*, *Argo*, and *Spotlight*.[2] Interestingly, Harvard Business School studied this and found that movies made from Black List scripts—controlling for all other factors—made 90% more revenue than all the other movie scripts.[3] So more novel stories generated new revenues. And it's worth noting that the Hunger Games film franchise—which Franklin spotted early on—had a global box office gross of approximately $3.3 billion, which ranks it among the top 20 highest-grossing film franchises worldwide, alongside Star Wars and James Bond.[4]

Kinda a big deal.

When I asked Franklin what he did well, he said, "I just shined a bigger light on the topic."

I didn't say it then, but I questioned that. If it *was* about bigger, someone—Spielberg, maybe—could have done it already.

By then, I'd studied hundreds of cases where the traditionally powerless used networks to scale ideas. And what stood out was this: Scale didn't come from size. It came from purpose.

You might not have caught it earlier, but Franklin was asking an entirely new question: *What scripts do you love?* Which got an entire industry to shift away from the question they were currently asking: *Will it make money?*

This is the power of generative questions, in action and in how they change the trajectory.

And value.

Change How We Relate, and We Change Reality

Franklin was doing *all* the right work to create change in his industry, but he described it using an outdated construct of power, which harms all those trying to replicate the approach.

That's why I'm pointing it out. (Not to be mean.)

"I just shined a bigger light" suggests that success is due to size, not the goal being served.

Size is a hallmark of how traditional power has worked for millennia, where success is to be constantly expanding (adding staff, projects, money) to be bigger or developing the ability to serve more people (regardless of how well it serves them). It's why the kings of old would conquer lands, ever expanding their kingdom because *bigger* and *more* are the measures of power. More land meant they could charge more taxes, which would fund the next expansion for bigger and more. Bigger and more are how power measures progress.

These metrics measure ways to *dominate* and do not capture *significance.*

This shift is not just words.

It is the difference between chasing *power* and chasing *purpose.*

Power asks: How much can I control?

Purpose asks: What are we creating together?

Power counts kingdoms. Purpose builds communities.

Power accumulates. Purpose accomplishes.

Shifting the focus from the player to the play unites us, because plays align our power and purpose. Moving away from the high-impact player norm means we no longer crawl *over* each other but stand tall as we run *with* each other, toward our common goals.

It's Not a Favor

The thing about leading something bigger than yourself is that most of us get it backward from the start. We ask people to collaborate, like we're asking people to carry our heavy backpack up a mountain they don't even want to climb.

But oof—that's not what's happening at all.

Here's what I've learned: People don't join your cause as a favor to you. They join because they care about the same outcome you do. The breakthrough comes when you stop asking, "Will you help me?" and start asking, "Do you care about this problem too?" It's a subtle shift, but it changes absolutely everything about how you show up and how others respond.

Because, again, it's not about you.

Now, this doesn't mean you disappear yourself from the equation. God no. You initiated this thing because you saw something from where you stand that others hadn't yet realized. That's not ego talking—that's your actual contribution to the world. You get to own that. The trick is learning the difference between ownership and possession. You own your part; you don't possess the entire outcome.

And here's where it gets interesting: There will come a moment when the conversations shift from "your project" to "the project." When this happens, don't panic. This isn't about you becoming smaller—it's about the idea growing beyond what any individual could achieve alone. Which is how I define purpose: that thing that none of us can do alone. Purpose is how your early vision achieves what I like to think of as escape velocity.

It's become something big because it belongs to everyone.

The credit aspect is also where people get really twisted up. Knowing how much goes into collaboration, you don't want to be that person who hogs credit. But you know that phrase "It's not bragging if it's true"? You get credit for seeing the opportunity, for bringing people together, for maintaining the vision, for making it actually happen, or whatever part you played. Obviously, you don't get credit for other people's contributions or for success that required the whole team. When you can say, "I initiated this, but it works because of what we've all built together," you're owning your piece without taking possession of everything.

That's the sweet spot.

You'll know you've got this figured out when someone asks, "Why should I get involved?" and your answer doesn't start with "you" but keeps the focus on "it"—the problem or opportunity. We can be connected in

many ways.⁵ For example, based on where we live or on our work expertise. Which are connections based on *place* or *profession*. But the connection
we're talking about is based on what matters to us, a connection based on
purpose. This is when we start seeing ourselves as co-creators of something
that we want to make happen. Not you, not them. But we. Which of course
includes each of us.

The trick is learning the difference between ownership and possession. You own your part; you don't possess the entire outcome.

In today's connected world, individuals can achieve what was once
possible only for massive organizations, all by tapping into the ideas that
unite them.

But to live into this, we have to overcome some powerful program-
ming. We've been told that competition is how we win. That our very
survival means outrunning everyone else—like that old story about the
bear in the woods: You don't have to be the fastest, just faster than the
slowest person. But that only makes sense if the goal is to save yourself
alone. Widen the lens, and the logic collapses. You can't outrun a bear if
you're carrying a child. You can't rebuild a town with one pair of hands.
At the level of the collective, cooperation isn't noble—it's necessary.
Competition turns everyone into a threat. It teaches us to get ahead by
taking others down. That may boost the firm's numbers, but it breaks
the bonds that let us actually build something together. And this is what
we have to remember.

As you learn to talk about the work in a way that unites and connects
in purpose, you do things that go beyond ordinary friendship—you propel
our best work. When you do, you'll have the tools to build momentum
and create lasting value, ensuring that what starts out as yours doesn't
die because it's yours alone.

INNOVATION PRACTICE
The Play

Goal: Define "the play" so many others
can join you in making a dent.

When we focus on the play, we stop chasing credit and start building flow. We move from singular performance to new possibility. And suddenly, what we're creating matters.

Now Do It:

- Ask yourself: **What is the deeper why?** Not just for you, obviously, but for this moment, for the people you're involving, for what the work could unlock if it succeeds.

- Realize that **naming a shared purpose isn't always easy**; it might take a few or many tries, over time, to get it clear(er).

- Clarify that you're not asking people for a favor; **you're asking them to join in something that matters** to them.

- Know that **the shared goal will evolve/refine** over time. This is part of how it goes from "your" project to "the" project.

- **Don't hog credit, but don't abdicate it either.** Take ownership for your part, own your responsibility, but don't possess the outcome as yours.

20

Forge A-Teams by Not Fixating on A-Players

Limiting Norm: Credentials
Leading Indicator: Capabilities

"Get the *right* people on the bus" is the prime directive when building our teams.

It's a key concept from Jim Collins's 2001 book, *Good to Great,* that describes how great organizations ensure that they have the right people in the right seats before deciding where to go. The idea is that if you have the right people, you can adapt to uncertainty and perform well no matter what happens. Collins says that great vision without great people is irrelevant, and that if you have the wrong people on the bus, it doesn't matter if you find the right direction.

It emphasizes *talent* as a—if not *the*—critical variant in doing "great" work.

Today, this is an invisible norm we accept as true.

While value starts with that original point of view each of us has, success is not about "high-impact" players but high-impact plays. As we just covered.

So why do we keep searching for stars in all the wrong places?

Circumstances

Hiring "A-players" can lead to hiring those who went to prestigious schools, had stellar grades, or worked at top brands; the chase for talent becomes hunting for *credentials*, not *capability*. These social metrics don't predict value creation. Just the opposite: They reinforce who has always led.

When we prioritize these trophies, we also miss out on the essence of what drives success: our ability to create value *together*.

Yet Collins's thinking informs every level of work. Think of interns as they join an organization on the first rung of the ladder. After a summer, they're assessed as A-, B-, or C-players, based on their supposed talent.

Or so we think.

Internships are often unpaid or pay very little, so only those with family resources can afford to do them. Access comes through connections—social capital. Screening uses SAT scores and grades, sorting for people who can afford to pay for test prep and tutors.

Then there's the daily reality. People who have cars or can get rides rather than use public transit might arrive on time more easily. People who don't have to do their laundry, cook, or clean can have more time and energy for "extra" projects, virtue signaling their commitment in ways others cannot.

Cultural capital matters too. People judge intelligence by vocal accents, so a British Oxford accent signals smarts. Someone's well-honed skills to appear professional and committed may have arisen, in part, because their parents invested in developing certain soft skills. (Kiddo still teases me that I signed him up for an etiquette class via our local Parks and Rec programs when he was 7 years old, long before a person who shows up for an internship has any ambitions of their own.) Charles Murray, the white nationalist who created the Bell Curve, famously called this "affirmative action for the advantaged."

These circumstances compound. A-player interns get permanent jobs, then recommendation letters for better education, then access to and from a top-tier school, and so on. What makes someone an A-player often marks their social *credentials*, not their *competence*.

Hierarchies reproduce themselves, becoming self-fulfilling prophecies. And get supported by those who have benefitted from those hierarchies, like Collins. He doesn't say so directly, but he clearly implies that some people have "talent" while others have none.

Yet look around.

Think of your family, your neighborhood, in addition to your colleagues. And you'll see that each person has *capabilities*. That's never the question. And we don't ever need to *compare* those talents because that is hierarchical and scarcity thinking. The only question is how we connect the talents in a way that adds up to more than the sum of the parts.

If you hire for talent instead of growing it, you lose actual capabilities. A cost to us all.

Passed Up Again

"We've decided to hire a CMO to do that work," Diana's boss told her. "You will be reporting to them."

As the head of marketing for a startup, Diana was used to working long hours. But when her boss asked her to take on even more responsibility, she did—because the team needed her to.

Then her boss called her into a meeting. To tell her this news.

Diana considered it and asked to discuss the decision to hire someone from outside when she was already delivering: "I've been thinking about the new role you're creating for managing the extra workload. I've been doing that for the past six months, and I believe I've shown I can handle it effectively. I'm really interested in taking on that responsibility officially and moving up in the company."

Her boss turned to her and said, "I have to be honest with you, Diana. We're looking for someone who can bring a certain level of experience and expertise to the table. It's time for us to hire an A-player."

Diana was being passed over. Some outside unknown stranger was seen as having more potential than she did.

Deciding whom to promote is tricky. Candidates need to excel at their current level, but they also need managers who believe they can succeed at the next. The problem? Potential is hard to measure, and the methods used to evaluate it (confidence, credentials, etc.) mean that among candidates with the same profiles, some people are seen as having higher potential. Recent research reveals that while women earn higher performance ratings, they receive lower "potential scores"—reflecting the way managers cannot assess talent or capabilities and thus fall back on old tropes.[1]

Diana was experiencing all of that. She could feel it. So she argued: "I've put in the time and effort to prove myself capable. Why bring in someone new when I'm already here, know the issues, and have all the relationships to jump right in?"

Her boss argued that an A-player would add something to the team. "We need someone with a specific background and qualifications, maybe someone who went to Stanford and worked at Google. Someone who can bring fresh perspectives and experiences to the role."

Diana's boss thought that hiring people with the "right" credentials would lead to freshness. However, hiring people who fit the mold of potential actually breeds homogeneity. The data on that is clear: Homogeneity never leads to innovation.[2]

Several months later, Diana went to her boss. "I couldn't help but notice that the new hire for the role I applied for seems like they're struggling."

Her boss had to admit it. "Yeah, it's been a bit of a rocky start. However, we knew there would be onboarding challenges with someone from outside the company."

Diana didn't say what she was thinking because she already had. She was *already* valuable, was familiar with the company culture, had a good relationship with the team, understood the workflows, *and* was doing the job well. Tired of being treated like she was anything less than a strong talent, she left the company a few months later.

When an employee quits after being passed over, the costs are substantial. Replacing an employee costs between 50 and 75% of their salary, according to the Society of HR Management.[3] A study by Glassdoor found that it takes around eight months for a new hire to reach full productivity, with the onboarding process typically lasting three to six months.[4] A demoralized team can experience up to a 34% drop in performance,[5] and losing an employee with significant internal knowledge can lead to a 30 to 50% reduction in efficiency in critical areas.[6]

This is the rippling economic effect of a talent search for A-players. It's lowered morale, disrupted projects, and the loss of institutional knowledge. Costing a company thousands, if not millions, depending on the role and industry.

Hyperfocusing on A-players signals a failure to build the A-team.

When the goal is to get everyone to be motivated, forward-thinking, and solutions-oriented collaborators who do great work together, setting up a false stratum of talent is counterproductive. The team members who have shown their capabilities and commitment feel less valued by this decision and so start to step back rather than step up.

Of course, this limits our best work.

Reinforcing the Archaic

Managers who seek these A-players show their hand: using credentials like a binky. This person must be "amazing"; they went to a "top-tier" school. When this happens, someone has used *credentials*—an external way to evaluate an individual's worth, usefulness, and benefits—to assess *character* or *capabilities*.

This behavior is rooted in an ancient view of what makes someone "A" quality. In 1642, six years after its founding, Harvard College held its first commencement exercise. The graduating class consisted of just nine students.[7] It probably goes without saying that they all were white, Christian, and male. Harvard reinforced the exclusive nature of higher education by not ranking its graduates by their grades or alphabetically. Instead, these elite men crossed the stage "according to the rank their families held in society."[8] Harvard continued to classify its graduates by their family status for 121 years until they finally switched to alphabetical order to seem more meritocratic. To say higher education began as a privileged institution designed to advance a certain kind of student and exclude others is an understatement.

Leaders who don't know how to discern capabilities use academic credentials as a proxy. Let's be clear. Often, hiring A-players is driven by insecurity. We've all seen leaders chase after the latest "expert" instead of rolling up their sleeves to figure it out themselves. But here's the catch: If they don't understand the task, how can they discern if the new hire does? A-player seeking is trying to compensate for that uncertainty. Worse, those doing the hiring lose precious time chasing an illusion.

Managers who seek these A-players show their hand: using credentials like a binky.

A better approach? Ask the talented people you already have on staff to figure out not only how to optimize their own work but how to make their teammates better. Coach on this; encourage this. This way, you're not just filling gaps—you're investing in and growing your team's capabilities over time.

It's counterintuitive that solidarity outperforms stardom. But it does. Every time.

Reward the Unseen Setup

I am a researcher at heart, and I sometimes feel like I read the internet so that no one else has to.

I've been obsessively reading vignettes about the US women's national soccer team (USWNT) for many years. And I've marveled at how this team has fundamentally changed how success is measured. Instead of tracking just the end-goal *outcomes*, they started to track the team *interplay*—the bad pass they forced the other team to make, the tee-ups that enabled future plays, and how teammates deferred to someone on a hot streak that day.

They started tracking the moments that don't make the highlight reel but make the team unstoppable. Unstoppable because they are playing not for individual success but for the team's.

By focusing on teamwork, they made the team work.

And that's how you win the gold medal.

By changing what we measure, we redefine what talent means.

Imagine the moment after a goal is scored.

In many sports, the scorer basks in the spotlight, the crowd chanting their name. But Abby Wambach of the USWNT introduced a simple yet revolutionary practice. "After every goal, I pointed to the player who assisted me."[9] People's eyes followed the finger. It shifted the focus from "Who scored?" to "Who all made this possible?" This made the tee-ups matter. It made the sacrifice to give the ball to the player on a hot streak matter. It made the teamwork count. For everyone to take pride in their part of the whole. Which is how teammates figure out how to play as a team. This "rush and point" moment makes the invisible labor visible.

By recognizing the unseen setup, we normalize the quiet work that builds success.

This is just one way the US women's soccer team expanded beyond measuring goals scored. It's about how the team's greatest victories came from *how* they worked together, not just *what* each star performer did alone.

Then they risked it all. Together.

"Tell them we're not playing." That's what Julie Foudy told the US Soccer Federation.[10] When the USWNT faced unequal treatment and pay disparities, the temptation to accept individual deals and break ranks was real. After all, each person had their own mortgage to pay, and they were being pitted against one another by being told, "There's only so much money to go around." But Foudy and the team, guided by Billie Jean King's strategic wisdom, chose something stronger: a collective refusal to show up to training.

Imagine boycotting the Olympics training camp.

The strength it would take to deny yourself the chance to work among the best athletes in the world to train for something you're dying to train for. But the boycott as a block was a powerful statement: No one gets rewarded unless everyone gets in on the action. This refusal to be divided by individual gain sent a clear message that the team's success and fairness would not be sacrificed for personal advancement. The team understood that fairness was not an individual commodity but a shared baseline. Which is what it looks like to create and then enforce a standard of behavior, as we talked about previously.

As the team evolved, so too did their understanding of leadership.

Instead of relying on a single captain or star figure to carry the mantle, the team rotated the captaincy. This wasn't about passing the baton; it was about distributing responsibility so that leadership became a shared and ever-evolving practice. Foudy explained that everyone, from the superstar forward to the greenest newbie, was held to the same standard. "Leadership comes in many different forms; it's personal, not positional."

Leaders often miss how much this helps teams to learn each other's capabilities. To see who is the most organized and prepared, the one who is the most inspirational, the one who is the most fun in how they lead. By letting leadership rotate, you learn how to actualize and lean on the gifts that each person has to offer.

By spreading and sharing leadership—from the rush of scoring a goal, the fight for equal treatment, and the passing of the captain's armband—the team put their emphasis on relational dynamics instead of individual metrics of who scored, who got the raise, and who holds the title.

They focused on the connective power that makes teams more than the sum of their players. That causes them to have exponential results.

The US women's national team isn't just successful—they've redefined what success looks like in international soccer. With *four* FIFA Women's World Cup titles (1991, 1999, 2015, 2019), they hold more than any other nation. They've also clinched *five Olympic gold medals* (1996, 2004, 2008, 2012, 2024), while the US men's team has never won a single World Cup and last stood on the Olympic podium for soccer over a century ago—in 1904, with a bronze. Across decades now, the USWNT has consistently ranked No. 1 in the world, setting records not just in wins but in goals scored, viewership, and cultural impact. In 2019 alone, they scored 26 goals in just seven World Cup matches and ignited a global movement around equal pay.

How they win is because of how they play game.

Quite literally.

A great soccer team is about how players—strikers, defenders, and midfielders—come *together* to form a winning squad. In business, leaders do the same when they stop focusing on individual heroes and A-players and design teams so that members learn to rely on each other to succeed. That can be done through cross-training, rotational roles, or project-based work. These practices do three things at once: (1) each player gets to improve their capacity development by switching things up; (2) by taking turns doing different work, the players build empathy for each other's needs; (3) the team learns shared interdependence—when to count on each other and for what. Plus, a team can optimize their overall performance by tapping each person's contribution.

We all need to realize that our teams are already made of the "right" people—all of them, regardless of their credentials. They are already talented. Our focus needs to be on building capabilities and connecting them together. Then rallying together around the goal that excites us all. That shared passion, that collective energy, that unstoppable will to win—those are the ingredients of success.

Let's *build* each other up. Let's *believe* in each other's talents. Let's do *our best work.*

INNOVATION PRACTICE
Rotate to Elevate

*Goal: Implement regular work rotations
and variety to teach team play.*

Anyone can start work rotations, because they don't require permission—just a shared commitment. When teammates agree to trade roles or shadow each other for a set period, they build mutual respect, deepen understanding, and grow skills across the team. It's a simple, self-organized way to break silos, spark learning, and make the whole team more adaptable—no sign-off needed, just support.

That said, there are three specific things that make it work:

1. **Name the give/get ratio.** Clarify what you hope to give—skill development, knowledge sharing, or increased engagement. Also be clear on what you want to get (visibility, access, a monetary upside in the future). The more explicit the expectations, the better they can be managed.

2. **Allocate sufficient time.** Is this a day rotation or a week or a month or six months? Determine how much time would be necessary to achieve the give/get.

3. **Create scaffolding.** The person doing the role often underestimates what they know as they pass on work to others. Training, onboarding, and written-down instructions can all be useful to communicate how it's done. Allow the asking of the "stupid questions" to learn what is often tacit to the one holding the job so the person assuming the work has a chance to succeed.

21

You Can't Bestow Power

Limiting Norm: Empowered
Leading Indicator: Powerful

"Is this your best work?"

Blake paused. Normally tall and lanky, he seemed smaller as he hunched in the doorframe. "Uh, well, I thought so. Did I miss something?" he replied.

"No, no," I said quickly, wanting to reassure him. "I just realized that by having you hand it off to me, I might be stepping in too much, not giving you the room to take it further yourself. That's why I asked."

His shoulders eased a bit. "I guess I've been trying to balance things. You usually handle this final stage of strategy better than I do, and then I can get my evening with my family."

I hesitated, torn. I wanted Blake to have his evening, but I couldn't ignore what my CEO peer group, Vistage, had pointed out just days earlier. I had gone to them wanting their help in getting my team to step up—and they had told me it was about my stepping back. I thought I was a responsible leader. The kind who rolls up her sleeves, digs in, and never lets the team fall. My CEO group helped me realize that my so-called supportive approach—empowerment—was actually holding everyone back.

They urged me to stop working so much *in* the business and start working *on* it.

With this conversation, I was exploring a new *how.*

"Your leaving this project on my desk at 5 p.m. the day before a client meeting means I miss time with *my* family. I am now the one in the hot seat. Maybe we can find a different way?" I asked, though it wasn't really a question.

Blake nodded, looking uncertain. "Of course. I just worry I'll never do it as well as you."

I sensed his hesitation. "I'm not asking you to be me. I'm asking you to bring the best of you. Because your best is already enough." I'd been training Blake on go-to-market strategy for years; I believed in him. But what I hadn't noticed before was that I was training my team on an entirely different thing, too. "I'm here to *support* you, but I realize that maybe I need to stop *doing* it for you. That way, you can step into more of who you are. How does that sound?"

Blake smiled, picking up the papers from my desk. "You asked if this was my best work . . ." He trailed off, then turned and walked away, the report back in his hands.

For years, I thought I was being a good leader by "helping" my team. I'd had too many terrible managers who'd left me to sink or swim. But maybe shielding my team from the hard stuff was equally imbalanced.

I was the one who took that final pass at our strategy recommendations, which meant the idea we presented to our client was nearly always more mine than ours. I'd tell my team to take it as far as they could, but I'd step in if things seemed wobbly to make sure no balls were dropped. What I had really shown them was that their best work wasn't worth doing; it would never get shown to the client. Because I'd *always* step in. And if that was the message, why would they bring their best work?

"Empowerment" made me feel good. But was it actually doing good?

Shift the Power

Empowerment is a beautiful word that often hides who's still in charge.

During COVID, remote work was hailed as "empowering" when it primarily served companies struggling to stay afloat, but those same flexible models were quickly denied after the crisis. Sheryl Sandberg's *Lean In* "empowered" women to fight for equal pay but shifted the burden to individuals who couldn't fix the problem rather than addressed systemic inequality at the corporate or national level. The conference TEDWomen was branded as an "empowering" platform for women, yet it first existed because TED wouldn't fully represent female voices on its main stage.

While some good surely came from remote work, *Lean In*, and TEDWomen, it's also true that empowerment is often used to package something as power-shifting when it mostly serves those already in charge so they feel good about themselves.

Empowerment didn't start out this hollow or symbolic.[1]

In 1968, the Brazilian academic Paulo Freire coined the word *conscientization*, empowerment's precursor, as the way in which an oppressed person *perceives* the structural conditions of their oppression so that they can subsequently act against their oppressors. (Not that dissimilar to what *Our Best Work* is doing, though I'm adding practices because it's not enough to have insight; we must act anew to shift things.) He taught us that shared consciousness enables power to grow.[2]

Eight years later, the educator Barbara Bryant Solomon wrote about American Black communities, applied Freire's notion, and gave it its current name: "empowerment." It was defined as an *ethos* for social workers in marginalized communities to discourage paternalism and encourage their clients to work together and solve problems in ways that worked best for them.

All ideas worth supporting.

Then, in 1981, Julian Rappaport, an American psychologist, turned the concept into a personal theory of power. In his construct, and likely due to his area of study, the focus shifted to the individual. Rather than seeing it as consciousness about structural conditions like Freire did or community-based like Solomon did, Rappaport advocated for more personal competency.

And this is where empowerment starts to fail us.

When power is made a construct for individuals, it isolates rather than connects. Disaggregating communities into singular units of one is how the powerful keep the less powerful unorganized and thus unable to create change. This strategy has been employed in various forms throughout history to maintain control over subjugated people, often by preventing different groups from uniting against a common ruler. Julius

Caesar used it in the first century to conquer and govern large parts of Europe.

We know it commonly as "divide and conquer."

It originates from the Latin phrase "Divide et impera," which translates to "Divide and rule." And as long as we're getting into language, let me add one geekier thing. The prefix "em" means "cause or put into." So "empowerment" promises to bestow power, but the fact that power has to be bestowed tells you everything—it assumes that power doesn't already exist within the person.

In the end, modern-day empowerment is a shiny-looking tool, promising to fix power dynamics. But it's like a hammer made of paper: useless in achieving its stated goal.

Open the Door from the Inside

"How many of you need more mentoring?" I asked, scanning the crowd at Thinkers50, a London-based conference packed with the top experts in leadership.

Crickets. No hands, no claps, just that awkward, polite silence.

I leaned in. "How many of you would rather have someone open the door from the inside so you can just walk in?"

The room exploded—applause, cheers, the works.

As the session wrapped up, I yanked off my mic and bolted for the bathroom. Caffeine was my ally in coping with jet lag, but it had consequences. The women's room? It was packed—at least fifty people. The moment I walked in, those near me clapped again, this time with laughter and a sense of shared relief. They let me cut to the front of the line.

"Finally, someone said it!" one of them exclaimed.

The question wasn't planned. It came out during a fireside chat with Tom Peters, the legendary management thinker whose book *In Search of Excellence* was the first business book to go mainstream and sit on grocery store shelves. I still remember the exact bench where I read his iconic article, "The Brand Called You." He's a giant in the leadership field, and I respect his work immensely.

So even I was surprised when I interrupted him.

As he spoke about mentoring women—proud of the many he'd helped—something didn't sit right. I thought about Blake, and how all my empowering talk hadn't helped until I finally stepped aside.

Mentoring might make Tom feel good. But it doesn't open the door.

Yes, there's a time and place for mentoring. Early in our careers when we're learning the basics, or when we're navigating new terrain, it's invaluable to learn from those who have more experience. But too often, mentoring is the go-to solution for addressing power dynamics, and it misses the mark.

Mentoring can easily reflect more on the giver than the gift. Another form of our old friend "servant leadership," where the focus is on caretaking rather than care.

We need to break these constructs. And we can.

Take a Hike

At first, no one left.

When Netflix announced its unlimited vacation policy, it didn't unleash a wave of Mediterranean sabbaticals or monthlong road trips. It triggered something stranger: silence. The offices stayed full. Calendars didn't change. And if you squinted, it looked like nothing had happened at all.

Which was exactly the problem.

Patty McCord, Netflix's Chief Talent Officer, watched this unfold with unease.[3] She'd co-written the now-famous Netflix Culture Deck that declared trust in employees and insisted on freedom with responsibility. But here was freedom staring everyone in the face, and no one was using it.

She realized what they'd missed and worked with her boss to fix it. "When you remove a policy," CEO Reed Hastings later explained, "employees don't know how to operate with the absence. If you don't tell them, 'Take some time off,' they won't."[4]

People's inaction wasn't about laziness. It was fear. In most companies, time off had been earned, tracked, approved. The calendar was policed. Now, suddenly, no guardrails. Even for a high-performance culture like Netflix's, this wasn't "empowering." It was paralyzing.

So McCord and Hastings tried something rare in corporate America: They didn't just trust people—they helped them know what to do with that trust.

The next policy had only two words: "Take vacation."[5]

But those words weren't the radical part. What happened next was.

Hastings began to model the behavior himself. Not token Fridays off or long weekends. Real vacations. Six weeks a year. Disconnected, in the wilderness, out of reach. "You often do your best thinking when you're off hiking in some mountain or something," he said.[6]

He knew what most leaders forget: What you model matters more than what you say. People don't follow management policies. They follow the socially accepted patterns they see.

Netflix shifted from the language of empowerment—"You *can* take time off"—to a powerful practice: "We'll do it, too."

This distinction is subtle but profound. Empowerment is the act of giving you the keys. Powerful is when you drive. To "empower" is to have a policy that sounds good but is never used, but powerful was when Netflix's PTO policy was used. It wasn't just words. It was policy, yes, but also the scaffolding, structure, and social support that enabled people to have more agency over their lives. McCord understood this. As she once said, great cultures are built on "extreme honesty coupled with the baseline assumption that people in the workforce are adults."[7]

Because, even for adults, modeling matters. Without it, the best policy is just a dare.

It took years to get this right. There were stumbles. Some managers clung to old norms. Some employees feared being seen as slackers. But over time, it stuck. And Netflix emerged with a policy that wasn't just permissive but powerful.

The lesson is bigger than vacation. It's about how change works. A policy can look like it's transformative, but it took McCord paying attention to what was stopping people to make it work. She could have easily said, *People are acting dumb or not acting in their best interest,* making individuals the problem. But she believed in her people, and kept looking for what blocked them.

And then she built what they needed. She didn't "empower" them; she created the infrastructure to unlock the power everyone *already* had.

In a world where overwork is a badge of honor, "Take vacation" might sound soft. But at Netflix, it's anything but. It's a line in the sand—a refusal to accept that productivity and burnout are the same thing.

To do our best work, rest isn't a reward. It's a requirement.

And it's not something we do until we have the power to do so.

Get Out of the Way

If we want to correct the power dynamic—so each of us is powerful—that becomes the direct goal.

And the lever of change isn't the individual; it's the relational structures.

The goal is to tap inherent power—so people grow into being more of themselves. It's one thing to say that you believe in people; it's another to act in a way that says people are already potent and able. If they cannot contribute fully, the goal is to figure out what is blocking them and fix that.

We all long to contribute and shine, like lotus flowers rising from the depths of dark mud, instinctively seeking the light. Lotuses emerge, untouched by the murky dark waters, and bloom magnificently on the surface. I have always loved that; my name, translated into English, means lotus flower. And so I am struck by their emergence. No one needs to instruct them or help them; they rise because it's in their nature to grow toward the light.

So the question at work isn't how we empower people. It's about how we get the hell out of the way, allowing the latent capacity in all of us to shine. That is the power we are activating—an aliveness that is inherent and unstoppable—a creative force within us all.

INNOVATION PRACTICE
Believe in Me Test

*Goal: Spot the difference between being
empowered and being believed in.*

Step 1: Marble Jar Reflection (5 Minutes)

Think of Brené Brown's marble jar metaphor—each act that builds trust adds a marble to the jar. Now ask yourself:

- Who in your life has consistently added marbles to your jar?
- What did they do specifically—listen without fixing, encourage without judgment, show up when things were messy?
- When did someone take a leap of faith by entrusting you with something big, advocating for you, or seeing potential in you that you didn't yet see in yourself?

Write down one specific moment when someone believed in you—not just helped or advised you but took a chance on you. What happened, and how did it change you?

Step 2: Mentoring vs. Believing (3 Minutes)

Reflect on two moments:

1. A time when someone mentored you.
2. A time when someone made it possible for you to do something you couldn't make happen alone.

   ○ Which felt more like someone believed in you?
   ○ What was the impact in each case?
   ○ What's the difference between guidance and belief?

Write three words to describe each experience.

Step 3: Share + Shift (20 Minutes)

With a trusted colleague:

- Share what came up for you.
- Reconsider what mentoring or empowerment is for. When is it useful? When might it unintentionally harm?

- Discuss: What might you do differently now—either in how you support others or in what kind of support you seek?

Optional:

Set up a marble jar system within your team.

- Give marbles to others who create the foundational support and infrastructure to enable each person to utilize their inherent power.

- Celebrate who has the most marbles every month. Reset the jars.

- Discuss what "caused" the marbles—what helps people to know someone believes in them.

22

A Hero Harms Us

Limiting Norm: Individualism
Leading Indicator: Individuation

Personal power is often described as something we summon from within—a kind of inner engine fueled by will and ambition.

But that framing misses a crucial paradox: Personal agency is never purely personal. Our ideas, our confidence, even our sense of Self are shaped by the people and places around us.

The myth of individualism—the idea that we rise by our own effort—flatters the ego but flattens the truth.

We are, all of us, entangled.

Which means that the most life-defining choice isn't what we do alone. It's who we let shape us. Power isn't something someone gives you (as we discussed in chapter 21). And it isn't something you do by ourselves (as we'll explore here in chapter 22).

Despite what the self-help aisle tells you, freedom isn't found through willpower. It comes from finding the people who invite you to become more of yourself.

That's how we gain real power—the kind that can walk away from proximity to power in service of something better.

Because it's not isolation that frees us. It's mutuality.

And still, we resist it.

Fiercely.

"If I have *her*, why do I need *you*? And if I have *you*, why do I need *her*?"

The newly appointed CEO of a tech company addressed his top 100 leaders at their first big gathering since his promotion from president and COO. And, for some crazy reason, I had become the topic of conversation.

Although I wasn't in the room when the CEO spoke, my colleagues-turned-friends had shared the story with me so uniformly that I finally had to believe it had happened.

But *why* it was happening was far less clear.

When this guy was promoted to CEO, I had worked with the company for nearly a decade.

I had helped them to outperform and eventually acquire their most significant competitor. I had designed their entire business/channel model, allowing the company to become more than a consumer-focused company and I had set the foundation for their lucrative data business. And I had helped with a product bundling insight that stopped the relentless price wars and allowed the product teams to focus on integration and workflow improvements.

I used "I" to individuate my role, yet I wasn't alone in this work.

I was part of a team, a word too overused at work to describe people reporting to a leader rather than the true meaning of a team—how we come together and work toward a common goal. But the team included Katie Keating, Gloria Chen, Hans Grande, and many others, along with my team at Rubicon. There were hundreds on the extended team. Together, we identified the problem statements, developed insights, debated options, made plans, and executed them.

We accomplished things. Stock-rising, value-creating, tectonic things.

And yet I was being voted off the island. I thought I must have done something wrong. This is often my first thought; a trauma response that many of us carry from our childhood to the workplace. But others have speculated that the CEO thought I was too influential or that he was perhaps establishing his power over others. Who knows?

What was observable? He threatened his team to show that he—and he *alone*—was in charge.

The Hero at Work

Throughout history, tales abound of leaders who take charge and create transformative successes, turning novel ideas into global change.

I saw it firsthand at Apple, a company born in the town I grew up in. Its first buildings were built on the land where I picked apricots for a summer job when I was super young—and where I had my first tech job in my twenties. There, Steve Jobs was widely celebrated for "singlehandedly" giving the world personal computers and, later, for "saving the company." While there's no doubt he played a pivotal role, he certainly didn't do it alone.

To describe Jobs as an individual hero ignores the inventive role of Douglas Engelbart, who designed the computer mouse in 1964 at the Stanford Research Institute. It also overlooks the inventors of the graphic interface technology that Jobs "borrowed" from Xerox PARC. Combined, it denies the value of the American government investing dollars in the Stanford Research Institute and Xerox PARC over many years, which incubated and led to our current tech-based economy. It renders invisible the team who worked with Jobs, including my friend Chris Espinosa, who started at Apple at age 14 and was one of the original 22 people who shipped the first Apple computer. It especially negates the contributions of Jobs's co-founder, Steve Wozniak, the technology innovator who designed Apple's first products, the Apple I and II computers, and helped create the Macintosh because he wanted something that didn't yet exist. And we shouldn't ignore how much the "solo hero" narrative obscures the legacy privilege of money, time, and network for these boys to have had the space to "tinker" while others with less privilege had to get summer jobs.

No one did it on their own. Many did it together.

Despite this ridiculous amount of evidence, the m of an individual hero persists—for Jobs and many who follow in those footsteps.

Which is downright crazy to me. And it should be to you.

After all, our ideas are shaped by those who have shaped us.

Our family, mentors, coaches, teachers, colleagues, and even the books we've read influence who we are and what we think. We bring this invisible network into every interaction. Then there are the back-and-forth exchanges among people about their ideas, adding the necessary friction to shape those ideas into a solid set of viable solutions. The team's collective intelligence emerges from how they interact to decide what makes the most sense to do next.

It's not just that our *best* work is collaborative. It's that *all* work is collaborative.

Yet our work cultures, especially in America, celebrate *individualism*, the notion of independent self-reliance where people make it "on their own."

Which is the very definition of how we limit our best work.

A company, isolated and disconnected from the place it operates in (or the earth it lives on), doesn't need to reinvest in the community that supports it. It needs only to be accountable to the shareholders and profits. It can use the countries' roads without paying taxes or use up the water supply as if others don't need it to live. It can plunder as long as it profits.

A colleague isolated from her peers can feel she has to throw her colleagues under the bus to win the boss's approval. Or steal their ideas if it means he gets ahead.

The CEO, earning 670 times more than their average worker, can feel impervious when they fire a team via email on a Saturday night.

And all this is by design.

Our ideas are shaped by those who have shaped us.

Individualism disconnects your success from reality. It denies how much your success depends largely on how you started—where you grew up and how much your parents earned.[1] Everything else— whether you attend college, your marriage prospects, your chances of landing a well-paying job, and even your health—hinges on this start.[2] Even today, children born poor in Canada, Denmark, or the United

Kingdom—nations that provide strong social safety nets and public investments—have a greater chance of economic success than children born poor in America.[3] This disconnection means we easily forget what gave us the stepping stones to upward mobility: public education, accessible childcare and healthcare, or even the low-interest mortgages given out when affirmative action was white that helped create the middle class.[4]

It should come as no surprise that individualism first became popular in the Andrew Jackson slavery era. Those actively oppressing an entire group's freedom used the language of individual rights.

Fall in Line

As we complete work, it completes something in us.

Work is a way we know we matter. I'm not saying it's because we accomplish things at work, though that is surely a part of it. No, it's more than that. Whether paid or unpaid, work is how we offer our particular gifts to the world. Which is why I use the term "work" and not "job"; while those can be linked, work is the way we are connected to those around us and to the world.

When I started a company to do strategic consulting, I tried to design it so everyone on the team could add their bit to the world. I certainly hired skilled and capable people. One guy was incredibly talented at imagining new uses for technology, and had designed and architected the first digital shopping cart, creating how e-commerce works today. Another ran competitive analyses for Palm and Apple and was brilliant at designing market moves. Another could do regression analysis like nobody's business. And so on. We each had gifts that contributed to our collective work.

And then one day, I shared the news that I had to step away from the firm for a bit. This was shortly after the school campfire incident and my decision to be there for Kiddo.

I told everyone as a group and then met with my leaders individually.

I asked them to take over the firm Rubicon. Which had enough money in the bank that if we brought in no new client work for six months, everyone's payroll would still be met. So taking over was about holding down the fort—doing the projects currently on our plate and doing them well. *Step up*, I asked my team, *so that I can step out for a minute.*

No, thank you, they each said.

A few years later, I ran into one of those leaders at a local coffee shop. We got to talking about how hard it was to walk away. To shut down something I had built from scratch. How I hated having to pick between different loves. That was when I learned that my leaders had kibitzed and decided I'd *have* to stay if they each turned down the offer to lead. They liked things just as they were, with me bringing out the best in them, and no one wanted to change their role on the team. They had also convinced themselves that I would judge them for not doing things as well as I could, so no one wanted to step up. They didn't believe me when I said they could lead *however* they liked. They didn't believe me when I said I *had* to take a break.

Well, that didn't work, did it? We laughed, even though it wasn't funny.

My team wanted me to *fall in line*, just like the CEO of that tech company wanted his team to *fall in line*.

We're collectively trapped by the norm of an iconic, individualistic hero rather than a collaborative team.

Individuation Instead of Individualism

Everyone wants to matter, to carve their own path, to leave a mark.

That's why individualism feels so resonant and is so popular. It feels like the path to making our mark. But like every other -ism, individualism takes a deep truth—in this case, that we are each *already* valuable as our own distinct part of the universe—and warps it to say we must make it on our own.

As if we're not already enough.

As if our value is based on what we do.

As if we must earn the right to be valued.

That's how individualism keeps us hustling, chasing something elusive. Because we can't find something we already have.

We believe we must *make it alone* because we're scared that *we are not already enough.*

Answering that fear? It's not done by simply *affirming* oneself as Al Franken did on *SNL* with his Stuart Smalley character: "I'm good enough, I'm smart enough, and doggone it, people like me." It's also not a matter of increased self-*awareness*, as if the issue is that you don't know how valuable you are. And certainly, it's not about emulating *another*, whomever else one sees as "enough." One of the weirdest things about individualism is how much it makes us copy each other as a way to leave our mark.

No, the answer to individualism isn't any of those things.

It is to go back to the basics, and it turns out we already have a word for it.

Individual.

The etymology of the word tells us what is relevant. An "individual" is the smallest measure of the whole. By definition, we are never isolated; we are always connected. The power of an individual comes not from freedom *from* others but by connection *with* others and what matters in common.

As an individual, *you* already matter. And you leave a mark by and with *your* people. You and yours: The two parts make the whole. Thus, the antidote to the heroic narrative of individualism—believing you must do it yourself—is to know how to individuate, the process by which an individual becomes distinct.

Unsurprisingly, that work is also never done alone.

Research in sociology, psychology, and anthropology reveals that isolated individuals tend to conform. If you're the "only" one in any group, you'll face three pressures to fit in: (1) hiding your true Self, (2) feeling self-conscious, and (3) feeling excluded. For example, a parent among childless friends might downplay their kids' doctor appointments to blend in. A Gen Z person in a group of Gen Xers might feel too self-conscious to say what the group says doesn't make sense. A quiet person might not be invited to important social gatherings where all the work gets done. Harvard's Rosabeth Moss Kanter's research found that the "only" conform—not by choice but because they feel alone.[5]

We all need social support to be fully ourselves.

Our capacity to matter and chart our life course is not simply personal but profoundly social. It's time we stopped trying to do it all alone.

Who Surrounds Us

The most consequential decision we make isn't about what to do—it's about whom we let shape us.

When Ava DuVernay walked away from her $100 million Warner Bros. deal, she wasn't just leaving money on the table. She was rejecting the entire premise of how power works in Hollywood. The unspoken norm is simple: Proximity to existing power is the path to more power. Get close to the gatekeepers, play by their rules, and eventually you'll get your shot.

DuVernay had already proven she could play that game. As a publicist working within Hollywood's machinery, she knew the systems and the gatekeepers intimately. She could have easily joined those already in charge.

Instead, she chose to do something radical: She chose to build power differently.

This choice cost her. Millions in guaranteed deals. The security of studio backing. The ease of working within established systems. When she needed $100 million to make *A Wrinkle in Time*, she couldn't just pitch a studio executive over lunch. When she wanted to make *Origin*, she had to convince the Ford Foundation director that, as he put it, she needed to be "untethered and unfettered" by the system that would probably constrain her.

But here's what she gained: the power to change not just her own trajectory but the entire landscape.

We've been taught that networking is about collecting connections. But the nature of those connections matters. Closeness doesn't just give you access to power; it reshapes you in its image.

Social science shows that our five closest relationships determine who we become.[6] If they get a tattoo, we will. If they lose weight or gain weight, we will. When they encourage us to become more or less ourselves, we do.

This is what I call the Five Forces. Not to be confused with Michael Porter's Five Forces—the well-known framework for analyzing competition in business, built around five threats: new entrants, suppliers, buyers, substitutes, and rivals. Porter's model assumes that power is something you defend. You build a moat, fend off competitors, defend what's yours. As with Share of Voice and Situational Leadership, I am reclaiming a name. To say that modern power isn't about protection but connection. You become what you surround yourself with. So be intentional about the five people closest to you.

Instead of collecting connections, DuVernay cultivated co-conspirators. She started small. With just a part-time assistant, she built a tight-knit team who shared more than skills—they shared a mission. "I don't just hire people for skill—I build teams with shared purpose. That's how the best work happens."

This commitment became the backbone of her company, Array. Founded in 2010, Array wasn't just a film distribution company—it was a platform for voices that Hollywood habitually ignored. Array isn't just about distributing films—it's about creating a network of artists who support each other and create change together.

But what does this kind of relationship actually look like? How do people help us become who we're meant to be? Through DuVernay's journey, we can see the Five Forces at work:

- They witness you into being.
- They don't sidestep the hard truths or doing the repair work.
- They want for you what you want for yourself.
- They are with you in Kleenex-times and Award-times.
- They encourage your growth without fear of losing you.

These kinds of relationships don't just happen. We choose them. We test them. We grow them. It takes guts to believe we need this kind of support—and even more to practice accepting it. To open ourselves to being seen and held. To name what we need instead of settling for what's offered.

These five qualities aren't just signs of love—they *are* love: active, attentive, alive.

We don't stumble into relationships like this; we shape them, choice by choice, word by word. They offer not perfection but something better: a steady, spacious support that lets us grow into ourselves. The Five

Forces function like an exoskeleton—outer support that helps us stand taller, move more freely. Without intentionality, our support system can become a corset: tight, rigid, designed to contain rather than expand. One holds us up. The other holds us in. One brings us home to ourselves—more whole, more fully seen. The other keeps us small.

The Five Forces are what leads to our then doing our best, biggest work.

DuVernay's films following *Selma*—including *13th* (a powerful documentary on mass incarceration), *When They See Us* (a miniseries about the Central Park Five), and *A Wrinkle in Time* (a major studio fantasy film)—all demonstrated how her agentic power grew as she moved fluidly between indie passion projects and big-budget productions.

Her ability to navigate these worlds was bolstered by her strong support network.

When DuVernay wanted $40 million for *Origin*, she didn't need a studio boardroom; her strategic alliances—notably with philanthropists and institutions like the Ford Foundation—committed $10 million, allowing DuVernay to stay true to her vision without compromising to accommodate industry norms. It was so notable that even the *Washington Post* wrote about it.[7]

This approach was a radical form of power-building. Instead of competing for scraps in Hollywood's usual arenas, she created her own "blue ocean"—a space where the rules were hers to write and she was surrounded by people who shared her goals and values.[8]

Her words echo this: "Surround yourself with the right people and ask for and accept support."

Her Five Forces aren't just a safety net. They're a launchpad.

As Ava teaches us: To direct our power, "If your dream only includes you, it's too small."[9]

INNOVATION PRACTICE
Five Forces

*Goal: Know how to surround yourself with
the exoskeleton of support.*

The question isn't whether you have the talent or the vision. Your agentic power comes not from going it alone but from cultivating your Five Forces: relationships with people who see you fully, challenge you honestly, support your deepest goals, stand by you through everything, and encourage your becoming over their personal interests.

Who are your Five Forces? And if you don't have them yet, how will you begin to get them?

This is a trial-and-error process. As we meet people, we ask:

- When I'm with this person, who do I become?

- Do I like myself in their presence?

- Do I feel expanded, or diminished?

Relationships are mirrors. Look for people who help you feel more yourself—not less.

Then, when conflict arises (which it will, from choosing what to eat to how we view a political issue), what happens:

- Do they allow you to have your own ideas, or do they need to be "right"?

- Can they handle closeness and give space for you to be exactly as weird as you are?

- Is there room for change, disagreement, play?

Relationships add complexity, which is to say friction, to our world. This is a good thing. The key is whether difference can be handled.

- Can we repair after rupture?

It's not about how much you like the same movies—it's about how you handle not liking the same things. Because what you want is someone stretching who you are through your exchanges. Not in a hard way, but in a *Wow, that's a new or surprising thought* way.

- Do I feel energized, even surprised, after we talk?

If the relationship feels like duty or work, that's not a friend; that's a coping mechanism.

And remember, people evolve. Relationships are living things. It's okay to outgrow people. Just do it kindly.

- If I met them today, would I still choose them?

Sometimes the most loving thing is not clinging tighter but letting someone go with grace.

23

Work Isn't Worthy of Worship

Limiting Norm: Productivity
Leading Indicator: Presence

Worship anything, and it changes you.

Worship money, and you will always need more. Worship beauty, and you will always feel ugly. Worship power, and you will find yourself amassing it and using it to oppress others—even if you hated this when it was done to you.

We know this. It's the foundation of every fable, parable, and Disney movie.

What we worship invisibly and intangibly shapes every decision. We find ourselves on roads we don't mean to be on simply because of what we devote ourselves to.

And we worship the hustle of work—of productivity—without much thought.

Which means we never question where our devotion could go instead.

Work as an Identity

Gina returned from work to find dinner dishes and food spread out over the kitchen countertop.

"Seriously? Can't you all just clean up after yourselves? I've had a long day, and the last thing I need is to come home to a mess."

"Hey, yeah, I was going to clean up after I finished my homework," her eldest kid, Beth, said as she sat up, alert. She had been lounging, but her mom venting like this always put her on edge.

"Okay, you do that. I'll just grab something to eat and go to my room. I've got some more work to do anyway. See you later."

As she got to her bedroom, where she had set up a workspace, Gina felt resentful—not of work and how it seeped into every minute of every day, but of her family. They didn't do what they could to support her so she could focus on work. She was, after all, the primary income earner by a long stretch. They needed the insurance, the pay. And they all needed her to keep working hard. Why did they not understand that? Support that?

She was venting to me via text. As was her daughter.

Beth wrote, "We need her, too, as a person. Mom is more than her job."

At the exact moment my heart went out to Beth, Gina's text came in. THIS IS WHO I AM.

At Work and Out of It

As we identify with our work, it becomes our religion, and we, its parishioners.

Benjamin Franklin—a founding father and patron saint of productivity—taught us this. Diligence is the mother of good luck. Defer pleasure in favor of labor. Get in early and stay late. Put forth an honest effort. Working hard is a virtue.

How we work today is thoroughly steeped in his ideas, forging the bars of our cage.

In hustle culture, work promises salvation: meaning, community, worth itself. We genuflect before our laptops, checking emails on Sundays to avoid the panic of Monday's inbox avalanche. We drag ourselves to work sick, celebrating the martyrdom as dedication. We resent our children's snow days—not for the lost wages but for the disruption to our devotional schedule. The pursuit of our goals is evidence of our passions. Home becomes a recovery station between shifts at the temple of productivity. And inbox zero is a moral victory.

In the constant presence of work, we lose our presence altogether.

This compulsion to always be "on," regardless of capacity, has a name: presenteeism. While absenteeism costs companies $150 billion annually, presenteeism bleeds $1.5 trillion in lost productivity.[1] This tenfold difference isn't an accident; it's architecture.

Exhausted, depleted workers can't organize and lobby for better; sure, they produce less, which isn't great. But they appear more committed, which is perfect for keeping everyone in line—the norm is clear. The economics expose the con: This isn't about productivity; it's about priorities.

Those benefitting from the system encourage this devotion to work. They will not ask if your family relationships are deteriorating as they give you the "most valuable player" award. They will not ask about your mental health as they give you the "opportunity" to take on more work, always more. They will not question why you send emails during your kid's birthday party.

They will celebrate you for how committed you are. Not for how joyous you are.

Complain? They will recite the scripture: *Work isn't supposed to be fun; that's why they call it work!* That's the Franklin doctrine—work is worshipped, suffering is virtue, exhaustion is character.

Hustle becomes a love language in the holy house of Work. It promises self-actualization while delivering self-annihilation. It sells freedom through productivity while constructing elaborate prisons of perpetual inadequacy. It insists that this is the Way.

We mistake the grinding of our own spirits for the sound of success.

Working for Free

"We're all volunteering" was how my 22-year-old stepdaughter described her weekend work.

After she finished her bachelor's degree, she started as a provisional employee at Google. Every weekend, she got out her computer and worked for four hours.

I asked about it because she was planning her life around this "volunteer" role. Google had hired her for a standard 40-hour-per-week job inspecting ads. But every weekend, for 50 or so weeks of the year, her ad support team worked an extra four hours—for free—for this multibillion-dollar company.

It seemed odd to me. But not to my stepdaughter.

Her explanation went something like this: Someone else would need to do the work if she didn't sign up for her four-hour block. And she didn't want to inconvenience her colleagues and peers, so she did her part. Not one of them questioned why another team wasn't hired to cover weekends—or why they weren't paid for the extra hours. Clearly, the work was needed. And it wasn't like Google was suffering for money.

Google was getting more than it was giving. The balance was off.

A few years later, the topic came up again, and this lovebug of mine now rolled her eyes at how much the company expected from people. The free evening food meant everyone stayed a few extra hours—leaving little time for friends. The expectation to always do work over the weekend left little time to develop a hobby. She wanted a richer life, she said. Yes, of course, she wanted work to provide her with meaning. Still, work shouldn't be so centered that it overtook everything—like an octopus, its tentacles smothering until there was no Self left.

We mistake the grinding of our own spirits for the sound of success.

Only after having kids did she start to set clearer weekend boundaries. She still works on weekends, when necessary, but not with the expectation that she will do it all the time. Having children gave her a reason to resist overwork—because she knows that neglecting those she loves isn't loving.

I notice that where once she gave 100% to work, she now splits that 100% between work, husband, and kids. She's still giving everything she has—it's just spread across more people.

I'm still not sure she's getting what *she* needs.

Her story shows a deeper pattern: When we give 100%—to work alone or to work plus family—we inevitably neglect something essential: our capacity to *be*, which is the wellspring of our capacity to *create*.

When we run all-out at 100%, there's no reserve left to create our best work. If our schedule is fully committed, we can't take the time to listen to a colleague and hear people out. If we're at full capacity, we can't pause and wonder if the question we're asking is our best formulation. If we're always busy, we're not building better.

The research says that if you leave just some slack—if you're operating at, say, 95% vs. 105%—you'll have the capacity to create value from a spacious place of *being*, rather than a tapped-out place of *doing*.[2]

We're human *beings*, after all, not human *doings*.

A cliché, yes—but one that reminds us of where our real power lies.

Now, for some, slack isn't a possibility. As we discussed in chapter 5, you can't sleep when you're dead. You can't choose presence when the economic model depends on your constant productivity just to survive. In that case, the lack of slack isn't a personal failing—it's a structural one.

Setting Yourself on Fire to Keep a Business Warm

Over the years, I've watched brilliant people trap themselves in this cycle.

One of my favorite people works so hard that she fantasizes about faking her own death or at least a coma—not because she hates her work, but just to escape the demands of it. Someone I work with felt guilty for "cheating" work when she prioritized her suicidal son. Another, a professor of strategy, said she won't consider throwing her hat in the ring for the newly open dean's role because she's sure that to do the job "well," she'd *have* to work 80-hour weeks. It's self-preservation, yes—but it's also denying her gifts.

I could keep going. So could you.

We know this all-out 100+% model in our bones.

As early as 1951, sociologist C. Wright Mills warned us otherwise. "Many whips are inside men," he wrote in *White Collar*, "who do not know how they got there, or indeed that they are there."[3] The lash is no longer on our backs, he argued—it's embedded in our identities. It looks like responding to Slack pings, or reaching inbox zero, or meditating to improve one's productivity, and doing weekend work for "just a few hours," to "be a team player." We have been taught to do it ourselves. In the name of commitment. In the name of purpose.

When I suggest to Gina or my stepdaughter that they take a step back, they resist.

But over the years, I've had colleagues try something out for size. I'd say, "See if you can find what 80% feels like. Just try it out for a week or two." The people I asked were hard workers, and so it seemed like I was asking them to be a slacker, lazy, or delinquent.

Going from 110% to 80% feels like an enormous dropping of the ball.

But you know what all of them realized?

No one noticed.

What's shifting isn't simply about hours or output. Though, of course, there's that. It's about finding a better way to define one's worth. And to redefine how to do our best work.

Worship work, and you'll set yourself on fire to keep a business warm.

Worship being a human person fully alive, and work becomes a way to do that.

Self or Work

There is a shift between work that imprisons us and work that sets us free—between labor that chains our days into units of obligation and labor that flows from our liberation.

When work is the organizing force, we become captives in our own lives, our spirits bound to rhythms not our own—we are efficient but caged. But when work is a way for the Self to contribute to the world, it becomes the pathway to our truest freedom—when our hands move not from compulsion but from choice, when our efforts break open like dawn across the horizon of possibility—then we discover what it means to be truly connected to the world.

The difference is what gets centered, prioritized: Self or Work.

This is an identity question. It's an organizing principle, too. And, also, our economic system. To assert that you are not your Work, you are your Self is to decide that our economy should work for us, not that we work for it. Where we don't do everything for "them" without also bene-fitting ourselves. Where we stop taking care of and being responsible for

something that isn't ours to manage, while neglecting the very person—
ourselves—that we *are* responsible for.

You cannot do great work from a place of servitude and submissiveness.

You can't create great work with a bent back.

You do great work when you stand tall with others, to contribute from
your fullness.

I recognize I write that with privilege. I know how hollow this can
sound when so many around the world are simply desperate for work—
any work—regardless of whether it fulfills them.

I am not ignoring that reality; I'm simply holding space for a better
one. To articulate a future vision. To believe in the possibility of better.

Creating value. I'm a big fan of it. But not of this slavish devotion to
work. Not of serving an entity that is ultimately just a shell. A business
is a legal entity, not the source of value creation. The source of value
creation is an original point of view, born from each of us, shaped by all
of us, and grown into realities by our collective efforts.

A business can die and be reborn. Anything that happens to it is,
therefore, survivable—even if painful. But the source of value—human
ingenuity—doesn't work that way. You can't tap into your energy if it's
all spent. If you've neglected your loved ones, they have already been
harmed. You can't get back your interests if you are a dry husk of a human
by the time you retire. Creating value is essential—but work cannot be
the central organizing force of your life.

What matters is how we can use our life energy to add value—at work.

The goal is to be fully alive. Period. At work, yes. But not just there.
Everywhere.

Now, back to Benjamin Franklin. Franklin argued that one's working
life could be, should be, the center of happiness. Some criticize him for
this belief while pointing out that he enslaved other human beings. He's
known to have purchased at least seven slaves, and he included adver-
tisements for the sale of people in his newspapers. In 2020, a statue of
Franklin in Philadelphia was vandalized with red paint on his hands—to
symbolize the blood on them.[4]

That criticism is valid. I want to add one more.

Franklin's worship of work didn't just cost him ethically. It cost him personally. He neglected his wife, Deborah, and was estranged from his son William. He is held up as a hero, as someone who said a job could be pleasurable. But beneath that is something more insidious. He promoted a vision of work that justified domination. That excused cruelty. That let him believe the value he produced—his inventions, his legacy—mattered more than the harm it caused to get there. Yes, we got a kite. But we also got a blueprint, a norm, that lets people build empires while denying the humanity *of* others and connection *with* others to do so.

That's the cost of worshipping work: not honoring human aliveness.

INNOVATION PRACTICE
The Four-Vote Strategy

Goal: To be fully alive at work and do your best work, not just work. Design for that.

You have one core responsibility: to apply that gift which is yours and yours alone. Not alone—but in relationship with many. Each day, you get to cast two votes. So does work. You can give both of yours to the work—to the team goals, the looming deadline, the hope of a raise. Or you can split the votes: one for the work, one for what fuels your ability to create value—your needs, your well-being, your ideas, your growth. This is not a private act. When enough of us stop giving away our votes, we stop playing a rigged game. We stop reinforcing systems that expect silence, reward self-sacrifice, and call it professionalism. When it works for all of us, the votes are equal. It works for work and our collective aliveness.

But we need to know how to place our votes:

Four Votes Framework

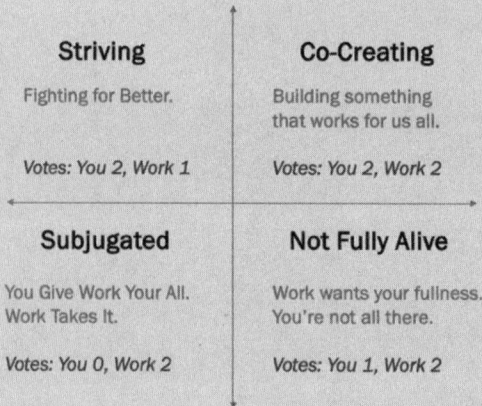

Striving

Fighting for Better.

Votes: You 2, Work 1

Co-Creating

Building something that works for us all.

Votes: You 2, Work 2

Subjugated

You Give Work Your All. Work Takes It.

Votes: You 0, Work 2

Not Fully Alive

Work wants your fullness. You're not all there.

Votes: You 1, Work 2

24

Change the Metrics

Limiting Norm: Success
Leading Indicator: Freedom

Success can create its own cage.

When we finally muster the courage to pursue that better life—following our joy, living with purpose, using our true talents—fear still looms. But it's not just failure we fear. It's what happens when we stray from the well-trodden path. We fear becoming the "lonely cat lady," the woman shamed for not doing what others expect, with only her cats to love. Or we dread ending up in our parents' basement, unable to provide for ourselves or stand on our own. Maybe we'll become the "struggling artist," passionate but unstable, living in small and shabby spaces, eating ramen noodles.

These stories—norms ingrained in our culture—tell us, show us, and ever so "humorously" pressure us to do what is expected of us: get an education, land a real job, create financial stability, be independent, get and stay married.

Follow the script, they say, and maybe, just maybe, you'll make it.

Success, as we've defined it, isn't just a trap—it's a lifelong payment plan.

When Success Metrics Collide

Firmly backing his workers, Howard Schultz stood up against stock market investors pushing to cut benefits and healthcare. "I'm not building a stock," he declared. "We are a performance-based company driven through the lens of humanity."[1]

It was classic Schultz—the kind of statement that positioned him as capitalism's conscience, the CEO who'd cracked the code on doing well by doing good.

But listen closely to that phrase: "a performance-based company driven through the lens of humanity." Notice how performance comes first. Notice how humanity becomes the lens, not the foundation. It's a subtle but revealing set of values, one that would come to define—and ultimately undermine—Schultz's legacy.

For decades, this formulation worked beautifully for Schultz. During the 2008 financial crisis, Starbucks shares plummeted to $2.93, but Schultz's turnaround plan—anchored in maintaining worker benefits— saw shares recover to $9.41 by the end of 2009, a 221% gain.[2]

The long-term numbers were even more spectacular.

From 2008 to 2017, Schultz oversaw nearly $100 billion added to the company's market capitalization while maintaining his progressive benefits philosophy. By 2023, Starbucks was generating $35.976 billion in annual revenue. It was a company built, as Schultz put it, through "the fragile balance of profit and conscience."[3]

As he explained to Walter Isaacson, "In 1987, when we had 11 stores, we decided early on that we were going to build a different kind of business model."[4] The costs were real: comprehensive health insurance for part-time workers decades before the Affordable Care Act, stock options for employees working more than 20 hours a week, and eventually free college tuition for all eligible employees. These weren't small gestures— they represented hundreds of millions in annual expenses that competitors avoided.

Schultz didn't just build the company; he built his identity through it.

He was the "good guy" of American capitalism, the CEO who proved that treating workers well was smart business. His success metrics were perfectly aligned: happy workers, loyal customers, growing profits, and a reputation as a moral leader in corporate America.

But success metrics have a way of calcifying.

Because there was a darker reality beneath the surface of this narrative.

In August 2014, *New York Times* reporter Jodi Kantor published "Working Anything but 9 to 5," a devastating exposé that followed Jannette Navarro, a 22-year-old Starbucks barista and single mother, through the chaos of algorithmic scheduling.[5] Kantor revealed how Starbucks used software to optimize labor costs that created unpredictable schedules that changed weekly—sometimes daily. Navarro would get her schedule just days in advance, making it nearly impossible to arrange childcare, pursue her education, or maintain relationships.

The software prioritized the company's efficiency over workers' lives.

The article had an immediate impact: Within hours of its publication, Starbucks announced it would revise scheduling policies for 130,000 workers.

Then, *dun, dun, dun*—the very people Schultz defined himself as protecting challenged Schultz directly.

Starbucks workers began organizing unions in 2021 and 2022. Suddenly, Schultz was being questioned not by greedy investors but by the workers themselves. They wanted higher wages, better scheduling, improved working conditions—the very things Schultz thought he was *already* providing through his benevolent leadership.

I can only imagine how hard that was for him.

He surely thought he was doing everything right and being underappreciated, maybe even thought that his staff were being too demanding, too needy, too much.

To his credit, he tried to address worker concerns. Schultz announced $200 million in additional investments in worker pay and training, including raises for employees with at least two years of service and nearly doubled training time.[6] The catch? These benefits were explicitly withheld from unionizing stores.

Workers said Schultz didn't understand how the country and their lives had changed. They were no longer grateful for Schultz's paternalistic care; they wanted their own agency, voice, and power.

And Schultz spent hundreds of millions of dollars to give them everything except that.

It was a threat to his life's work, as one *Washington Post* profile put it.[7]

The guy who valued the metric of being a good guy, a fair employer, and a conscious capitalist leader was being challenged on all three measures.

Rather than seeing unionization as a natural extension of workers flourishing, he saw it as a rejection of everything he'd built. The National Labor Relations Board found that Howard Schultz violated federal labor law by telling a barista in California who questioned the coffee chain's response to union organizing to "go work for another company."

Even more revealing was the pattern of economic coercion. A federal judge ruled that Starbucks violated labor law when it increased wages and offered new perks and benefits only to nonunion employees. The company was using its financial resources—the very benefits Schultz had pioneered as progressive—as weapons against workers seeking collective bargaining power. Union organizers noted the obvious: "If you can add these benefits now, then we could have had them all along. So why is it so important to add them now?"[8]

The same financial flexibility that had once made him a *hero* for defying investors now made him a *villain* for defying workers' right to organize.

The transformation is instructive; it reveals something fundamental about how we measure success.

When Schultz appeared before the Senate in March 2023, he unequivocally denied that the coffee giant had broken the law in its fight against unionization during tense questioning from Senator Bernie Sanders. Here was a man who had spent decades building his reputation as a worker-friendly CEO, now being grilled about labor violations while sitting on a $3.9 billion personal fortune built partly on the narrative of being capitalism's conscience.

We all live this paradox, though obviously at a different scale.

Because once we commit to a success identity, we can use that identity to shield ourselves from changing.

Good guy.
Hard worker.
Entrepreneur.

These labels can help us and hurt us. An entrepreneur who has defined themself by that metric will pound at the door of success to keep their enterprise alive even if it's killing them to do so. A hard worker who gets their worth celebrated by pulling all-nighters will become a workaholic. A good guy will shut down anyone who is telling him there is still room to grow, to avoid a threat to Self.

In business, we create heroes out of CEOs who treat workers better than they have to, and then we're surprised when those same CEOs resist workers who want to be treated better than any CEO thinks they should be. The norm is to measure success by the gap between what employers could do and what they choose to do, rather than the gap between what workers need and what they actually get.

The irony in the Schultz case? The metric for success—being seen as the good guy—had become more important than the underlying values that originally made him good.

Break Chains

If "success" is a terrible metric, what is a good one?

I hate to tell you this—I don't know. In fact, no one does. If you're seeking answers for this, chances are you've been grappling with this question for quite some time. You've likely scoured books, magazines, and Google or compared your achievements to those on lists like "30 Under 30" or "40 Under 40." Some of you might even wonder if your absence from these lists means you'll never amount to anything.

I urge you to stop.

You're looking outside yourself, and that needs to end. The best measure of your worth isn't found in comparisons to others or defined by external standards. The feelings and desires we chase in our pursuit of success or fulfillment don't originate from any places or anyone outside of ourselves.

In fact, to chase success as defined by others is to chain ourselves to a life that can never be our own. We hand over the keys to our freedom, measuring our worth by standards we did not create. In doing so, we shrink, feeling perpetually inadequate, forever racing toward a finish line that keeps moving.

The truest act of power, the one that sets each of us free, is claiming the metric that matters. It doesn't define you; you define it. It's stepping off the well-worn path and daring to craft our own perspective, guided not by the eyes of others but by the quiet, undeniable truth that only we can hear—a truth that whispers, *What is it that we seek?*

While specifics will differ for everyone, some universal desires exist. What we seek isn't in approval or the roles we've been handed. It's in the radical act of living as our truest, fullest Self—the Self with a capital S. This Self holds our history, honors our experiences, celebrates our dreams, and fuels our passion. It doesn't seek to be small or to serve others at the cost of its own essence. This is the Self that builds, creates, and connects with those who share our values. It's the Self that moves forward, even when the path is unclear. To live as our whole Self is to embrace the joy of showing up in this world on our own terms, shaping our surroundings, and insisting that we belong just as we are. This is what we seek: the power to stand tall, unbound, and to meet the world without flinching.

The Self seeks freedom.

Freedom is not the absence of restraint but the presence of choice, self-determination, and the ability to live with integrity. It means being valued and creating value with the systems, scaffolding, and structures in place that allow each of us to do just that. We can engage in work that shapes us as we shape it. When we are free, we recognize that each of us is worthy—not because we've earned it or met some arbitrary metric, but because we've acknowledged our inherent value.

It's our faces "lit up," as Toni Morrison and Oprah would say.

From the inside, I would add.

It doesn't define you; you define it.

The way we measure this freedom isn't about success or failure.

It's measured by progress toward our own objectives. Which is both simpler and more profound than we think. Teresa Amabile of Harvard

Business School studied what drove engagement at work, and 76% of participants reported that their best days at work were when they made progress, any kind of progress.[9] Making progress was the most significant contributor to positive emotions and motivation. This is in stark contrast to how most managers view what matters—only 5% of 669 surveyed by Gallup ranked supporting progress as the top motivator for their teams. Instead, most placed more value on recognition, incentives/pay, and interpersonal support.

Practice doesn't make perfect, as is commonly said.

No, practice makes progress.

So *what is it you seek?*

Only when you answer this question for yourself can you begin to live into who you are. Only then can you join with others to create the most value. And it's not a onetime decision. It's a decision you'll make again and again because each day invites you to choose your own freedom. When you do, you'll know the "right" measures of progress.

Not because there is one right or wrong. But because it is *yours*.

The Tree of You Is Withering

As we tied ribbons to balloons, arranged sunflowers in vases, and placed cupcakes just so, Marian began telling me about her marriage. We were throwing a party together for someone we both loved, our hands busy while we talked.

"He's trying," she said, more to herself than to me. "He said he's willing to do whatever it takes. To learn how to be better for me. To show me the love I need, not just the distant comfort of being on the couch and in the same house together."

Her friend Susan, folding napkins nearby, confirmed this. "Paul's 100% in," she said.

I nodded. Paying attention as if my life depended on it.

Later, sweeping up crumbs after all the guests had gone, I replayed Marian's words in my mind.

Our situations weren't the same: Her husband was vulnerable instead of justifying his behavior. He owned his part instead of casting one person as the villain of the story. He was open to changing, while mine kept insisting that he was a "good guy."

I both loved and hated hearing her story. Loved that she named for me what I wanted—the shared commitment, repair, a way forward. Hated that my relationship was headed another way.

I resorted to mental gymnastics, an inner script running to try to make both things true.

Everyone can grow. Be patient; he'll get past his defensiveness. Stop wanting what he can't give. Maybe I am too needy, like he says. He's seeing his own therapist now—good sign. I'm too sensitive to the yelling. And if I speak even more carefully, maybe he won't feel the need to cut me down. Some days, one person only has 20% to give, and the other carries the rest. Better to work on a 25-year relationship with the father of our children than let it fall apart.

I remembered how he brings me coffee in bed, that mug warm in my hands.

Who cares if the pillow is still wet from last night's tears?

This is what love is, right? Holding on until there's nothing left to hold?

I must admit, I didn't know.

My parents split when I was just a year old, and I grew up with my mother telling me it was my fault. What I didn't understand as a child was how my father, dark-skinned under British colonial rule in India, had directed his pain and oppression toward my mother. That's why she had to leave her homeland to provide for us because, as a divorced woman, she couldn't support us there. My mother's parents didn't help her—though they could have done so—because she was seen as rebellious for having married without her father's approval. She had arranged for me to stay with a cousin's family, who cared for me until I had to leave them, too, at four and a half, to reunite with a brother, sister, and mother I didn't recognize. In a new country. With a language I didn't know.

Which is all to say that relationships were always complicated for me. Due to personal trauma, yes. But that trauma was shaped by the invisible and intersecting forces of white supremacy, patriarchy, and colonialism.

But I wanted to learn. To get good at relationships. To prove that the love and connection I saw in my friends' families and read about or saw on TV wasn't some fantasy—it was possible for me, too.

Yet Marian's story had me spinning.

I took the question to my pastor and friend, Dave.

"What is the most loving way?" I asked.

He looked at me kindly but directly. "You're always looking for growth," he said. He and I had been meeting for over a year on this topic, so he knew the situation. "And every time you see the tiniest sprout of it, you get hopeful things will get better."

And then he paused, meaningfully. I could hear the "but" in his tone.

"While you've been waiting patiently and sacrificially for that 'tree of us' to flourish, you haven't noticed your own."

I stared at him, confused and just wanting an answer to my question.

He waited for the words to sink in before continuing. "Your tree," he said quietly. "It's been withering. For some time now. You've been holding on and working and working, but you're not meant to live this way. You deserve to grow in a space where your value isn't constantly questioned, and your worth doesn't need to be proven. Your tree is withering as you keep focusing on the tree of us."

His words sat there between us like heavy branches I hadn't seen before.

I left that meeting not exactly clear, but clearer. Somewhere along the way, I had internalized specific ideas about success: Keeping the family together was paramount, marriage was hard work, sacrifice was essential, and so on. I thought I was saving my son from a "broken home," not seeing that a home where people feel unsafe is broken its own way. I couldn't see that a broken home is not about how many people live there but about whether peace lives there.

And that the more we fight to be valued by someone else, the more our own value withers.

Question the Metrics

When we define ourselves by common success metrics like the length of a marriage or the salary we earn, we forfeit the opportunity to live authentically.

This is an intangible decision. Picture a wild animal born into captivity: Even when the cage door swings open, the animal remains inside, conditioned to stay in place. It's not about choosing to escape; it can't even grasp the concept of freedom. As economist John Maynard Keynes said, "The difficulty lies not in the new ideas but in escaping from the old ones." Our mental cages are built from familiar ideas that feel comfortable, even as they hold us back.

In this way, success metrics shape us—as they are intended to.

The first known metrics date back to ancient civilizations like Egypt and Mesopotamia, where standardized measures managed labor on monumental state projects. These systems broke down colossal tasks, like building pyramids, into measurable units, assessing the output of enslaved workers and the effectiveness of their overseers.

It's crucial to recognize that the rulers, like early pharaohs, didn't live by metrics; no one asked if they were "performing productively." The powerful design and impose metrics on others, and a leader's departure doesn't disrupt the measures; a pharaoh might die, but the metrics continue.

People are measured by what they do for the powerful, while their own needs go unvalued.

It's easy to mistake metrics for a genuine desire to track or maximize productivity, but they serve a far more strategic purpose. Metrics aren't just numbers; they shape economic and social order, defining value. Metrics are the intersection of value and values, the line between financial gain and human worth. Success metrics like year-over-year growth, profit margins, shareholder returns, and employee performance ratings reinforce hierarchies: Those who produce more are deemed more valuable, while those who manage production reap the rewards—all defined by those at the top. Even in the nonprofit sector, which aims to "do good," metrics often ask how many people are served rather than about the quality of the work. In education, teaching to the test has overtaken the learning context to "prove" that something of value is being done.

Until we create metrics that integrate our own needs, we remain trapped.

What Is Worth Your Life

I never stopped loving Hubster—I still do—I just started loving myself, too.

From a distance, the shift seems like self-worth or self-love.

But this oversimplifies how power works.

Each of our lives has been shaped by domination and control, supremacy and patriarchy. We can feel *inadequate* as we are told to speak up instead of having the room change to allow us to be heard. We can lack *self-worth* as we seek out mentoring because the world has told us that we're missing something when the fact is more that the door is being blocked from the inside. We can feel *tenuous* as we demand equal pay because pay issues cannot be fixed one person at a time.

Insecurity or self-worth issues are, more correctly, tensions between the Self and the powerful. The Self knows our value, yet the powerful signals otherwise. Insecurity is when we are encouraged to think we are broken, when the reality is that we're living in structures designed to break us.

I realize now that my relational struggle within the marriage wasn't about him or even about me. It was always about what I valued and how I was being valued, and the success metrics that fuse the two.

And so, too, at work.

Once you know your value and values—specific to you—you can start to shift power. And when you do, it will liberate not only you but us.

For, as one of my favorite authors says, there is no such thing as one-way liberation.[10]

Howard Schultz's story is not really about Howard Schultz. Just as my marriage story isn't about my marriage.

These stories are about all of us.

Every definition of success carries within it the seeds of its own contradiction. Define friendship as always being there, and you can find yourself caring for others and not yourself. Define marriage as preserving the family unit, and you might endure what diminishes you. Define work success as earning loads of money, and you will feel betrayed when your ideas are taken but your paycheck arrives on time. Define joy as having a successful exit, and you will be crushed when the VC doesn't fund you.

The very metrics that guide us toward one kind of flourishing can obscure the ways in which we're failing.

This is why the work of defining our metrics is unfinished work. What we measure shapes what we do, and what we do shapes who we become—which means we must constantly return to the question of what we're measuring and why. The future is always being written by the definitions we choose today, and the only way to avoid traps is to hold those definitions lightly enough that we can change them when they begin to change us in ways we didn't intend.

THE PRACTICE TO BREAK FREE

Redefine the Metrics

Goal: Make the invisible visible.

What you measure inevitably becomes what you optimize for. If your team measures only outcomes, you'll optimize for short-term results. If you also measure progress, you'll build the capabilities that create sustainable success. There are no right answers, just aligning questions.

Step 1: Establish Values

As a team, write down what you care about most in your work together. Not what the company says you *should* care about—what you actually *do* care about. It could be: "We value learning from our mistakes, creating elegant solutions, and making our users' lives genuinely better." It could also be "Our work has to be zany or we'll die from boredom."

Step 2: List Metrics

Be honest about what your team actually tracks, reports on, or uses to judge if you're winning. Example: "We measure success by quarterly revenue, number of features shipped, and whether we hit our deadlines."

Step 3: Mind the Gap

Compare your values (Step 1) with your measurements (Step 2). Most teams get trapped measuring outcomes (features shipped, revenue) instead of the *progress* that creates those outcomes (learning, problem-solving, user understanding). Example: "We value learning from mistakes, but we never measure whether we're actually getting smarter. We value elegant solutions, but we only count how many we ship, not how well they work. We value helping users, but we track revenue, not user satisfaction."

(cont.)

Step 4: Design a Better Metric

For each value, create one or two simple ways to measure both the outcome *and* the progress. Make them specific enough that your team will know if you're succeeding. Examples? Learning: "What did we discover this month that changed how we approach problems? How many experiments did we run?" Elegance: "How many user complaints did we solve with our solutions? How much code did we delete while adding functionality?"

Step 5: Check and Adjust Regularly

Every few months, ask as a team: "Are our measurements still serving our values, or are they starting to drive us in directions we don't want to go?"

Remember: There's no perfect measurement system. The goal isn't to measure everything perfectly—it's to ask the questions of what you value and then make sure your measurements of that are pulling you toward your best work.

CONCLUSION

The Jaws of Life

When the only thing you have to change is everything, it can be overwhelming.

I've been there.

When I was 18 years old, I was supposed to enter into an arranged marriage. I wanted so much to support my mother—to give her what she needed. She had raised three kids on her own, doing night shifts and overtime to keep us afloat. How could I not want to help her?

What no one in my family knew was that I'd secretly applied to UC Berkeley—and gotten in. But I couldn't go there on my own, so I signed a one-year deferral, started community college, and hoped I could somehow stitch my dreams to hers.

Then one day I came home from school to find an engagement party already underway. My aunties and uncles were all gathered. The house was filled with the scent of biryani and the clatter of celebration.

I asked if anyone had talked to the man I was to marry about my desire for an education.

No, they hadn't. They didn't plan to. The focus was on negotiating a house for my mother. I knew—even at 18—that this wealthy widower, with a housekeeper and nanny, wouldn't mind if I got my education. But if I waited until after the marriage, I might lose another year. Or more.

I wanted them to ask on my behalf.

My mother refused. My uncle, handling the negotiations, refused. What I wanted didn't matter.

You should know something else. In high school, I was part of a club called Future Business Leaders of America—FBLA for short. It's a little ironic how much I now challenge how business works.

But that experience shaped me. And the words I chose next.

I told my mother: I'm the product. No deal could be made without me. I would move out unless they agreed to ask about my education. I didn't need them to guarantee the outcome—just the dignity of the question.

She didn't believe me. Why would she? I had no money. No independent checking account. No family or community support. She thought she had all the power. And she did.

But I acted anyway.

I packed five books and two outfits into a soggy grocery store box. No toothbrush—this was theater. The box didn't even have a lid.

I was sure she'd stop me before I got to the front door.

She didn't.

I was sure she'd stop me before I made it down the driveway.

She didn't.

And that's when it hit me: I had no idea where I was going.

But I still walked forward.

I spent that night in a small office at the community college where I worked. I had a key. I wasn't supposed to be there. But I was.

I thought maybe she would come around the next day. She didn't.

Turns out I'm stubborn. But I learned it from her.

She never relented.

And I never returned.

That's how my life—as I know it—began. Not with certainty. But with one step. Alone, destitute, scared. But walking anyway.

If this story resonates, it's not because it's about arranged marriage. Or culture. Or even gender. It's because it's about power—who gets heard, whose needs are ignored, and what happens when you stop participating in your own oppression.

I've lived this reinvention process many times. Leaving my family. Leaving corporate life. Leaving my company. Leaving a 20-year-long marriage. Losing a best friend. Even surviving an attack by a serial rapist. Each time, the pattern was the same. My mother wanted me to be her belonging. Corporate life wanted my insights but not my agency. My team wanted me to stay when I couldn't. My husband of more than 20 years wanted the marriage—but not my desires. My best friend wanted me to do what she wanted for me. My rapist simply took what he wanted.

What they all had in common was this: My needs weren't valued. Only their needs were centered.

Each time, I thought I was walking away. But I was really walking toward something: the life that could be built only by my naming and then acting on my interests. It did not solve everything right away, but it shifted everything over time.

When you decide what matters to you and act on your interests—not theirs alone—the power dynamic changes instantly.

You don't have to fix what failed you. You can build what frees you.

That's not just a personal truth. That's a pattern.

Today, in my family, kids are not treated like extensions of their parents. They are seen as whole people with agency and autonomy. I'm not saying I was the change. I'm saying: This is how change happens.

We don't need to fight the old system. When we create what works for us—so filled with aliveness—it becomes irresistible. And the old becomes increasingly irrelevant. And it always begins the same way: not with clarity, or safety, or assuredness. But with the refusal to accept the status quo. By seeing and challenging the norms that hold us in place.

So when someone tells me that work is unfixable, I understand. I've lived in systems that felt immovable. But I've also lived what happens when we decide they will move.

We can believe what we're told: Things at work suck and nothing can fix it. When a system feels too big and too broken to fix, the instinct often is to check out or wait for someone else to fix it—not to believe that a small act on our part could make a difference.

But it can.

The system doesn't change because someone at the top issues a memo. It changes when someone in the middle does something different—and others follow.

Our expectations of one another spread faster than any policy. One act of humanity, repeated, is how every better *whatever* has ever started.

Let me put it more simply: You don't have to fix the system. You just have to refuse to pass it on. You say, *I am not interested in fixing the past but building our next.*

That act of future-building? It's contagious.

The way we invite others to play. The way we ask a generative question. The way we define better metrics. The way we stop accepting that our fates are ranked but see them as linked. The way we stop pretending that individualism is strength. All of it—is leadership.

You don't have to fix what failed you. You can build what frees you.

It's that quiet, persistent refusal to submit to what harms us that makes change possible.

Nothing changes until something does.

Some will call this hopefulness.

Some will call it bravery.

Some will say it's naïve.

History will decide what it is.

What I know is this: Nothing is preordained. The path ahead isn't marked. It is made by walking. By acting. By stepping out the front door, down the driveway, and onto a path that doesn't yet exist—until we go there.

And yes, I acknowledge that it will be hard.

But it's a good kind of hard.

And yes, it will require hope. Which sounds light and easy. But hope isn't light. It isn't passive. It doesn't wait for the right time. Hope is like the Jaws of Life—that powerful hydraulic tool firefighters use to pry people from wreckage. Hope is the force that breaks through, that opens what's crushing you, so a new future is possible. It is not comforting, that soft thing we want. It is, instead, solid and strong. And it creates the crack where the light gets in.

And when we dare to hope like that—with the raw power to break ourselves free—they lose their power over us.

Because in that act, we are already free.

Acknowledgments

No book is ever written alone, but this one required spotters. A brain injury bent my world sideways for more than two years, and yet, with the help of many, I found my footing here on the page. Thank you to my Concussion Care Circle! Including Dr. Michael Collins, without whom I'd never have recovered.

To **Lara Love**: Your gift is not just seeing the best in people but witnessing them into being. That is rarer than rare—the grace to let people unfold their brilliance. Thank you, my Lotused Love.

To **Hollis Heimbouch** and the entire team at Harper: Thank you for believing in this work when it was nothing more than a possibility. For collaborating in every way—from the big-idea clarity to the eleventh-hour final debates—until it became what it is now.

To **Cheryl Strayed**: for teaching me to seek out the truthiest truth at the bottom of the lasagna pan—and for showing me that the mess is not a detour but the path of freedom.

To my **Five Forces—Marie Cameron, Tim Kastelle, Alex Krasne, Tammy Madsen, Kristell Rivaille, Jean Russell, and Kathleen Warner (yes, I know, I'm lucky to have more than Five Forces)**: Thank you for the tea-leaf salad, french fries, and ratatouille; for the mind-melds; for the kind of nurturing that left fingerprints not just on my heart but on my imagination. Just look and you'll see your love pressed like ink into every page of this work.

I am talking here about reimagining work not as what limits us but as what can liberate us. These ideas are not mine alone. We are what shapes us, and I stand in a lineage of thinkers who carved the path through stone and lit the way forward. To **Angela Davis**, **Barbara Smith** and the **Combahee River Collective**, **Heather McGhee**, **Tressie McMillan Cottom**,

Michelle Alexander, Jamia Wilson, and **bell hooks**: Thank you for the road you carved and the torch you left burning. If this book carries even a fraction of your brilliance, it is because you made the way.

To **Omega Institute**, which invited me to write this work in the same spaces where Pema Chödrön and Gloria Steinem wrote: Thank you for the residency, the quiet, and the reminder that place can be teacher, too.

And finally, to **all who let me tell your stories here**: Thank you. Your lives, in all their mess and magnificence, are sure to help others. You hold the intangible, invisible vision of what could be.

Notes

INTRODUCTION: Caged

1. Urban studies theorist Richard Florida estimates that roughly one-third of US jobs (fewer, globally) fall within the "creative class"—including 12% in a "Super-Creative Core" and another ~20% in creative professions—leaving approximately two-thirds (≈67%) of jobs in roles with little to no creative component. Richard Florida, *The Rise of the Creative Class: And How It's Transforming Work, Leisure, Community, and Everyday Life* (Basic Books, 2002), chap. 2.

2. Nilofer Merchant, "Sitting Is the New Smoking," TED Talk, Long Beach, CA, February 2013, 3 min., 14 sec., https://www.ted.com/talks/nilofer_merchant_got_a_meeting_take_a_walk.

3. Sarah Ponczek, "Epic S&P 500 Rally Is Powered by Assets You Can't See or Touch," Bloomberg, October 21, 2020, https://www.bloomberg.com/news/articles/2020-10-21/epic-s-p-500-rally-is-powered-by-assets-you-can-t-see-or-touch.

4. Tim Kastelle, Nilofer Merchant, and Martie-Louise Verreynne, "What Creates Advantage in the 'Social Era'?," *Innovations* 10, nos. 3–4 (2015): 81–91, https://direct.mit.edu/itgg/article/10/3-4/81/9812/What-Creates-Advantage-in-the-Social-Era.

5. For more on the cage metaphor, see Marilyn Frye, "Oppression," in *The Politics of Reality: Essays in Feminist Theory* (Crossing Press, 1983).

6. Emily K. Carian and Amy L. Johnson, "The Agency Myth: Persistence in Individual Explanations for Gender Inequality," *Social Problems* 69, no. 1 (2022): 123–47, https://doi.org/10.1093/socpro/spaao72. While this study was gender-focused, it applies to power.

7. David Whyte, *Consolations: The Solace, Nourishment and Underlying Meaning of Everyday Words* (Many Rivers Press, 2014).

1: Trade Comfort for Change

1. Paraphrased from Octavia E. Butler, *Parable of the Sower* (New York: Four Walls Eight Windows, 1993).

2. Nilofer Merchant, *The Power of Onlyness: Make Your Wild Ideas Mighty Enough to Dent the World* (Viking, 2017), 45. Research conducted at the Martin Prosperity Institute at the University of Toronto's Rotman School of Management indicates that "one-half to as much as 70% of fresh new ideas are ignored."

3. In 2017, researchers Adam Galinsky and Joe C. Magee of Columbia University described how power and status act as self-reinforcing loops: How much status a person has directly affects whether their ideas are heard. Joe C. Magee and Adam D. Galinsky, " Social Hierarchy: The Self-Reinforcing Nature of Power and Status," *Academy of Management Annals* 2, no. 1 (2008): 351–98, https://doi.org/10.1080/19416520802211628.

4. Elizabeth Gilbert, "Your Elusive Creative Genius," TED Talk, Long Beach, CA, February 2009, 19 min., 29 sec., https://www.ted.com/talks/elizabeth _gilbert_your_elusive_creative_genius.

5. Jonathan Fields, *Uncertainty: Turning Fear and Doubt into Fuel for Brilliance* (Portfolio/Penguin, 2011).

6. Multiple lines of neuropsychological and trauma-informed research indicate that blame and shame elicit a physiological cascade. See Sarah B. Lupis, Natalie J. Sabik, and Jutta M. Wolf, "Role of Shame and Body Esteem in Cortisol Stress Responses," *Journal of Behavioral Medicine* 39 (2016): 262–75, https://doi.org/10.1007/s10865-015-9695-5; Bessel van der Kolk, *The Body Keeps the Score* (Viking, 2014), chap. 13; Kishani Townsend and Nerina Jane Caltabiano, "The Extended Nervous System: Affect Regulation, Somatic and Social Change Processes Associated with Mindful Parenting," *BMC Psychology* 7, no. 41 (2019), https://doi.org/10.1186/s40359-019-0313-0.

7. Studies demonstrate that anxiety limits cognitive flexibility—hindering creative problem-solving. See Michael W. Eysenck, Nazanin Derakshan, Rita Santos, et al., "Anxiety and Cognitive Performance: Attentional Control Theory," *Emotion* 7, no. 2 (2007): 336–53, https://doi.org/10.1037/1528-3542.7.2.336; Henk van Steenbergen, Guido P. H. Band, and Bernhard Hommel, "Threat but Not Arousal Narrows Attention: Evidence from Pupil Dilation and Saccade Control," *Frontiers in Psychology* 2, no. 281 (2011), https://doi.org/10.3389

/fpsyg.2011.00281; and Kaplan et al., "Attention Dysregulation Accounts for Cognitive Variation in Anxiety," *Scientific Reports* 13 (2023).

8.   Stefan G. Hofmann and Aleena C. Hay, "Rethinking Avoidance: Toward a Balanced Approach to Avoidance in Treating Anxiety Disorders," *Journal of Anxiety Disorders* 55 (April 2018): 14–21, https://doi.org/10.1016/j .janxdis.2018.03.004.

9.   Tim Kastelle, "A Conversation Is the Smallest Unit of Change," *The Discipline of Innovation* (blog), September 26, 2020, https://timkastelle.org /blog/2020/09/a-conversation-is-the-smallest-unit-of-change/.

10. My understanding of how we resist change—often unconsciously, and in service of protecting our identity, purpose, and social standing—is deeply influenced by the work of Robert Kegan and Lisa Laskow Lahey, who explore the hidden commitments that block transformation in *Immunity to Change: How to Overcome It and Unlock the Potential in Yourself and Your Organization* (Boston: Harvard Business Press, 2009).

2: The One with the Pain Is(n't) the One with the Problem

1.   Ross LaJeunesse, then Google's head of international public policy, spearheaded the company's 2010 decision to stop censoring search results in China and helped create a human-rights-focused program to champion free expression and data privacy. "Google and China," Opinion, *New York Times*, March 23, 2010, https://www.nytimes.com/2010/03/24/opinion/24wed2.html.

2.   Ross LaJeunesse, "I Was Google's Head of International Relations. Here's Why I Left," Medium, January 2, 2020, https://medium.com/ @rossformaine/i-was-googles-head-of-international-relations-here-s-why-i -left-49313d23065. LaJeunesse describes how he discovered that he was considered "problematic" after being "accidentally copied on an email from a senior HR director."

3.   Irving L. Janis, *Victims of Groupthink: A Psychological Study of Foreign-Policy Decisions and Fiascoes* (Houghton Mifflin, 1972). Janis observed that when dissent is discouraged or punished, individuals conform to group consensus, resulting in suppressed creativity and decision errors.

4.   Nilofer Merchant, "Don't Demonize Employees Who Raise Problems," *Harvard Business Review*, January 30, 2020, https://hbr.org/2020/01/dont-demonize-employees-who-raise-problems.

5. Charlan J. Nemeth and Jack A. Goncalo, "Finding Value in Dissent," in *Rebels in Groups: Dissent, Deviance, Difference, and Defiance*, ed. Jolanda Jetten and Matthew J. Hornsey (John Wiley & Sons, 2010). Nemeth and Goncalo reported that even when wrong, dissenting minority viewpoints can enhance team performance by approximately 30%.

6. Alexia Fernández Campbell, "Google Employees Say the Company Is Punishing Them for Their Activism," *Vox*, April 23, 2019, https://www.vox.com/2019/4/23/18512542/google-employee-walkout-organizers-claim-retaliation.

3: Disrupting Value

1. Christopher A. Bartlett, "Unilever's New Global Strategy: Competing Through Sustainability," Harvard Business School Case 916414 (November 2015; revised August 2016).

2. Michael Skapinker and Scheherazade Daneshkhu, "Can Unilever's Paul Polman Change the Way We Do Business?," *Financial Times*, September 29, 2016.

3. Myriam Sidibe illustrates how a simple bar of soap became a high-impact intervention when it was made affordable for daily budgets, local kiosks could profit, and a campaign was launched—in partnership with UN agencies, NGOs, competing brands, and governments—to change social norms and drive adoption. Myriam Sidibe, *Brands on a Mission: How to Achieve Social Impact and Business Growth Through Purpose* (Routledge, 2020), chap. 3.

4. Paul Polman and Andrew Winston, *Net Positive: How Courageous Companies Thrive by Giving More Than They Take* (Harvard Business Review Press, 2021).

5. "Paul Polman: In His Own Words," *Financial Times*, December 3, 2017, https://www.ft.com/content/2209d63a-d6ae-11e7-8c9a-d9c0a5c8d5c9.

6. "How Dove Empowered 60 Million Young People—and Counting," Unilever, July 29, 2020, https://www.unilever.com/news/news-search/2020/how-dove-empowered-60-million-young-people-and-counting/.

7. Jonathon Porritt, "Unilever: Profits Up; Purpose Down," JonathonPorritt.com, February 23, 2024, https://jonathonporritt.com/unilever-sustainability-commitments-abandoned/.

8. Sarah Kaplan, "The Promises and Perils of Corporate Purpose," *Strategy Science* 8, no. 2 (2023): 288–301, https://doi.org/10.1287/stsc.2023.0187.

9. Anand Giridharadas, *Winners Take All: The Elite Charade of Changing the World* (Alfred A. Knopf, 2018).

10. Kaplan, "Promises and Perils."

11. Milton Friedman, "The Social Responsibility of Business Is to Increase Its Profits," *New York Times Magazine*, September 13, 1970, https://www.nytimes.com/1970/09/13/archives/a-friedman-doctrine-the-social-responsibility-of-business-is-to.html.

12. Adam Smith, *An Inquiry into the Nature and Causes of the Wealth of Nations* (W. Strahan and T. Cadell, 1776), book I, chap. II, https://www.gutenberg.org/ebooks/3300.

13. Michael E. Porter and Mark R. Kramer, "Strategy and Society: The Link Between Competitive Advantage and Corporate Social Responsibility," *Harvard Business Review* 84, no. 12 (2006): 84–92, https://www.fsg.org/wp-content/uploads/2021/08/Strategy_and_Society.pdf.

14. Qian Wang, Junsheng Dou, and Shenghua Jia, "A Meta-Analytic Review of Corporate Social Responsibility and Corporate Financial Performance: The Moderating Effect of Contextual Factors," *Business & Society* 55, no. 8 (2016): 1083–1121, https://doi.org/10.1177/0007650315584317.

15. George Serafeim, "Social-Impact Efforts That Create Real Value," *Harvard Business Review*, September–October 2020, https://hbr.org/2020/09/social-impact-efforts-that-create-real-value.

16. "Brand Purpose as a Competitive Advantage," Global Marketing Trends 2022, Deloitte Insights, October 19, 2021, https://www.deloitte.com/us/en/insights/topics/marketing-sales/global-marketing-trends/2022/brand-purpose-as-a-competitive-advantage.html.

17. "New Meta-Analysis from NYU Stern Center for Sustainable Business and Rockefeller Asset Management Finds ESG Drives Better Financial Performance," NYU Stern School of Business, February 2, 2021, https://www.stern.nyu.edu/experience-stern/faculty-research/new-meta-analysis-nyu-stern-center-sustainable-business-and-rockefeller-asset-management-finds-esg.

18. This view is grounded in the work of adrienne maree brown, *Emergent Strategy: Shaping Change, Changing Worlds* (AK Press, 2017); Ursula K. Le Guin, "The Carrier Bag Theory of Fiction," in *Dancing at the Edge of the World* (Grove Press, 1989); and Indigenous scholar–activists like Deborah

McGregor, Cristina Eisenberg, Melissa K. Nelson, and Ochy Curiel, whose work spans ecological justice, traditional knowledge systems, and decolonial feminist theory. It also resonates with management thinkers such as Renée Mauborgne (coauthor of *Blue Ocean Strategy*), Linda Hill (on collective genius and leading from behind), Herminia Ibarra (on identity and leadership development), Zeynep Ton (on operational excellence with human dignity), and Sanyin Siang (on relational intelligence and values-based leadership).

19. Katrine Marçal, *Who Cooked Adam Smith's Dinner?: A Story About Women and Economics*, trans. Saskia Vogel (Portobello Books, 2015), chap. 1.

4: If You Don't Ask, You Don't Get

1. Daniel J. Simons and Christopher F. Chabris, "Gorillas in Our Midst: Sustained Inattentional Blindness for Dynamic Events," *Perception* 28, no. 9 (1999): 1059–74, https://doi.org/10.1068/p281059.

2. David W. Pearce and R. Kerry Turner, *Economics of Natural Resources and the Environment* (Johns Hopkins University Press, 1989); Kate Raworth, *Doughnut Economics: Seven Ways to Think Like a 21st-Century Economist* (Chelsea Green Publishing, 2017).

3. Roger Fisher and William Ury, *Getting to Yes: Negotiating Agreement Without Giving In*, 3rd ed. (Penguin, 2011).

5: You Can't Sleep When You're Dead

1. Jason A. Okonofua and Jennifer L. Eberhardt, "Two Strikes: Race and the Disciplining of Young Students," *Psychological Science* 26, no. 5 (May 2015): 617–624, https://edens.berkeley.edu/PDF/2strikes.pdf.

2. Cheryl Strayed, "The Ghost Ship That Didn't Carry Us," *The Rumpus*, April 21, 2011, https://therumpus.net/2011/04/21/dear-sugar-the-rumpus-advice-column-71-the-ghost-ship-that-didnt-carry-us/.

3. This is my recall of a story I read shortly after Donald Trump was elected president in 2016 but unfortunately can't relocate.

4. "Highest-Paid CEOs," AFL-CIO, https://aflcio.org/paywatch/highest-paid-ceos.

5. Dominick Reuter, "Walmart's CEO Made 976 Times the Median Employee's Pay Last Year," Business Insider, April 29, 2024, https://www.businessinsider.com/walmart-ceo-made-976-times-median-employee-pay-last-year-2024-4.

6. "Waltons Remain Top of Global Richest Families List," Family Wealth Report, January 2, 2025, https://www.familywealthreport.com/article.php/ Waltons-Remain-Top-Of-Global-Richest-Families-List.

7. S. Rep. No. GAO-21-45 (2020), https://www.sanders.senate.gov/wp-content /uploads/taxpayers-subsidize-poverty-wages-at-large-corporations-gao-finds.pdf.

8. Zeynep Ton, *The Good Jobs Strategy: How the Smartest Companies Invest in Employees to Lower Costs and Boost Profits* (New Harvest, 2014).

9. ADP Research, "Over Half of Global Workforce Living Paycheck to Paycheck," ADP People at Work 2025 Report, June 17, 2025, https://adp.com/about-adp /press-centre/over-half-of-global-workforce-living-paycheck-to-paycheck.aspx.

10. Approximately 160 million adults in the United States are living paycheck to paycheck, according to the US Senate HELP Committee's 2025 estimate. (60% of the adult population; 78.3% of the 340 million total US population.) US Senate Committee on Health, Education, Labor and Pensions (Minority Staff), "The Impact of Living Paycheck to Paycheck: Shorter Lives, More Stress," March 7, 2025, https://www.sanders.senate.gov/wp-content/uploads/3.7.2025 -Life-Expectancy-Working-Class-Report_final.pdf.

11. Helen Pearson, "How to Make America Healthy: The Real Problems—and Best Fixes," *Nature* 642, no. 8069 (2025): 857–60, https://www.nature.com /articles/d41586-025-01969-1.

12. *Mirror, Mirror 2021: Reflecting Poorly*, The Commonwealth Fund, August 4, 2021, https://www.commonwealthfund.org/publications/fund-reports/2021 /aug/mirror-mirror-2021-reflecting-poorly.

13. *International Comparison of Health Systems*, KFF, May 28, 2024, https:// www.kff.org/health-policy-101-international-comparison-of-health-systems/.

14. Melissa Norton, "Sharecropping, Black Land Acquisition, and White Supremacy (1868–1900)," Durham Food History, World Food Policy Center (Duke University Sanford School of Public Policy), accessed June 2025, https://wfpc .sanford.duke.edu/north-carolina/durham-food-history/sharecropping-black -land-acquisition-and-white-supremacy-1868-1900/.

15. Mark Templeton, quoted in Bob Sutton, "Hierarchy Is Good. Hierarchy Is Essential. And Less Isn't Always Better," LinkedIn Pulse, January 12, 2014, https://www.linkedin.com/pulse/20140112221140-15893932-hierarchy-is -good-hierarchy-is-essential-and-less-isn-t-always-better/.

16. Joel Makower, "Walmart Sustainability at 10: The Birth of a Notion," Green-Biz/Trellis, November 16, 2015 (updated July 24, 2024), https://trellis.net/article/walmart-sustainability-10-birth-notion.

17. Walmart Corporate, Twenty-First Century Leadership (press release, October 23, 2005), https://corporate.walmart.com/news/2005/10/23/twenty-first-century-leadership; Walmart 2009 Global Responsibility Report, https://corporate.walmart.com/content/dam/corporate/documents/purpose/environmental-social-and-governance-report-archive/2009-sustainability-report_129823716349292605.pdf (2005 sustainability baseline; prototype stores were designed to be 25 to 30% more energy efficient with up to 30% lower GHG emissions).

18. Walmart Coop, "Project Gigaton," Walmart Sustainability Hub, accessed June 2025, https://www.walmartsustainabilityhub.com/projectgigaton.

19. Ibid.

20. Matthew Boyle, "Ikea Lost $5,000 When Each Worker Quit. So It Began Paying More," Bloomberg Law Daily Labor Report, June 11, 2024, https://www.bloomberglaw.com/daily-labor-report/ikea-lost-5-000-when-each-worker-quit-so-it-began-paying-more.

21. Wikipedia, "Level of Analysis," accessed June 2025, https://en.wikipedia.org/wiki/Level_of_analysis; see also "Micro, Meso, and Macro Approaches," Saylor Academy, accessed June 2025, https://saylordotorg.github.io/text_principles-of-sociological-inquiry-qualitative-and-quantitative-methods/s05-01-micro-meso-and-macro-approache.html.

22. Jonathan Levy, "Accounting for Profit and the History of Capital," *Critical Historical Studies* 1, no. 2 (2014): 171–214, https://economicsociology.org/wp-content/uploads/2014/12/accounting-for-profit-and-the-history-of-capital.pdf. In this article, Levy argues that profit is not merely a neutral accounting metric. Accounting practices do more than record economic activity—they actively shape our understanding of value and success within capitalist systems. By framing profit as a psychological construct, he shows how it both reflects and reinforces societal expectations and power structures.

6: Serve Progress, Not Power

1. Kate Manne, *Down Girl: The Logic of Misogyny* (Oxford University Press, 2017), 197, https://global.oup.com/academic/product/down-girl-9780190604981.

2. Susan Cain, *Quiet: The Power of Introverts in a World That Can't Stop Talking* (Crown, 2012), https://susancain.net/book/quiet/.

3. Sheryl Sandberg, *Lean In: Women, Work, and the Will to Lead* (Alfred A. Knopf, 2013); Sheryl Sandberg, "Why We Have Too Few Women Leaders," TEDWomen, December 2010, https://www.ted.com/talks/sheryl_sandberg _why_we_have_too_few_women_leaders.

4. Gretchen McCulloch, referencing Dale Spender's classroom study, *All Things Linguistic*, July 2015, https://allthingslinguistic.com/post/145374253955/do -women-talk-too-much-hint-science-says-no.

5. Alice H. Eagly and Steven J. Karau, "Role Congruity Theory of Prejudice Toward Female Leaders," *Psychological Review* 109, no. 3 (2002): 573–98, https://doi.org/10.1037/0033-295X.109.3.573.

6. Pursuing power for its own sake is seen as undermining communal goals—an association that has especially damaging consequences for women and other groups denied access to power. Barbara Schneider, *Power, Conflict and Community: Understanding the Dynamics of Power and Conflict in Organizations* (Cambridge University Press, 2016), 112.

7. Wikipedia, "Benevolence (Tax)," accessed June 2025, https://en.wikipedia .org/wiki/Benevolence_(tax).

8. *Britannica*, "Ella Fitzgerald," accessed June 2025, https://www.britannica .com/biography/Ella-Fitzgerald; Ashley Angelucci, "Ella Fitzgerald," National Women's History Museum, accessed June 2025, https://www.womenshistory .org/education-resources/biographies/ella-fitzgerald.

9. Nilofer Merchant, "Is Bias Fixable?," *Harvard Business Review*, August 28, 2013, https://hbr.org/2013/08/is-bias-fixable.

10. "Need to Know: What Is Share of Voice?" Nielsen Insights, March 2025, https://www.nielsen.com/insights/2025/what-is-share-voice/.

11. Robert I. Sutton, *The No Asshole Rule: Building a Civilized Workplace and Surviving One That Isn't* (Business Plus, 2007), https://bobsutton.net/book /no-asshole-rule/.

7: There Are Limits to Logic

1. Itai Yanai and Martin J. Lercher, "It Takes Two to Think," *Nature Biotechnology*

42, no. 1 (2024): 18–19, https://doi.org/10.1038/s41587-023-02074-2. Yanai and Lercher's argument highlights the inherently social nature of thinking and how dialogic interactions deepen insight and creativity—an idea that parallels the relational, collective view of intelligence in this chapter.

2. Wikipedia, *"Phronesis,"* accessed June 2025, https://en.wikipedia.org/wiki /Phronesis; Wikipedia, "Episteme," accessed June 2025, https://en.wikipedia .org/wiki/Episteme.

3. Immanuel Kant, as quoted in Paulinus Chikwado Ejeh, "Kant's Racial Views and the Categorical Imperative," *Philosophy International Journal* 5, no. 2 (2022): 3–4, https://doi.org/10.23880/PhIJ-16000238.

4. Howard Gardner, *Frames of Mind: The Theory of Multiple Intelligences* (Basic Books, 1983).

5. Teresa J. Frasca, Emily A. Leskinen, and Leah R. Warner, "Words Like Weapons: Labeling Women as Emotional During a Disagreement Negatively Affects the Perceived Legitimacy of Their Arguments," *Psychology of Women Quarterly* 46, no. 4 (2022): 420–37, https://journals.sagepub.com /doi/full/10.1177/03616843221123745.

6. A foundational paper demonstrated the now-famous inverted-U relationship between arousal (stress) and performance, providing clear evidence that too much stress impairs optimal functioning. Robert M. Yerkes and John D. Dodson, "The Relation of Strength of Stimulus to Rapidity of Habit-Formation," *Journal of Comparative Neurology and Psychology* 18, no. 5 (1908): 459–82, https://doi.org/10.1002/cne.920180503.

7. One of my colleague's research partners, Mike Cole of Hatch, said, "It's not actually herding cats; it's more like herding butterflies."

8. Weihua Li and Hongwei Zheng, "Expertise Diversity of Teams Predicts Originality and Long-Term Impact in Science and Technology" (preprint, arXiv, October 10, 2022), https://doi.org/10.48550/arXiv.2210.04422.

9. Amy Edmondson, "Psychological Safety and Learning Behavior in Work Teams," *Administrative Science Quarterly* 44, no. 2 (1999): 350–83, https:// doi.org/10.2307/2666999.

10. Christopher W. Alexander, *The Timeless Way of Building* (Oxford University Press, 1979), chap. 9, "The Flower and the Seed," sec. "The Quality Without a Name."

8: Go Out Beyond Absolutes

1. Marissa Mayer, "Marissa Mayer on Life and Leadership Lessons," posted by Stanford Graduate School of Business, talk dated January 26, 2017, YouTube, 52 min., 41 sec., https://www.youtube.com/watch?v=PMnkxdWUvLw.

2. Karim R. Lakhani, Lars Bo Jeppesen, Peter A. Lohse, et al., "The Value of Openness in Scientific Problem Solving," Working Paper No. 07050 (Harvard Business School, 2007), https://www.hbs.edu/research/pdf/07-050.pdf.

3. Matthew Fisher, Joshua Knobe, Brent Strickland, et al., "The Influence of Social Interaction on Intuitions of Objectivity and Subjectivity," *Cognitive Science* 41, no. 4 (2017): 1119–34, https://doi.org/10.1111/cogs.12380.

4. Robert Lindsay Hakan et al., "Social Judgments as a Measure of Right Mindfulness," *Sage Open* 7, no. 1 (2017), https://doi.org/10.1177/2158244016686811.

5. Sherry Turkle, *Alone Together: Why We Expect More from Technology and Less from Each Other* (Basic Books, 2011).

6. Nilofer Merchant, "MurderBoarding," June 20, 2011, https://nilofermerchant.com/2011/06/20/murderboarding.

9: End Rank and Yank

1. John Dujay, "Eighty-five Per Cent of Workers Inclined to Quit After 'Unfair' Performance Reviews," Canadian HR Reporter, September 1, 2019, https://www.hrreporter.com/focus-areas/performance-management/eighty-five-per-cent-of-workers-inclined-to-quit-after-unfair-performance-reviews/304985.

2. "Madeline E. Heilman, Aaron S. Wallen, Daniella Fuchs, et al., "Penalties for Success: Reactions to Women Who Succeed at Male Gender-Typed Tasks," *Journal of Applied Psychology* 89, no. 3 (2004): 416–27, https://doi.org/10.1037/0021-9010.89.3.416.

3. David Gelles, *The Man Who Broke Capitalism: How Jack Welch Gutted the Heartland and Crushed the Soul of Corporate America—and How to Undo His Legacy* (Simon & Schuster, 2022).

4. Joe Nocera, "Netflix's Firing Culture Works for Netflix, but Would It Work for You?," *Financial Review* (Australia), October 30, 2018, https://www.afr.com/technology/netflixs-firing-culture-works-for-netflix-but-would-it-work-for-you-20181028-h17729.

5. B. F. Skinner, *Science and Human Behavior* (Macmillan, 1953).

6. James K. Harter, Frank L. Schmidt, and Theodore L. Hayes, "Business-Unit-Level Relationship Between Employee Satisfaction, Employee Engagement, and Business Outcomes: A Meta-Analysis," *Journal of Applied Psychology* 87, no. 2 (2002): 268–79, https://doi.org/10.1037/0021-9010.87.2.268.

7. Carol S. Dweck, *Mindset: The New Psychology of Success* (Random House, 2006).

8. Amy Edmondson, "Psychological Safety and Learning Behavior in Work Teams," *Administrative Science Quarterly* 44, no. 2 (1999): 350–83, https://doi.org/10.2307/2666999.

9. Donna Morris, "Check-In: Reinventing Performance Management at Adobe," Adobe Blog, 2014, https://blog.adobe.com/en/publish/2014/03/10/lessons-learned-with-check-in.

10. Drake Baer, "Why Adobe Abolished the Annual Performance Review and You Should, Too," Business Insider, April 10, 2014, https://www.businessinsider.com/adobe-abolished-annual-performance-review-2014-4.

11. Peter Cappelli and Anna Tavis, "The Performance Management Revolution," *Harvard Business Review*, October 2016.

12. Drake Baer, "Performance Reviews Don't Have to Be Absolutely Awful," *Fast Company*, December 2, 2013.

13. Donna Morris, "Why Businesses Should Rethink the Annual Performance Review," *Forbes*, May 29, 2014, https://www.forbes.com/sites/adobe/2014/05/29/why-businesses-should-rethink-the-annual-performance-review/.

14. Nathan Sloan, "Performance Management Redesign," Deloitte Insights, February 27, 2015.

15. Shane McFeely and Ben Wigert, "This Fixable Problem Costs U.S. Businesses $1 Trillion," Gallup, March 13, 2019, https://www.gallup.com/workplace/247391/fixable-problem-costs-businesses-trillion.aspx.

16. Toni Morrison, in conversation with Oprah Winfrey on *The Oprah Winfrey Show* (television broadcast, May 2000), posted May 2000, YouTube, 1 hr., 5 sec., https://www.youtube.com/watch?v=4iIigAgDp2Q.

17. Louise L. Hay, *You Can Heal Your Life* (Hay House, 1984).

18. Glen Lubbert, CEO of Stamina Lab, has a model of performance improvement that is behaviorally based. Instead of doing root-cause-analysis-type work (identifying what's not working), his solutions-based model identifies what is working so that people can continue that momentum. He ideated this practice with me.

10: Never Fake It

1. Herminia Ibarra, *Working Identity: Unconventional Strategies for Reinventing Your Career*, rev. ed. (Harvard Business Review Press, 2023), 92–93.

2. Stacy London, "Stacy London on Her Year of Going Broke," Refinery29, February 2, 2018, https://www.refinery29.com/en-us/2018/02/188983/stacy -london-managing-money-heartbreak.

3. Stacy London, interview on *The Tamsen Show*, podcast, April 24, 2025, https://www.instagram.com/p/DI1_d6-SmPm/.

11: Strategy and Execution Are One and the Same

1. Nilofer Merchant, *The New How: Creating Business Solutions Through Collaborative Strategy* (O'Reilly Media, 2010), 27.

2. Ibid.

3. Carole Cadwalladr, "This Is What a Digital Coup Looks Like," TED Talk, Vancouver, BC, April 2025, 17 min., 41 sec., https://www.ted.com/talks /carole_cadwalladr_this_is_what_a_digital_coup_looks_like/transcript.

4. "The Demise of Applicant Tracking Systems," Talview, January 21, 2016, https://blog.talview.com/en/demise-of-applicant-tracking-system.

5. Carolyn Crist, "AI-Using Managers Rely on the Tool to Decide Who Gets Promoted or Fired, Survey Shows," HR Dive, July 9, 2025, https://www .hrdive.com/news/managers-use-ai-to-decide-who-gets-promoted-or -fired/752528/.

6. Philip Roth, "The Art of Fiction No. 84," interview by Hermione Lee, *Paris Review*, no. 93 (Fall 1984), accessed June 2025, https://www.theparisreview .org/interviews/2957/the-art-of-fiction-no-84-philip-roth.

12: Trust the Present, Not the Past

1. Damian A. Stanley, Peter Sokol-Hessner, Mahzarin R. Banaji, et al., "Implicit Race Attitudes Predict Trustworthiness Judgments and Economic Trust Decisions," *Proceedings of the National Academy of Sciences* 108, no. 19 (2011): 7710–15, https://doi.org/10.1073/pnas.1014345108.

2. Victor Luckerson, "Uber CEO Promises to Make Company 'More Humble' as It Raises $1.2B," *Time*, December 4, 2014, https://time.com/3618349/uber-ceo-travis-kalanick-40-billion/.

3. Katie Richards, "Uber Promises to Do Better in a New Brand Campaign Featuring the Company's CEO," *Adweek*, May 14, 2018, https://www.adweek.com/brand-marketing/uber-promises-to-do-better-in-a-new-brand-campaign-featuring-the-companys-ceo/.

4. Uber disclosed $1,960,000 in US federal lobbying expenditures in 2022. "Client Profile: Uber Technologies—Total Lobbying Expenditures, 2022," OpenSecrets, accessed June 2025, https://www.opensecrets.org/federal-lobbying/clients/summary?cycle=2022&id=D000067336.

5. Peter Sims, "The Immaturity and Arrogance of Uber," Medium, October 2, 2014, https://petersimsie.medium.com/the-immaturity-and-arrogance-of-uber-eea64bcfa5bf.

6. Sam Frizell, "What Is Uber Really Doing with Your Data?," *Time*, November 19, 2014, https://time.com/3595025/uber-data/.

7. Nilofer Merchant, "Dismantling Tech's Sexist Culture Isn't Easy, but Deleting Uber Sure Is," *Time*, November 19, 2014, https://time.com/3595318/uber-sexism-tech-delete-app/.

8. Frances Frei, "How to Build (and Rebuild) Trust," TED Talk, Vancouver, BC, April 2018, 14 min., 56 sec., https://www.ted.com/talks/frances_frei_how_to_build_and_rebuild_trust?language=en.

9. Angus Maddison, *Contours of the World Economy, 1–2030 AD* (Oxford University Press, 2007), tables showing India's share: 24 to 30% during the 17th century and only ~3.7% in 2025; Wikipedia, "List of Countries by Largest Historical GDP," accessed June 2025, https://en.wikipedia.org/wiki/List_of_countries_by_largest_historical_GDP.

13: Don't Mistake Paternalism for Leadership

1. Inga Jóna Jónsdóttir and Kari Kristinsson, "Supervisors' Active-Empathetic Listening as an Important Antecedent of Work Engagement," *International Journal of Environmental Research and Public Health* 17, no. 21 (2020): 7976, https://doi.org/10.3390/ijerph17217976.

2. Martina Pansini, Ilaria Buonomo, and Paula Benevene, "Fostering Sustainable Workplace Through Leaders' Compassionate Behaviors: Understanding the Role of Employee Well-Being and Work Engagement," *Sustainability* 16, no. 23 (2024): 10697, https://doi.org/10.3390/su162310697.

3. Robert K. Greenleaf, *The Servant as Leader* (Robert K. Greenleaf Center for Servant Leadership, 1970), accessed via Internet Archive, https://archive.org/details/20200601-the-servant-as-leader.

4. Jeffrey Pfeffer, *Power: Why Some People Have It—and Others Don't* (Harper Business, 2010).

5. Wikipedia, "Pro-Slavery Ideology in the United States," accessed June 2025, https://en.wikipedia.org/wiki/Pro-slavery_ideology_in_the_United_States.

6. Wikipedia, "Patriarchy," accessed June 2025, https://en.wikipedia.org/wiki/Patriarchy.

7. A useful article about how to say the right thing during a health crisis, and to whom: Susan Silk and Barry Goldman, "How Not to Say the Wrong Thing," *Los Angeles Times*, April 7, 2013, https://www.latimes.com/opinion/story/la-timeless/how-not-to-say-the-wrong-thing.

8. Mary Parker Follett, "The Giving of Orders," in *Dynamic Administration: The Collected Papers of Mary Parker Follett*, ed. Henry C. Metcalf and Lyndall Urwick (Harper & Brothers, 1941); also summarized in "Mary Parker Follett: The Law of the Situation," Panarchy.org, https://www.panarchy.org/follett/lawsituation.html.

14: Stop Fighting for the Emperor's Pleasure

1. Tarpley Hitt, "A Hedge-Fund Founder's Obsessive Storytelling," *New Yorker*, November 16, 2023, https://www.newyorker.com/books/under-review/a-hedge-fund-founders-obsessive-storytelling.

2. Lee Chong Ming, "Steve Ballmer Explains His Viral, Sweaty 'Developers!' Chant from the Early 2000s," Business Insider, June 2, 2025, https://www.businessinsider.com/steve-ballmer-viral-sweaty-developers-chant-microsoft-2025-6.

3. Jyoti Mann, "How Satya Nadella Created a 'Learn-It-All' Culture at Microsoft to Help It Become a $3 Trillion Powerhouse," Business Insider, July 31, 2024, https://www.businessinsider.com/satya-nadella-microsoft-powerhouse-ai-investment-openai-2024-7.

4. Felix Richter, "Microsoft's Share Price Surged 10-Fold Under Satya Nadella," Statista, accessed June 2025, https://www.statista.com/chart/16903/microsoft-stock-price-under-satya-nadella/.

5. Aditya Soni, "Microsoft Briefly Overtakes Apple as World's Most Valuable Company," Reuters, January 11, 2024, https://www.reuters.com/technology/microsoft-overtakes-apple-worlds-most-valuable-company-2024-01-11/.

6. Gabrielle Treanor, "Reframing the Story of ADHD," Substack, accessed June 15, 2025, https://substack.com/@gabrielletreanor/note/c-114421379.

15: Labels Limit More than Liberate

1. Myers-Briggs Type Indicator (MBTI) one-page overview (PDF), the Myers-Briggs Company, accessed June 2025, https://shop.themyersbriggs.com/pdfs/ICON_onesheet_MBTI.pdf.

2. Interestingly, MBTI has a "what this tool can/can't do" section and specifically says the assessment cannot be used for career placement, etc. "All About the Myers-Briggs® (MBTI®) Assessment," Myers-Briggs Company, accessed October 2025, https://www.themyersbriggs.com/en-US/Campaigns/All-About-the-MBTI-Assessment. This is their response to the criticism. The thing is, the assessment is used that way. As their own case studies on that same website show.

3. David J. Pittenger, "Cautionary Comments Regarding the Myers-Briggs Type Indicator," Consulting Psychology Journal 57, no. 3 (2005): 210–21, https://doi.org/10.1037/1065-9293.57.3.210.

4. Kenji Yoshino and Christie Smith, "Fear of Being Different Stifles Talent," Harvard Business Review, March 2014, https://hbr.org/2014/03/fear-of-being-different-stifles-talent.

5. "MBTI Stands Out Among Personality Tests," Pepperdine Graphic, citing CPP Inc., accessed June 2025, https://pepperdine-graphic.com/mbti-stands -out-among-personality-tests/.

6. Murray R. Barrick and Michael K. Mount, "The Big Five Personality Dimensions and Job Performance: A Meta-Analysis," *Personnel Psychology* 44, no. 1 (1991): 1–26, https://doi.org/10.1111/j.1744-6570.1991.tb00688.x.

7. Pittenger, "Cautionary Comments."

8. William L. Gardner and Mark J. Martinko, "Using the Myers-Briggs Type Indicator to Study Managers: A Literature Review and Research Agenda," *Journal of Management* 22, no. 1 (1996): 45–83, https://doi.org/10.1177 /014920639602200103.

9. Wikipedia, "Barnum Effect," accessed June 2025, https://en.wikipedia.org /wiki/Barnum_effect.

10. C. G. Jung, *Psychological Types*, vol. 6 of *The Collected Works of C. G. Jung*, trans. H. G. Baynes, rev. R. F. C. Hull (Princeton University Press, 1971), accessed June 2025, https://archive.org/details/Vol06PsychologicalTypes . Originally published as *Psychologische Typen* (Rascher, 1921).

16: You Are Not for Sale

1. Lauren F. Friedman and Kevin Loria, "Elizabeth Holmes Fires Back at Her Critics," Business Insider, October 15, 2015, https://www.businessinsider .com/elizabeth-holmes-fires-back-at-her-critics-2015-10.

2. John Carreyrou, *Bad Blood: Secrets and Lies in a Silicon Valley Startup* (Vintage, 2020), https://www.penguinrandomhouse.com/books/549478/bad -blood-by-john-carreyrou/.

3. Timothy Noah, "The Dark Lesson of Elizabeth Holmes's Theranos Is That Corporate Bullying Works," *New Republic*, September 2, 2021, https://new republic.com/article/163522/elizabeth-holmes-theranos-corporate-bullying.

4. Elizabeth Holmes, "An Evening with Elizabeth Holmes," Stanford Graduate School of Business, April 17, 2013, YouTube video, 1 hr., 6 min., 9 sec., https://www.youtube.com/watch?v=uJDc4tOU3zo, quote at 58:48.

5. Wendell Berry, *The Art of the Commonplace: The Agrarian Essays of Wendell Berry*, ed. Norman Wirzba (Counterpoint, 2002), 140.

6. Caitlin Rosenthal, *Accounting for Slavery: Masters and Management* (Harvard University Press, 2019), https://www.hup.harvard.edu/catalog.php ?isbn=9780674241657.

17: Cease and Desist Bad Behavior

1. Lillien M. Ellis, "The Interpersonal Consequences of Stealing Ideas: Worse Character Judgments and Less Co-Worker Support for an Idea (vs. Money) Thief," *Organizational Behavior and Human Decision Processes* 171 (July 2022), https://www.sciencedirect.com/science/article/pii/S0749597822000498.

2. "The Real Story Behind Apple's 'Think Different' Campaign," *Forbes*, December 14, 2011, https://www.forbes.com/sites/onmarketing/2011/12/14/the -real-story-behind-apples-think-different-campaign/.

3. Robert I. Sutton, *The No Asshole Rule: Building a Civilized Workplace and Surviving One That Isn't* (Business Plus, 2007).

4. The concept that once you defend yourself with the same tools used to harm you, the clarity erodes is from Esther Perel's *Mating in Captivity* and various interviews. Esther Perel, *Mating in Captivity: Unlocking Erotic Intelligence* (Harper Paperbacks, 2017), https://www.harpercollins.com/products /mating-in-captivity-esther-perel.

5. Monica Lewinsky, "The Price of Shame," TED Talk, Vancouver, BC, March 2015, 22 min., 16 sec., https://www.ted.com/talks/monica_lewinsky_the _price_of_shame.

6. D. Lynn Hawkins, Debra J. Pepler, and Wendy M. Craig, "Naturalistic Observations of Peer Interventions in Bullying," *Social Development* 10, no. 4 (2001): 512–27, https://doi.org/10.1111/1467-9507.00178.

18: New Solutions Need New Questions

1. Gloria Steinem, *My Life on the Road* (Random House, 2015), 204.

2. Case study of Mayekawa from Ikujiro Nonaka, Ryoko Toyama, and Toru Hirata, *Managing Flow: A Process Theory of the Knowledge-Based Firm* (Palgrave Macmillan, 2008).

3. "The Four Stages of Competence," Mercer County Community College, accessed June 2025, https://www.mccc.edu/~lyncha/documents/stagesof competence.pdf.

19: Stop Making It All About You

1. Riya Vinayak, "Chasing Stars: The Myth of Talent and the Portability of Performance," *Vikalpa: The Journal for Decision Makers* 42, no. 1 (2017): 58–60, https://journals.sagepub.com/doi/full/10.1177/0256090916686712.

2. Wikipedia, "The Black List (Survey)," accessed June 2025, https://en.wikipedia.org/wiki/The_Black_List_(survey), citing compiled data.

3. Michael Blanding, "Crowdsourcing Is Helping Hollywood Reduce the Risk of Movie-Making," Harvard Business School Working Knowledge, September 16, 2019, https://www.library.hbs.edu/working-knowledge/crowd-sourcing-is-helping-hollywood-reduce-the-risk-of-movie-making.

4. Wikipedia, "*The Hunger Games* (Franchise)," accessed June 2025, https://en.wikipedia.org/wiki/The_Hunger_Games_(franchise); also confirmed by Box Office Mojo's franchise ranking table.

5. Nilofer Merchant, *The New How: Creating Business Solutions Through Collaborative Strategy* (O'Reilly Media, 2010).

20: Forge A-Teams by Not Fixating on A-Players

1. Kelly Shue, "Women Aren't Promoted Because Managers Underestimate Their Potential," Yale Insights, Yale School of Management, September 13, 2021, https://insights.som.yale.edu/insights/women-arent-promoted-because-managers-underestimate-their-potential.

2. Celia de Anca, "Why Hiring for Cultural Fit Can Thwart Your Diversity Efforts," *Harvard Business Review*, April 25, 2016, https://hbr.org/2016/04/why-hiring-for-cultural-fit-can-thwart-your-diversity-efforts.

3. Regina Dyerly, "The Myth of Replaceability: Preparing for the Loss of Key Employees," Society for Human Resource Management, SHRM Executive Network, January 21, 2025, accessed June 2025, https://www.shrm.org/executive-network/insights/myth-replaceability-preparing-loss-key-employees.

4. Aleks Peterson, "The Hidden Costs of Onboarding a New Employee," Glassdoor, February 27, 2020, accessed June 2025, https://www.glassdoor.com/blog/hidden-costs-employee-onboarding-reduce/.

5. Ryan Pendell, "Employee Engagement Strategies: Fixing the World's $8.8 Trillion Problem," Gallup, June 14, 2022 (updated September 11, 2023), https://www.gallup.com/workplace/393497/world-trillion-workplace

-problem.aspx. This Gallup report underscores that low employee engagement (a demoralized team) can result in "$8.8 trillion in lost productivity"—equivalent to a 20 to 34% drop in performance across global organizations.

6. Nataliya Galan, "Knowledge Loss Induced by Organizational Member Turn-over: A Review of Empirical Literature," *The Learning Organization* 30, no. 2 (2023): 117–36, https://www.emerald.com/insight/content/doi/10.1108/TLO0920220107/full/html.

7. Annika Neklason, "Elite-College Admissions Were Built to Protect Privilege," *Atlantic*, March 18, 2019, https://www.theatlantic.com/education/archive/2019/03/history-privilege-elite-college-admissions/585088/.

8. "The First Harvard Graduate," *Harvard Crimson*, December 9, 1890, https://www.thecrimson.com/article/1890/12/9/the-first-harvard-graduate-the-following/.

9. Abby Wambach, *Wolfpack: How to Come Together, Unleash Our Power, and Change the Game* (Celadon Books, 2019).

10. Rich Nichols and Sam Yip, "'Tell Them We're Not Playing': Inside the USWNT's Fight for Equal Pay," *Guardian*, June 7, 2024, https://www.theguardian.com/football/article/2024/jun/07/us-womens-national-team-equal-pay-us-soccer.

21: You Can't Bestow Power

1. Jia Tolentino, "How 'Empowerment' Became Something for Women to Buy," *New York Times Magazine*, April 12, 2016, https://www.nytimes.com/2016/04/17/magazine/how-empowerment-became-something-for-women-to-buy.html.

2. Paulo Freire, *Pedagogy of the Oppressed* (Bloomsbury Academic, 2018).

3. Patty McCord, *Powerful: Building a Culture of Freedom and Responsibility* (Silicon Guild, 2018).

4. Justin Bariso, "Netflix's Unlimited Vacation Policy Took Years to Get Right. It's a Lesson in Emotional Intelligence," *Inc.*, September 14, 2020, https://www.inc.com/justin-bariso/netflixs-unlimited-vacation-policy-took-years-to-get-right-its-a-lesson-in-emotional-intelligence.html.

5. "The Best Work of Our Lives," Netflix, accessed October 2025, https://jobs.netflix.com/culture.

6. Jeff Cox, "Netflix CEO Reed Hastings: Why I Take 6 Weeks' Vacation," CNBC Net Net, November 3, 2015, https://www.cnbc.com/2015/11/03/netflix-ceo -reed-hastings-why-i-take-6-weeks-vacation.html?.

7. Bruce Daisley, host, *Eat Sleep Work Repeat*, podcast, "The Netflix Culture Document 'We're Not a Family,'" January 30, 2017, https://eatsleepworkrepeat .com/netflix/.

22: A Hero Harms Us

1. Richard V. Reeves and Eleanor Krause, "Raj Chetty in 14 Charts: Big Findings on Opportunity and Mobility We Should All Know," Brookings, January 11, 2018, https://www.brookings.edu/blog/social-mobility-memos/2018/01/11 /raj-chetty-in-14-charts-big-findings-on-opportunity-and-mobility-we -should-know/.

2. Pablo A. Mitnik and David B. Grusky, *Economic Mobility in the United States* (The Pew Charitable Trusts and the Russell Sage Foundation, 2015), https:// www.pew.org/-/media/assets/2015/07/fsm-irs-report_artfinal.pdf.

3. https://www.stlouisfed.org/-/media/project/frbstl/stlouisfed/files/pdfs /community%20development/econmobilitypapers/section1/econmobility _1-1chetty_508.pdf?d=l&s=tw.

4. Ira Katznelson, *When Affirmative Action Was White: An Untold History of Racial Inequality in Twentieth-Century America* (W. W. Norton, 2006), https://wwnorton.com/books/9780393328516.

5. Rosabeth Moss Kanter, *Men and Women of the Corporation* (Basic Books, 1977), in which she examines how individuals in underrepresented groups often conform—not out of agreement but due to isolation and fear of being the exception.

6. A well-known longitudinal study by Nicholas Christakis and James Fowler found that behaviors like smoking and weight gain spread through social networks—not just because of influence but because of identity. Nicholas A. Christakis and James H. Fowler, "The Spread of Obesity in a Large Social Network over 32 Years," *New England Journal of Medicine* 357, no. 4 (2007): 370–79, and "The Collective Dynamics of Smoking in a Large Social Network," *New England Journal of Medicine* 358, no. 21 (2008): 2249–58.

7. Geoff Edgers, "Budgets for 'Prestige' Films Dried Up. So Ava DuVernay Found a New Way," *Washington Post*, December 4, 2023, https://www

.washingtonpost.com/entertainment/2023/12/04/ava-duvernay-origin
-caste-financing-philanthropists/.

8. Nilofer Merchant, "How Ava DuVernay Is Finding Blue Oceans in Hollywood," *Harvard Business Review*, August 7, 2019, https://hbr.org/2019/08
   /how-ava-duvernay-is-finding-blue-oceans-in-hollywood.

9. Julie Walker, "Ava DuVernay at SXSW: 'If Your Dream Only Includes You, It's
   Too Small,'" *Root*, March 14, 2015, https://www.theroot.com/ava-duvernay
   -at-sxsw-if-your-dream-only-includes-you-1790859101.

23: Work Isn't Worthy of Worship

1. Sandy Smith, "Presenteeism Costs Business 10 Times More than Absenteeism," *EHS Today*, March 16, 2016, accessed June 2025, https://www
   .ehstoday.com/safety-leadership/article/21918281/presenteeism-costs
   -business-10-times-more-than-absenteeism.

2. Louis W. Fry, "The Numinosity of Soul: André Delbecq's Legacy for MSR,"
   Journal of Management, Spirituality & Religion 17, no. 1 (2020): 5–21, https://
   doi.org/10.1080/14766086.2019.1583597.

3. C. Wright Mills, *White Collar: The American Middle Classes*, rev. ed. (Har-
   court, Brace and Company, 1952), 110.

4. "Benjamin Franklin and Slavery," Benjamin Franklin House (London), accessed June 2025, https://benjaminfranklinhouse.org/education/benjamin
   -franklin-and-slavery/; Franklin Li, "Ben Franklin's Personal Flaws Should
   Not Diminish His Achievements," *Daily Pennsylvanian*, October 25, 2023,
   https://www.thedp.com/article/2023/10/benjamin-franklin-legacy-reflection
   -flaws-achievements.

24: Change the Metrics

1. Howard Schultz, quoted in Micah Solomon, "Starbucks CEO Howard Schultz's
   Strategy to Boosting Profits and Building Our Country," *Inc.*, April 8, 2016,
   https://www.inc.com/micah-solomon/starbucks-ceo-howard-schultz-boost
   -profits-build-our-country-through-corporate-a.html.

2. "Starbucks—33 Year Stock Price History," Macrotrends, https://www
   .macrotrends.net/stocks/charts/SBUX/starbucks/stock-price-history.

3. "Through the Lens of Humanity," Aspen Institute, September 1, 2016,
   https://www.aspeninstitute.org/magazine/through-the-lens-of-humanity/.